ESSAYS ON THE THEORY OF CONSTRAINTS

Eliyahu M. Goldratt

North River Press

North River Press
Publishing Corporation
P.O. Box 567
Great Barrington, MA 01230

Phone: (800) 486-2665 or (413) 528-0034
Fax: (800) 266-5329 or (413) 528-3163

www.northriverpress.com

Copyright ©1987,1988,1989,1990
Eliyahu M. Goldratt

All rights reserved. No part of this book may be reproduced or utilized in any form or by any means, electronic or mechanical, including photocopying, recording, or any information storage and retrieval system, without permission in writing from the publisher.

Manufactured in the United States of America

TABLE OF CONTENTS

Chapter 1
Hierarchical Management - The Inherent Conflict   1
Modine - The McHenry Plant   19

Chapter 2
Laying the Foundation   1
APOLOGIA* or In The Move Toward The Third Stage   23

Chapter 3
The Fundamental Measurements   1
When Quoted Lead Times Are The Problem   23

Chapter 4
The Importance Of A System's Constraints   1
Looking Beyond The First Stage; Just In Time (Fictional Visit - Real Plants)   13

Chapter 5
How Complex Are Our Systems   1
Looking Beyond The First Stage; Just In Time - Part Two   15

Chapter 6
The Paradigm Shift   1
Looking Beyond The First Stage; Just In Time - Part Three   25

Chapter 1

Hierarchical Management—The Inherent Conflict

1. Every Organization Uses A Pyramid Structure

What is common to Roger Smith, Margaret Thatcher, Ghengis Khan, the Pope and holy Moses? It doesn't take long to find the answer. They all were at the top of a hierarchical pyramid of command. It seems a little bit strange that such diverse organizations with totally different purposes and separated by tremendous distances and time, are all structured in basically the same way.

A very precise description of this basic structure was documented as early as the Old Testament. When the Israelites fled from slavery it didn't take long (less than three months) for their leader to find that the only effective way to manage his newly created organization was by building a hierarchical pyramid of command. "And Moses chose able men out of all Israel and made them heads over the people, rulers of thousands, rulers of hundreds, rulers of fifties, and rulers of tens" (Exodus 18:25).

Managing large organizations is of particular interest in this century. In the past, large organizations were restricted to basically three types of organizations—governments, armies and religions. By their nature, only a very limited number of such large organizations could exist. This is not the case anymore. From a modest beginning in the nineteenth century we have witnessed an explosion of new types of large organizations—the industrial and service companies. If we chose as a measurement the number of employees, the number of industrial companies that exceed ten thousand employees is probably at least two orders of magnitude greater than the handful of such large companies in existence during the previous century.

This explosion is even more startling when we examine the service companies. The only large service companies that were in existence before this century were the banks. Today, not only are there many more banks that are much larger than the biggest bank of the last century, but new types of large service organizations have emerged. Insurance companies have grown from modest beginnings to surprisingly large businesses. The small world traders have grown into huge distribution organizations, which in some cases encompass enough people to create an entire army. Individually owned shops have given birth to the mammoth chains, and even the once modest accounting profession which was previously operated by individuals or very small groups has produced the "big eight" companies, each encompassing more than ten thousand people.

At first glance it is quite surprising that this tremendous explosion in the number of large organizations didn't break the boundaries of the ancient organization structure, especially since it was accompanied by an unprecedented growth of new technologies and an immense effort in management science. All the current organizations are still based on a hierarchical pyramid of command. The different organizations may have varying numbers of levels of command, more or less autonomy in local decisions, "dotted" lines of reporting on top of the main "solid" line of command, but the basic pyramid structure is still the back bone of all these organizations. Maybe a good way to uncover the reason for this across-the-board uniformity is not to delve into the small details that distinguish organizations from each other, but to do exactly the opposite, to look for uniformity, even in the micro-fine structure.

2 The Underlying Reason For The Pyramid Structure

As we have just seen, the basic ratio in the structure that Moses developed was 10 people reporting to one. This same number was used as the base ratio of the Roman Empire's army and Genghis Khan's Mongolian army. If we examine other old and modern organizations we see that the pyramids are built on repetitions of a few people—in most cases between 5 to 15—reporting to one person. The commonalty of this phenomena, which is independent of culture, time or even the tasks that the organizations have to fulfill, lead me to believe that it represents the fundamental capabilities of humans.

> *We cannot conclude anything about the pyramid's effectiveness just from the fact that it is so widely used*

A person is probably able to manage directly and effectively only about 5 to 15 other people. Attempts to manage directly a substantially larger number of people proves, in a surprisingly short time, to be totally ineffective. If that is the case, it is quite obvious why the only solution to managing an organization of more than a few dozen people is unequivocally found in the form of an hierarchical pyramid of command.

Organizations are not built exactly like a pure pyramid. As we look toward the top of the pyramid we find some people reporting directly to a high level manager, who have very few people reporting (directly or indirectly) to them. This phenomenon is probably an unavoidable result of the fact that most organizations need to carry out a variety of supporting tasks that require very few people compared to the main task of the organization. We call the people responsible for the supporting tasks "staff" while we refer to the people at the same level who are involved with the organizations's main tasks, and are thus in charge of a much "deeper" pyramid, as "line" managers. In this respect there is no basic difference between an industrial company, a government or an army.

A very quick calculation reveals that the need for extensive staff does not lead to a very deep management structure. This is contrary to the belief that I have found among top managers. Take for example an organization of about 30,000 people that uses the highest practical management ratio—1 manager per 15 subordinates—across all levels. This

> *The net effect is that each link, on the average, increases the chance for distortion*

organization will need four management levels to operate. Now let's compare this organization to an equivalent one using the same ratio but where at each management level (remember, the lowest level of the pyramid is not a management level) two thirds of the people are staff and only one third are line managers. This is certainly a very high proportion. Carrying out a simple calculation shows that this second organization requires six levels. Heavy reliance on staff for such large organizations does increase the organization's depth, but not as dramatically as might be expected.

Organizations that have too many management levels and seek to shallow this structure should not search for a solution in reducing staff—it won't help reduce the number of management levels. Rather the organization should search for management levels that have a low ratio of line managers to subordinates. Low ratios of one manager to two, or even three, may inflate the organization's structure turning any approval process into an ineffective and extremely cumbersome one. In our example, a ratio of 1 to 3 in line management levels will inflate the number of organization levels from 4 to 9.

We just concluded that the uniformity of the management method used by all organizations throughout time, stems from the basic ability of individuals to directly handle only a relatively few people compared to the number of people in the organization. This means that organizations are using the hierarchical pyramid of management not because it is the best method but because it is probably the only workable method.

Does it mean that the hierarchical pyramid is good? Not at all. It just means that we cannot conclude anything about the pyramid's effectiveness just from the fact that it is so widely used. There simply are no other apparent alternatives. It also does not mean that substantial improvements are not possible. It only means that the most promising places to look for improvements are *within* the framework of a hierarchical pyramid and not outside it. The first place to look for a significant improvement is to find the biggest flaw in this method. Only by identifying flaws will we be able to devise improved ways. The bigger and more fundamental the flaw the greater the possibility of a substantial improvement.

3 Local Optimums Distort Information Flowing Upwards

In order to find a fundamental flaw—if one exists at all—we should seek to define, in the broadest terms possible, how the hierarchical pyramid functions. It looks as if information must constantly circulate up and down the pyramid's chain of command in order to ensure a workable organization. Information must stream upward and instructions must stream downwards. How is this done? Every link (manager) in the pyramid asks for information from his subordinates, which he "massages" before passing on to his boss. Let's clarify this process. Each manager does not ask for and pass on just mere data. If this was the case, the amount of data that would reach the top would be so voluminous as to make it totally indigestible. Instead a manager asks for information—basically an evaluation—rather than data. "Give me a one page summary" is certainly a request for information, not data.

After gathering information from all subordinates, a manager employs his intuition, some guidelines and his own first-hand data to formulate the evaluation that he will pass to his boss. This process is repeated throughout the pyramid in order to supply decision makers with the crucial ingredients for making reasonable decisions. Lets remember, all managers, without exception, are decision makers. What distinguishes them from each other are the subjects and magnitude of the decisions they are expected to make.

Now we can spot a possible flaw. How does a manager make his evaluation? Does he examine the information forwarded to him from the viewpoint of the entire organization? Is it possible that he is equipped to look on his area of responsibility and make his evaluations while taking the bigger picture into account? Let's ask this question in a clearer way. If the president of the entire organization, with his knowledge and perspective, was substituted for our middle level manager, would we witness the exact same evaluation? And what about personal considerations? Can we take for granted that the evaluations of a manager are not colored by what he thinks would be the best for his "kingdom"? Are biased evaluations such a rare phenomena?

4 The Longer The Chain The Greater The Distortion

I think that we have to conclude that in most such evaluations a distortion is introduced due to the local point of view of the respective manager. Since we are dealing with chains of command we should expect that the longer the chain—the more links involved—the bigger the accumulated distortion.

Let's analyze this last statement for a moment. There is always the possibility that a manager will reach a correct evaluation even if the evaluations forwarded to him by his subordinates were distorted by their local points of view. True, but what is the chance that in every case a manager will be able to sift through distorted evaluations and reach the right one? Is it a 100% probability? Certainly not, even for talented and intuitive managers. Moreover, a higher level manager is liable to introduce his own distortions. Let's remember, the ability of a link in the chain is limited, at most, to correcting distortions that have been passed to him, but he cannot ensure that new distortions will not be introduced above him. On the other hand, he can certainly accept distorted evaluations, magnify them and pass them on, reducing the probability of his boss reaching a correct evaluation. The net effect is that each link, on the average, increases the chance for distortion rather than reduces it.

Since we cannot escape the validity of the above statement, we should proceed to derive the full magnitude of its ramifications.

A decision made does not mean yet a decision executed. The decision has to be turned into instructions and communicated to the proper person for execution. If a decision is made at the upper levels of the pyramid it cannot be broken down at that level into specific instructions. Take for example a decision made by a president of a company. He cannot possibly translate his decision into direct, detailed instructions to all employees that are going to be involved in carrying it out. Rather, the president will formulate it as a policy which will be broken down by his direct subordinates into finer guidelines—each for his area of responsibility. In turn their direct subordinates will do the same refining and specifying the details, until the last level of management eventually gives direct instructions to be carried out by the bottom level of the pyramid.

This is, in broad terms, the way information flows from the top down. But once again, the same problem occurs. When the broad guidelines are interpreted by a middle level manager and converted into finer guidelines, or even instructions, the manager again basically interprets the broad guidelines according to his local understanding. Local perspective, rather than a global one, comes once again into play. The middle level manager is very likely to lack the global perspective and he might be influenced by what he thinks is best for his kingdom. We should expect distortion to creep into the interpretation, and once again the longer the chain, the more distortion to the original intent by the time the president's policy is executed.

5 Some Indications On The Magnitude Of Distortion

How severe are these distortions? To what extent is the performance of an organization affected by them? It is probably very hard to give a global answer and certainly almost impossible to quantify it. But maybe the following hypothetical case will help to clarify its order of magnitude.

It is not a coincidence that the expression "do it by the book" is an army one.

Imagine a chess game in which the white pieces are played, not by a single player but by a hierarchical pyramid of command. We have the president in charge of the white pieces. He does not look on the board, rather he has two vice-presidents, one in charge of attack and one in charge of defense. They too do not look on the board, they have their directors. One director is in charge of the bishops while attacking, another is in charge of the defense for the two far left columns, and so on.

These directors gather information from their people who are actually look on the board, and based on what they see, they formulate their evaluations which they pass upwards. Finally, information reaches the president who formulates the global policy—"attack from the right!" This guideline is now converted by the various management levels into finer and finer guidelines until the actual move is made on the board. Quite amusing—but do you think that this hierarchical pyramid has a chance of winning even against a small child? It looks as if their only hope of winning is to play against another hierarchical pyramid.

6 Stating The Inherent Conflict

Hopefully, this last analogy was helpful in illustrating the degree to which distortions in the flow of information circulating in hierarchical pyramids can impede the performance of an organization. What is also alluded to, is the inherent conflict that is built into the pyramid structure. The pyramid was developed to answer the problem of limited span of control. Using a hierarchical structure we extend the span of control of the person at the top from managing a handful of people to managing any desired number. Unfortunately, this increase in the span of management is achieved through intermediate links that introduce distortions into the picture. The larger the span, the larger the number of intermediate links and thus the greater the distortions.

The distortions are a result of the basic difference between a local—one department, one product, one function—point of view and the global—the entire system—considerations. The severity of the effect of the accumulated distortions is in direct proportion to the validity of the following statement:

The total of local optima is not equal to the optimum of the total.

When organizations are built in a way that the difference between a local optimum and the global optimum is large, then distortion due to the pyramid structure is great. The overall performance of this pyramid is far from the performance attainable by a pyramid that succeeded in minimizing the difference between the local and global considerations.

The recognition of the existence of the inherent conflict is as old as the creation of the pyramid structure. Every organization struggles—intentionally or intuitively—to find its answer. Let's review some stereotype solutions used in different organizations. It should be stressed that no organization uses just one solution. Actually everyone uses a blend where one solution is dominant but where at least traces of other solutions exist.

7 The Army Solution

Probably the most known and ancient solution is the army one—discipline. Discipline is an attempt to minimize the distortions introduced when interpreting guidelines into finer guidelines and detailed instructions. The pyramid is used mainly as a convenient channel of distribution and not so much as a management structure. The use of discipline as the main behavior pattern is an attempt to neutralize the lower management levels from making any significant decision on their own, leaving the task to decide to the very top of the pyramid. This

These rules are supposed to define what is right and what is wrong. Thus, if it is desirable to quantify them, they justifiably are referred to as measurements.

method cannot work unless it is accompanied by a predetermined translation of each and every guideline to very specific and detailed instructions. The task of the lower management ranks is basically to carry out the current guideline according to the respective predetermined process. It is not a coincidence that the expression "do it by the book" is an army one.

Discipline does not deal with the other stream of information, that of passing information upwards. No wonder that in ancient armies, where the discipline method was used even more extensively then in modern armies, the supreme commander always located himself in a high place. There he could see the battle first hand, even if it meant taking a personal risk and possibly a fatal exposure for the entire army. The discipline method tries to avoid the need to rely on local optimums and works very effectively when the situation encountered has been precisely predicted. The "book" has an appropriate detailed breakdown of how to act and the lower parts of the pyramid have been trained to carry out these detailed instructions. In its pure form it is a stiff mechanism that cannot possibly cope with the constantly changing environments faced by industrialized and service companies.

8. The Religion Solution

The approach used by religion-based organizations is almost the antithesis of the army method. Religions also use a pre-determined "cook-book", but what a vast difference in concept between their cook-books and the army books. Religion based organizations do not use a predetermined, strict translation between a guideline and instructions. Rather they have developed a very detailed code of what is right and what is wrong. This code is the connection between a situation and the appropriate guideline rather than between a guideline and a detailed instruction.

The best and most widely known example was mentioned previously—Moses and the Israelites. The Bible tells us that Moses first instituted the hierarchical pyramid and nominated the intermediate management links. The very next chapter is about Mount Sinai and the Ten Commandments. The Ten Commandments are given to all levels of the newly created organization. The next chapters contain more details and specific rules. What are these rules? They are not how to execute a guideline given from the top of the pyramid, they are the rules by which the lower levels can *deduce* guidelines without waiting for a decision from the top of the pyramid.

This method tries to give maximum autonomy and decision power to the lowest possible rank in a pyramid, preferably to the base level itself. What a contrast to the army way, which asks for blind discipline from the lower ranks. The religion way of solving the inherent conflict of local and global view points is through institution of predetermined rules that cause a local optimum to coincide with the global optimum. The Ten Commandments themselves are not just a set of rules, they are at the same time a very precise statement of the goal of the entire organization. The inherent conflict between local and global optimums is simply eliminated.

9 The Goal Dictates The Solution

The conceptual solution adopted by the religious organizations is clearly superior to that adopted by army organizations. The fact that all armies, without exception, use basically the same method indicates that there is a basic difference between armies and religious organizations. This difference prevents the army from using the solution of the religion

But we refused for quite a long time to admit that a tool cannot replace a method, it can only help in carrying it out.

based pyramids. The reason for the difference is probably in the means that have to be used in order to achieve each organization's goal.

The goal of a religious based organization is achieved when each individual behaves separately in a certain way. The goal of the army can be accomplished only though a synchronized effort of many individuals. Thus for religion it is sufficient to find the rules that will guide the individual. The higher levels of the pyramid are necessary only to interpret those rules in situations where their ramifications are not clear. Since the army goal can be achieved only through group effort, in addition to individual effort, rules appropriate for all levels must be found—rules that are appropriate to every existing subgroup. This is certainly a bigger and more difficult task.

Industrial and service organizations suffer from the army's basic problem even though usually not to the same degree. In order to achieve the goal of industrial or service organizations, synchronized mutual efforts of at least subgroups is vital. These organizations are not oblivious to the benefits inherent in the methods of religion based organizations. It is not surprising that we can trace the efforts of industrial and service organizations to formulate such rules to the beginning of this century, when these organizations started to emerge. We all are very aware of these attempts, even though we usually refer to them by a different nomenclature—measurements. These rules are supposed to define what is right and what is wrong. Thus, if it is desirable to quantify them, they justifiably are referred to as measurements.

The next chapter will deal more rigorously with the measurement subject. For this discussion let me postulate that our efforts to formulate measurements to judge—and thus to guide—a business as a whole (the financial statements) were much more successful than our effort to formulate measurements for the lower ranks of the pyramid (management accounting).

An indication of this situation can be observed in the restless shifting of organizations between centralized and decentralized modes of operations. It seems that whenever an organization can be split vertically so that each subsystem interacts just with the external world, decentralization tends to increase the performance of the entire organization. The quite successful rules of judging an entire business can, by this vertical split, be used by a lower level of the pyramid. This is not the case when splitting is done horizontally. In a horizontal split we create subsystems that are interacting not just with the external world, but with each other. Services or materials are supplied by one subsystem to another subsystem within the same organization. In such cases the global measurements—the financial statements—have proven to be ineffective when used for subsystems. Not only are they distorted by "transfer prices", they intensify rather than diminish the tendency for local optima.

10 Computers—A Method Or Just A Tool?

So far it seems that only two avenues are open to deal with the inherent conflict of hierarchical pyramid—discipline and measurements. The first does not utilize the initiative and intuition of the lower ranks and by definition is stiff and unable to accommodate changing environments. The second is limited by our ability to find and institute appropriate measurements. In retrospect, the efforts to find appropriate measurements hasn't yielded any new fruits since the thirties. No wonder that when the computer came on the scene, bringing with it a tremendous capacity to store data and impressive calculating power, we thought that at last a new avenue was opened up to use the army method without suffering from its rigidity.

Three decades ago it looked like the computer could be used to bypass the inherent conflict of the pyramid. The organization could load the raw data to the computer without any interpretation or evaluations being done by the lower ranks. Top managers could input their wishes, dictating the desired policies, and the computer would process them into detailed instructions for all appropriate people. In this way no local optimum could creep in—discipline would prevent misreporting—thus securing the channel of information streaming up. Once again discipline to carry out the computer generated instructions would secure the channels of information flowing down. The computer would basically generate instantly the appropriate instruction books, removing the major obstacle of the discipline method, that of rigidity.

Organizations in the Western world have invested inordinate sums of money to achieve this solution. Now, after more than twenty years of extensive efforts, almost everybody shares the disappointment. The basic target was not achieved. Computers are not the management arm of the top of the pyramid. Instead they have turned out to be quite helpful as data banks and for automating clerical—not managerial—work.

What went wrong? Why in spite of all the money and efforts did this avenue turn out to be such a disappointment? My belief is that this avenue was not open to start with. A hidden assumption underlies that dream of using a computer to bypass the pyramid—the assumption that somewhere in the computer's guts there will be a mechanism to translate data and broad policies into instructions. Who is going to put this mechanism into the computer? Do we know what this mechanism is? As a matter of fact isn't this mechanism just a different name for "appropriate measurements" or "the right rules"? It looks to me as if we became frustrated in our unsuccessful effort to find these rules and then embarked on using a tool, that by itself might be effective in exploiting them. But we refused for quite a long time to admit that a tool cannot replace a method, it can only help in carrying it out.

Moreover, it seems to me that when satisfactory rules—measurements—are found and instituted, the way to use the computer will not be to enhance the discipline method by bypassing the lower ranks of the pyramid, but exactly the opposite. There will be no need to bypass the lower ranks because local optima are going to coincide with the global optimum. Thus the computer will become a tool for enhancing the rules method, not bypassing it. Each individual at each level, could then expand his ability to use his initiative and know-how through the access to the data banks and the supreme power of the computer to perform voluminous, simple calculations. The enormous sums invested in the computer were not wasted. They will benefit us once we find and institute the essential basic requirement—the organization's rules.

Even if we cross these two immense obstacles a third one is waiting for us.

11 Another attempt

At the time that the Western world has chased a pie-in-the-sky solution, the Japanese made a much less ambitious, but more effective attack, on the inherent conflict of the pyramid. If evaluations are distorted due to the local point of view of the lower management levels, let's expand this point of view. Every manager in the large Japanese industrial and service organizations goes through a many year training period. During those years he moves through a wide spectrum of different functions. After that training period his ability to evaluate a situation is not dictated by just his "kingdom", but by his intimate knowledge of the impact of a situation on other parts of the organization. To a large extent the individual manager's local optimum is expanded to come closer to the president's view of the entire organization.

This is not enough—the Japanese carry it a step further and are careful not to make a decision until a "consensus" has been reached. This is a lengthy process and basically consists of a "rubbing shoulders"—extensive formal and informal communication up and down the organization. This process' almost guarantees that the decision finally made will not be based entirely on local optima, but will be closer to meeting the needs of the organization as a whole. This process is a slow and not effective for daily decisions. The fact that the Japanese cumbersome and time consuming method yields much better overall results, than those achieved in Western countries, is a frightening testimony to the unadvanced state of the Western methods.

12 Obstacles To Instituting A Better Way

It seems that the only promising avenue is to try once again to find the appropriate rules—measurement—that will remove the difference between local and global optima. These rules will have to be good not just at one level or for one function, they will have to be appropriate for all management levels and for all the various tasks that mangers carry out. The difficulties are not restricted to just finding these rules, there is another set of immense obstacles. Suppose for a minute that we have found a very satisfactory set of rules. These rules, by definition, will demand that a middle level manager conduct his evaluations, decisions and actions along the global perspective of the entire organization rather than the way he is doing it today—concentrating more on what is good for his local kingdom. This means, by definition, that these rules will demand a drastic change of behavior by all management levels. The magnitude of the required change certainly borders on a "cultural revolution". We are not just dealing with a technical or logical problem—finding the rules. We are dealing with an immense psychological problem—a drastic change in the ingrained behavior of all managers.

Even if we cross these two immense obstacles a third one is waiting for us. How much data is needed in order for each manager at every level to see the global picture of the entire organization at any given point in time? If the data required is too extensive or if it changes faster than the digestion period of the managers, then the rules will not be effective since the managers will not have sufficient information to enable them to use these rules. This book will deal with all of the above obstacles, trying not only to derive the rules but also to deal with the psychological and data problems.

A Visit

MODINE—THE MCHENRY PLANT

"As time went on through the early 80's the plant was continuing to improve, both financially and as far as reputation was concerned. We started to do some of the right things. In early 1986 we were faced with entering into some new business with Chrysler Corporation and had some gentlemen from Chrysler coming en masse—two groups of eight to ten people —to review our facility. I don't know if you are familiar with a psychologist by the name of Maurice Massey. He talks about significant emotional events as a very powerful tool for changing your life. Chrysler came here and they gave us one of those! They really laid it on the line for us in terms of—'if you think you are even close to being a decent supplier for any domestic or certainly any foreign automobile manufacturer you are sadly mistaken'... I walked out underneath the door without even having to open it.... One of Chrysler's largest complaints about our facility was that you have so much in-process material, how can you ever hope to keep track of anything?'... When I think back, the biggest complaint was that we were doing everything [ ] backwards... They were here on a Friday and I think it was the following Monday that we all got together and said ' my God, what are we going to do?' We had all read *The Goal* but without that real shock, without that something slamming you right in the teeth, telling you that you won't have any business with them or anyone else unless you get off your [ ] and do something. We decided all right, let's try what's in *The Goal*."

"We approached it first as an experiment, just to see if it's going to work and literally what we did was to turn off the front of the factory and just drained all the in-process inventory. Once the inventory disappeared, we handcuffed the supervisors to produce just what was needed. It took us about three-four weeks to drain the plant (the throughput time then was about three-four weeks). Our total in-process inventory dropped by 65%, but remember, we classify as work-in-process anything that is not raw material. We made press room parts two years ago using our 'have a hunch, build a bunch' approach and they were still in our warehouse and we considered them obsolete, but we were going to punish ourselves and call them work-in-process. The result of turning off the faucet shows better in condensers, the core of our work-in-process inventory, and they dropped by more than 75%".

Bob and I are sitting in the office of Jim Rulseh. He is the plant manager of a small plant, about 150 employees, in McHenry, Illinois. This plant is producing heat exchangers for the automotive industry, or in more understood terms, car radiators. This plant is one of the many that actually implemented the fictional story described in *The Goal* and made it into reality. Jim even looks, to a large extent, like Alex Rogo— he's in his late 30's, 6 foot plus, blonde hair and radiates confidence without even a trace of arrogance. I met Jim about a year ago, in July of 1986, when I came to spend a half day at his company's headquarters. At that time he told me about the turn-around that his plant had made. When I heard what he had achieved and in what time frame, I was a little skeptical. Such results cannot be sustained for more than a month or two without active participation of workers on the floor. If the results quoted were real, the active participation of workers would be manifested in a different attitude toward the plant. The most obvious ramifications would have been a drop in absenteeism. Thus I asked Jim if there had been such a drop. He said he didn't notice any. To tell the truth, judging from such a reply I more than suspected his story.

'have a hunch, build a bunch'

About two months later I received a letter from Jim in which he elaborated on and quantified in much more detail his results and also addressed directly the absenteeism subject. I probably wasn't too good in disguising my disbelief because his letter read as follows: "...During our dinner conversation in July you told me to check our absenteeism figures for the plant. You felt, that by reducing work-in-process inventory we will notice a 10% drop in absenteeism. Well, on this point I am happy to say you were mistaken. For the past six month period our absenteeism rate has dropped by over 20% over any other six month period. Our current absenteeism rate is the lowest level in our plant's 25 year history."

You can imagine my pleased reaction toward such a letter. At that time I was aware of only a handful of plants who had implemented successfully the saga of Alex Rogo. Learning about such *Goal* implementations was quite a surprise. After years of trying so hard to convert plants to these semi-controversial concepts it was delightful, but a bit hard to accept, that a book can succeed where frontal lectures, a computer system with its simulation capability and so much one-on-one persuasion produced only limited success. These first testimonials forced me to predict what will happen to a plant that has turned the corner just because of *The Goal*. Moreover, the first testimonials clearly showed that the changes adopted by plants were exactly the ones that were outlined in detail in *The Goal*. I was concerned about stagnation, since *The Goal* contains only about 1% of the knowledge we have developed. Moreover, *The Goal* does not stress enough that the key to a long standing implementation of a process of on-going improvement is a thorough understanding not just by the top of the pyramid, but also by every manager, engineer and staff member of the organization and preferably every worker.

I predicted, since such a thorough understanding was not available, that after the initial huge jump in performance, there was a danger that the plant would stabilize and as market and product conditions changed would then deteriorate. This fear was so strong that I hurriedly brought out the revised edition of *The Goal* where Alex Rogo warns in the epilogue that *The Goal* is not a story of a success but of exactly the opposite.

Since that time more and more testimonials of *Goal*

implementations—literally hundreds—have reached me. Even though some of them carried some symptoms of stagnation I started to suspect—and hoped—that my gloomy predictions would not come true. Nevertheless I couldn't shake the fear, since if a plant reverts back it may be virtually impossible to start the process again. When the Israeli Army shortened my reserve duty and I found myself with a week of unscheduled time, I decided to devote some time to a personal check of the process that a plant goes through when it embarks on implementing *The Goal*.

These were the circumstances that Bob and I found ourselves in as we sat in Jim Rulseh's office. Jim was certainly delighted by his achievements and rightly so, but the numbers he was quoting us now were only slightly better than the ones he mentioned in his October 1986 letter. As Jim was continuing to describe the various steps he had taken and the actual results achieved, I started to have a sickening feeling that one has when his Cassandra predictions turn out to be true. I asked myself how was I going to delve into it without offending this proud, enthusiastic and gentle person. I decided to concentrate first on the time of the change, basically on the first half of 1986.

The first step this plant had taken was a drastic one. Probably under the vivid impression that the Chrysler visit had left, they had decided not to reduce the work-in-process gradually, but abruptly. They simply didn't release anything unless it was needed for the very near future—draining the high work-in-process inventory that jammed the plant. Such an abrupt, drastic action should have left, for the initial two or three weeks, most workers without sufficient material to work on. I ask Jim how his actions were received by the workers on the floor. Jim chuckles and with a broad smile answers, "They thought we were going out of business."

The plant had succeeded to sustain extremely low levels— approximately 3 1/2 days on the floor since then.

I knew that this would not be a lasting problem because after three weeks, as

— 22 —

the existing work-in-process inventories were drained, more and more work would be released to the floor. Workers would regain their confidence in the future of the plant and at this stage, even a somewhat artificial explanation would be sufficient to reduce fear. I also knew that this drastic action should have a major impact on improving delivery performance, leading to a less chaotic mode of expediting orders. This would of course be very noticeable to the workers and, coupled with the visual impact of work-in-process evaporating from the floor, would create the proper atmosphere to gain the support of the shop floor workers.

Jim, of course, was concentrating more on his management efforts and continued, "The deep understanding that all the superintendents had—they all had read *The Goal* and had thoroughly enjoyed it—and the conscious effort by management to explain the reasons for their actions not only restored the workers confidence but gained their active support as evident by the drop in worker absenteeism."

No wonder that the drop in work-in-process was not just a short term drop. The plant had succeeded to sustain extremely low levels—approximately 3½ days on the floor—since then. We discussed the drop in absenteeism. Jim said that the work-in-process is so low that a worker who does not show up for even one day causes a severe disruption. The workers now feel that they are needed and that's why the absenteeism rate has dropped.

Hearing such an explanation causes all the alarm bells to go off in my head. If the plant would have instituted the proper mechanism of Drum-Buffer-Rope*, a worker's absence of one day would have caused much less of a disruption than previously, even though more noticeable. I'm looking at Bob and I see a dark cloud go over his smiling face. He probably noticed the same thing. If Jim thinks that currently a no show for one day is much more disruptive than before it means that he probably implemented the drum and the rope but didn't put the buffer mechanism in place. If this is the case the only way that

---

*A detailed description of Drum-Buffer-Rope can be found in *The Race*. (Goldratt; Fox).

the plant made any additional progress, after the first few weeks, was through an across-the-board assault on all perturbations in the plant—a very exhaustive drain on management, even if the plant is successful.

Bob and I are bothered because we know that if this is how Jim achieved his improvements, then the relatively small incremental improvements in the last year are now understandable and the success is very fragile and depends on the existence of a few persistent, strong people at the top of the pyramid. We are both now looking closely at Jim and are hesitant to ask the next obvious questions, but we must verify to what degree the local process improvements are diffused rather than focused. I start by asking Jim about the plant's efforts in preventive maintenance. Jim rushes to answer my question with confidence. Here's another area where he is proud of the plant's progress. He tells us that preventive maintenance really becomes a key area now. Since work-in-process was so low they couldn't afford any malfunction of machines and thus embarked on an aggressive program of preventive maintenance. He states that over 90% of the machines are now under the preventive maintenance program. "Things have improved substantially and, even though it's not easy, we can live with this low level of inventory."

I glance at Bob and we nod to each other. Yes, as far as the preventive maintenance program is concerned, the plant has probably unnecessarily put itself into a hazardous and fragile situation. Now I'm sure that this plant hasn't implemented buffer management. Having 90% of the machines under preventive maintenance translates, in our minds, to lack of focus. If you concentrate on everything, you haven't concentrated on anything. Certainly the buffer management technique that highlights the very few problems in the plant

If you concentrate on everything, you haven't concentrated on anything.

that must be regulated and improved is not implemented here. But maybe we are wrong. Maybe Jim has implemented the technique in a very early stage—after the inventory had been drained—and moved so aggressively that by now he has covered 90% of the machines as they appeared in their turn at the top of the list. The probability that this has happened is very low since the plant's gain in performance since last October certainly does not support such a hypothesis. The gain should have been at least tripled.

At this stage, Bob and I are not smiling anymore. Jim looks at us a little bit puzzled and probably in order to regain the positive atmosphere—the sense of enjoyment that we have radiated because of his achievements—he plunges full speed into describing their efforts in improving quality and reduction of setups. Once again, the same shotgun approach is revealed. Jim states that they are now the internal showcase for Modine for preventive maintenance, setup reduction and statistical process control. Many other plants within the corporation send their people to his plant to see how these efforts are conducted. It certainly is a source of major pride with Jim. I decide not to dig further at this stage, especially when now the situation is quite clear, since Jim ends his comments by stating that these efforts are the most difficult part of the implementation and any further reduction in work-in-process is dependent on continued success in this broad and exhausting effort. Despite the effort Jim feels they have been well worth it. As evidence Jim cites a serious battle they are having with the State of Illinois because of a pollution problem inherent in one of their processes. It seems that because of the plant's improved performance corporate has decided to do battle with the state agencies rather than transfer the production to another plant, causing the McHenry operation to be closed.

It's very hard to tell a person that much of this mammoth effort was unnecessary and moreover, that this exhausting year could have been relaxing and inspiring by dealing with no more than two or three problems at a time and enjoying seeing each time physical, concrete evidence of improvement. At this stage we're quite sure that Jim did not implement buffer management at all. Otherwise he would have mentioned it when describing his efforts in local improvements. I see that Bob still hopes to find the opposite, as he asks Jim, "What is the size of the plant's time buffers?" Jim does not really understand the question and answers that his buffers are about ½ to 1 hour. After a few more questions its totally obvious. Jim, probably affected by what he's heard about KANBAN, has spread the inventory throughout the plant rather than concentrating it to protect the constraints.

I am silent for awhile, bothered by another puzzle. Jim has repeatedly mentioned the achievement of 3½ days of work-in-process on the floor. Is it possible that Jim doesn't know that after a significant reduction of lead time, a plant should capitalize on it through an increase in sales. When sales increase lead time and thus work-in-process should be increased in order to maintain the same level of protection against disturbances. If the plant is so proud of its achievement—3½ days—they're certainly not going to increase it deliberately. The only way that I can understand maintaining a constant 3½ day work-in-process is if the increase in sales didn't yet absorb all the excess capacity uncovered by instituting the rope and the process improvements. But this is a remote possibility since if the proper actions are taken, the excess capacity is absorbed within a few months. Any increase in sales then eats into the protective capacity which translates into the need to increase lead time or slip rapidly back into the expediting mode throughout the plant. But Jim's plant is already a year and a half into this process—something does not match.

On a daily basis his delivery performance is over 95% he informs us.

Bob has just finished verifying that Jim's plant just implemented the drum and the rope so I signal to Bob that I would like to continue the questioning and ask Jim about the plant's situation regarding available capacity. Jim answers with delight since even in this area the plant has made impressive progress. "We don't have any bottlenecks right now. Initially we had a tremendous bottleneck in one of our first operations, which was our press room. A huge bottleneck, always working overtime and never having the parts when we needed them. It was almost a classical comparison to *The Goal*. We started to reduce batch sizes and we found that we had machine capacity coming out of our ears. We were so busy running parts that we didn't need, that we never had time for the ones that we did need. So we cut our batch size in the press room."

"We used to produce 40 days of demand. Now, while our material people do release a whole month's worth of work, the superintendent, and really the plant supervisor of the press room who is also the supervisor of the assembly area, actually release to the floor much smaller lots. The setups were three to four hours long. We reduced them to about 20 minutes, still far from the 15 seconds of the Japanese quick die change. But on all our big volume products the supervisors are releasing only daily batches and for the very low volumes—remember we have products that range in demand from hundreds per day to a few per month—they release in weekly batches. Overall I would say today we don't have any real bottlenecks in the plant."

I store in my mind the inconsistency between the formal release done by the material people and the actual release done by the production people and decide to continue on to sort out the puzzle. The first step is established, capacity is not viewed as a problem. Still there's the question of whether there is enough protective capacity. If there isn't the plant would be in a tremendous expediting mode—which is clearly not the case here—or it would be totally unreliable in its deliveries to customers. So naturally my next question to Jim is about the plant's delivery performance. Jim is now really on

"Margins based on what?" I say with a sharp tone.

a high. For most of his products the plant is now on daily deliveries and he doesn't find any difficulty in coping with them. On a daily basis his delivery performance is over 95% he informs us.

Then with a big smile he bends and picks up a quite complicated looking radiator and asks, "Who is the most demanding automobile producer today?" Hating to be on the questioning side I fidget in my chair and answer—"The Japanese." Jim nods his head and says, "This is a product we are beginning to deliver in large quantities to Honda."

Victory is written all over his face. I don't dare to mention Chrysler since I don't want any diversion in the conversation. The plant certainly has enough protective capacity if it can sustain such a high level of delivery performance on a daily basis and without too much management effort on the floor. How can they support large increases in sales without oscillating the lead time? Maybe the plant increased machine and worker capacity during the last year, but Jim denies it. I don't believe in miracles and thus there must be a flaw somewhere in my logic. I decide to go over each component of the equation separately with Jim.

"How much did you increase sales last year" I ask. "Just a small increase," he answers. Ok, there it is! I was so sure that the plant has capitalized on its new found potential to increase sales that I took it for granted. I'm a little bit angry with myself and thus my irritation is probably noticeable when I press Jim too aggressively. "Why haven't you increased sales substantially!" Jim reacts as if I don't understand his markets and answers that his markets are very price sensitive and competitive, as if explaining the basic economics. To support it he tells us about a case where they reduced the price by a few dollars, cutting their margin to zero in order not to lose a major client. With continued improvement they succeeded in both regaining their previous margin and giving the client another $1 reduction in price.

"Margins based on what?" I say with a sharp tone. Jim, with the expression of a man who has just put his hand in the fire replies, "Conventional cost Eli, conventional costing." Now, it's apparent! Because of conventional ways of estimating margins the plant has not been able to use its new potential to substantially increase its bottom line performance. I decide to lay it on Jim. "How much excess capacity do you have," I ask. "It's very hard to answer", he replies. "Would you say 20%, even on your most heavily loaded resources?" "Might be," Jim responds. "To what extent is your market sensitive to price?" I probe. I see he has difficulty in answering so I say, "What if you drop your price by 20%?" "I can easily double my sales," Jim answers with the expression of someone who talks about an improbable scenario. I'm waiting for Jim to jump to the obvious conclusion, but he doesn't.

This plant is producing to a very segmented market. There is no problem to drop the price on a new bid without affecting the other products' prices even to the same customer. The plant has excess capacity everywhere and thus any additional sales would not require any significant increase in operating expense —the only additional expense would be the energy cost at the ovens. The raw material cost is about 50% of the current selling price. Any increase in sales, even if achieved by a drastic 20% drop in price, will generate significant net profits, since almost the entire difference between the selling price and the raw material cost will fall directly to the bottom line. Nevertheless, even after all my questions, it looks to us that Jim is still unaware of this opportunity. In *The Goal* I made Alex Rogo capitalize on his potential by turning his vastly reduced lead time into sales. This was intended to be just an example of one of the many, many avenues of how a plant's newly uncovered potential can be turned into a bottom line increase. I continue to hint in that direction by asking Jim if marketing reports directly to him. His answer is exactly like in *The Goal*, marketing does not report to the plant but to corporate.

It looks as if what I succeeded to impart in *The Goal* is the explicit case described, not the thinking process itself. Jim is certainly very bright, able and a doer. Nevertheless he hasn't developed the appropriate procedure to capitalize on his opportunity. "Can you affect sales if you suggest a drop in price and convince corporate that it is a profitable proposition?" I ask.

"Yes", Jim replies but without any flickering of understanding of where I'm going. I turn, uneasy, in my chair. Bob, sensitive to what I am going through, but not like me also sensitive to the fact that Jim is not smiling anymore suggests a break. Modine has recently instituted a no-smoking policy and I excuse myself to go outside for a smoke. Jim is relieved since he probably thinks that my irritation is from the long hours without smoking—which is partially true.

I pace up and down the parking lot puffing on my cigar trying to summarize what I have found so far. Certainly lack of knowledge not only prevented this plant from capitalizing on its potential but also put the plant into a potentially hazardous situation. A significant increase in sales is probably unavoidable since customers must be already aware of the superior quality and response of this plant. An abrupt growth in sales—which is very typical in this type of bid environment—cannot be compensated by gradual increases in capacity but only by an abrupt, matched increase in the buffers. Thus the plant could unexpectedly be thrown into a downward spiral that could cause its workers, management and most importantly its customers to lose confidence.

Eventually the plant would have to increase lead time but by then the rope concept would be blamed and the plant will find itself in the same situation as they were before the "Chrysler visit," but without the courage to change the system itself once again. If knowledge is the only thing lacking, since this knowledge is available, I assume that it would be enough just to expose its existence and explain my Cassandra prediction. The plant should then be motivated enough to acquire the needed knowledge and put it to use before the situation goes out of control.

The real problem bothering me is that this plant is not unique. How to identify and warn the other plants that, due to *The Goal*, have placed themselves in exactly the same situation. I force myself to stop

> *Over there a mammoth new line is being built.*

thinking about these open questions and concentrate on the visit at hand. Something still bothers me. In *The Goal* I certainly emphasized strongly the importance of throughput. Can it be that Jim has concentrated so much on reduction of inventory that he didn't put enough emphasis to increase sales? I find it hard to believe and decide to put Jim through the "third degree" to find out what he has done in the last 1½ years to increase his market. Returning to the lobby, Bob points to the bulletin board and the *Success* magazine editorial that describes *The Goal* and mentions this plants achievements in implementing it. Jim returns with two pairs of safety glasses and leads us onto the production floor for a tour. The third degree will have to be postponed.

We are walking through a typical shop floor and Jim is explaining the production process. Right from the start it's apparent that this plant went through a huge change. All the areas designated for interim work-in-process storage are virtually empty or are filled with non-production items like picnic benches. The contrast with the pictures of the plant prior to 1986 that Jim showed us in his office are startling. The plant has gone from being totally full to quite empty. It doesn't take long to see that it is a very well laid out plant. Every Group Technology advocate would be delighted. Bob and I try to question some of the workers about the changes that occurred, but the noise is too loud for any meaningful conversation. We soon give up.

After 10 minutes it is obvious that the plant has spread the buffer rather than using inventory to protect the constraints. The plant is using effectively the rope concept—timing and controlling the actual release of material. The Just-In-Time control of inventory between operations does not add anything and in fact reduces the plants abililty to sustain disruptions. Since there aren't any internal constraints, the only buffer to be monitored and controlled should be located in front of the external constraint.

Marketing is the constraint of

I probably have opened another Pandora's box.

the plant and the buffer should be in finished goods. Nevertheless, we see many small buffers scattered and monitored throughout the production process. This not only verifies our previous prediction that just the drum and rope concepts have been implemented in this plant but also shows that the plant has additionally implemented the small buffers of KANBAN. We are not amazed to find only a small amount of finished goods inventory and that most of it was actually released to the floor five days before the needed shipping date. Judging from what we have already seen about the products and processes we know that if the Drum-Buffer-Rope procedure had been implemented we would have found over two days of finished goods and even less work-in-process on the floor.

Discussing the content of the small pile of finished goods immediately reveals that some of the customers have not taken advantage of the plant's capabilities to supply in very frequent deliveries. One of these clients is Modine's After-market Distribution operation. We exchange with Jim some comments about the distribution systems large inventories and the fact that corporate hasn't yet bridged between the new capabilities of his plant and the vastly reduced inventories they could now hold in the distribution warehouses without hurting customer service.

We don't see any new surprises on the floor and I suggest that we end the plant tour. "No", says Jim with a grin on his face and points to the corner of the plant. Over there a mammoth new line is being built. This line will produce a new family of products based on a new technology that among other advantages will eliminate environmental problems. Once completed it will account for a very significant portion of the plant's production.

Jim says that this line represents the new confidence of his corporation in the improved capabilities of his plant. It is a very large investment and certainly Jim had to fight quite hard until the decision was made to put it in his plant. In my heart I curse myself for jumping to hasty conclusions. Now I know that Jim did not concentrate only on reducing inventory but was also aggressively looking for more sales. He simply used the plant's remarkably improved capabilities to attract the new technology from his corporation. This would not only increase sales but will secure the future of the plant from the threat of being closed due to environmental problems. To expect Jim to develop the necessary procedure to increase his current product sales and at the same time to fight for new technology was maybe too much to expect from a person.

We return to the cafeteria rather than Jim's office since its lunch time and smoking is allowed in the cafeteria. Now I have the impression that the picture is complete. I don't see any inconsistencies. Relaxed and enjoying the cigar and coffee I allow myself to deviate from the original purpose of our visit to get some technical details about the construction of the new line. "Where have you decided to locate the bottleneck of the line?" I ask. The only answer I get from Jim is just a blank look. "Where did you decide to put Herbie?" Still no answer. Oh, oh! I probably have opened another Pandora's box. A few more questions and answers and its apparent that I have. Even though Jim completely understands that balancing capacity prevents balancing flow, the new line is built along the conventional rules of line balancing. All plant management is even mentally prepared for a long and tedious process to debug the line—to turn a balanced capacity line into a functioning, balanced flow line.

While Bob is using lunch time to explain how a line should be built along the rules of flow I try to clarify to myself why, once again, I feel uneasy. Let's summarize what actions I had hoped to find and didn't. First, I haven't found the buffer concept implemented—leading to over-exposure of the plant. Second, I haven't found buffer management—leading to unfocused efforts of process improvement. Third, I haven't found the needed actions that can bring greatly increased sales by exploiting the new capabilities of the plant. Fourth, I haven't found the attempts to build the line to

Since then they have continued to change, but only within the existing traditional framework of industrial systems.

support flow. Rather the line is being built to balance capacity, seemingly to save cost. None of these specific situations were explained explicitly in the *The Goal*, but some have been elaborated on in *The Race*.

I interrupt quite rudely Bob and Jim's conversation to ask Jim whether or not he has read *The Race*. Jim says yes and that he even enjoyed it but had not yet spread it to the rest of management. I can't understand it. Keep on thinking I tell myself, there must be a core reason. Is it once again this old and unlikable problem of inertia? My thoughts go into a loop. I don't know where to look for an answer since I can't precisely formulate the question. I notice that Bob and Jim are now talking about how Jim can dramatically increase the plant's sales just because the plant's market is very price sensitive. Probably Bob has seen on my face what my friends call the "autistic look" and he explains these important things to Jim to buy me some uninterrupted thinking time.

Now I feel obliged not to let go and force myself to continue my attempts to clarify the core problem. I try to attack it from another angle. Maybe this plant management is so proud and happy with their achievements that they don't want to allow anything to alter it? Maybe the attitude of "don't rock the boat" has taken hold of this plant? From what I have heard from Jim it doesn't look like it, but once again I feel I must check it. Again I interrupt Bob and Jim's conversation. "Jim, try to answer this question very honestly. Are you really open for more changes in this plant?" Jim answers proudly, radiating sincerity and total honesty, "Eli, it's not only that I am determined to continue to improve the plant, I do believe that all my top people are determined to the same degree."

Now I'm lost. The only possible explanation that I can find is that Jim is mistaken in his evaluation of his peoples' readiness to change. It's a very remote possibility but I don't see any other avenue. I ask Jim to assemble the same people that participated in the decision to drain the plant after the Chrysler meeting. The "we" that Jim periodically refers to when he talks about plant management.

It turns out that they are all out in the plant and Jim steps to the phone to call Les Johnson, the Plant Superintendent, Joe Petrie, the Manager of Manufacturing Engineering, and Robert Schneider, the Production Control Manager. I know that my hypothesis has a very slim chance of being right and since I don't want the conversation with the plant management to be just be a social, polite one I go back to try to find a more plausible hypothesis. Bob and Jim continue their conversation. I ask myself what are the activities that the management of this plant have occupied themselves with since last October. Certainly they have made a tremendous effort in preventive maintenance, set-up reduction, statistical process control, and in persuading corporate to chose their location as a site for the new technology. It is this new line that they are all now immersed and involved in—testing and modifying the various sections of the line. Despite this impressive effort by a small staff, I sense stagnation. I'm looking for a common denominator of all these activities to contrast with the abrupt change they made in early '86. Once I formulate it in this way, the answer becomes obvious.

In early '86 this plant instituted a change to the system itself. Since then they have been totally immersed in changing within the system. I search my mind to see whether, except for that special event following the Chrysler visit, they ever changed the system itself and I can't find any. This significant emotional event in one's life as Jim described the Chrysler visit was sufficient to provoke this plant management to change the system once. Since then they have continued to change, but only within the existing traditional framework of industrial systems. If this hypothesis is right then what I wrote in the epilogue has become a reality.

This plant has instituted improvements, but not a process of ongoing improvement. How to check it? The first thing of course is to find out if all plant management really feel the basic difference between changing the system itself or changing within the system. I decide not to use these terms in my future questioning but rather to try to find if the plant management see their efforts to change as a continuing process or whether they distinguish a sharp break in their efforts in early '86. If this hypothesis is verified I still have to inquire what will cause them to take the next step to change the system. Is it just lack of knowledge of the huge leverage of such a change and how to do it or is it a psychological barrier? When Jim's management group arrives, I'm ready.

After the handshakes Jim explains to his people the purpose of our visit and I start my line of questioning. First I want to check to see if they verify Jim's opinion that the plant is eager to change. Only then will I try to focus the questions to find out what they really mean by the word change. I begin by asking, "According to what Jim has explained to me there is now here an openness to accept change. You are not satisfied with where you are and want to continue to improve. Is it true in all levels of your plant?" "Pretty much! Different levels adapt quicker than others," Jim answers. I want to hear Jim's peoples' reaction so I rephrase the question. "What would you say— change becomes here the exception or the norm?" I ask by looking at Joe Petrie, the Chief Engineer. "I'd say it's more norm than exception," he answers quite confidently. "We're changing all the time," Robert Schneider, a Production Control Manager, adds with a broad smile.

No surprises so far, so I decide to press a little bit more. "What is today the reaction? 'Oh, oh another change, or good, let's continue to improve and improve.'" A little bit of both they all admit. I decide that the time has come to highlight the experience that they had in another form of change. "Jim told me that he can almost pinpoint when the attitude towards change has been drastically improved," I lie. "He says that three events happened about the same time. One was that *The Goal* was read by all of you. Then the "Chrysler" punch in the nose and then it was your decision to try *The Goal* ideas and they did work. What's your opinion about his description?"

After the pause Joe summarizes my question. "Do you mean when did change become more acceptable as a rule than as an exception?" I nod and he continues. "I think that we started the process earlier and that there was much more resistance at that time than now." He seems to confuse between changes within the system. and changing the system itself, probably because it doesn't represent his main job. So I immediately push forward. "But would you say that the attitude changed gradually or at that time it changed more like a step function?" A very long silence follows—everyone was thinking. At last Joe answers very slowly. "I think that it was more gradual." Everybody continues to think.

Interestingly, they probably feel that both descriptions of change are right at the same time and it bothers them. Yes, there was always the pressure and action to change. Productivity improvements did not start in just early '86, they are as old as the plant itself. Preventive maintenance was not invented in this decade even though the pressure today is much greater for it. The national emphasis to improve quality as a prime target is probably three or four years old already. Nevertheless something more significant as far as change is concerned happened in early '86. They all feel it, but since it was never verbalized they have trouble articulating it. How should I continue? The temptation to explain it at this stage is large, but unless they can be provoked to deduce and verbalize it themselves, such an explanation would be totally useless.

I notice that the only one who is not troubled is Robert. That surprises me since the change of the system in '86 occurred through a drastic change in the method of material release. Robert should have been a major figure in this effort and thus he should be very sensitive to the different type of change that occurred in early '86. It doesn't take more than a few seconds to combine this puzzle with another open question that I still have—the difference between the formal release of material (two weeks before the order and in batches of two-four weeks) and the actual release by the

An improvement, but not enough to expose the idle time inherent in almost any plant

production people (five days before the order and mostly in daily batches). Probably due to computer limitations that are controlled by corporate and not in the plant, Robert is actually not at the heart of this change. The full load of timing the release is on the production people themselves. Maybe here is the way. If I can cause Robert to claim that the process of change was always in the plant, maybe the others will succeed to verbalize the difference between change within the system or changing the system itself.

I bring the tape recorder closer to Robert and leaning forward I ask in a demanding voice, "What is your opinion?" With a matching tone he answers, "We were always changing. I myself started to cut the lead time when I first came to the plant." Interesting. Maybe I've misjudged the situation, but the current procedure indicates the opposite, so I ask, "What was the reaction of other departments to your changes?" "No reaction at all," comes the reply. "The changes were procedural changes internal to my own department." Interesting to think that changes in material release procedures are considered to be just internal to the material people and that they do not have any effect on the production departments.

Robert continues, "When I came here we were releasing material for a month in the future. I cut it to three weeks and then to two weeks." "Do you tell me that previously when ten people in a department didn't have work that there wasn't pressure on you to release more work?" "No," comes the answer. Jim and Les Johnson, the Plant Superintendent, plunge into the conversation and start to talk at the same time protesting that previously (before '86) the release was in such big quantities that the problem of insufficient work never arose (Jim would certainly know since his prior job was as a Plant Superintendent).

Here I make a huge mistake. I didn't continue with the Socratic method

I'm afraid that the orderly conversation we've had so far is starting to get out of hand, so I ask to clarify the time table of these changes. It turns out that when Robert came to the plant, the convention was to release four weeks ahead of the order and in batches that covered two-four months. Around '84—no one remembers exactly—the release was cut by the material people to three weeks ahead of time and was associated with a slight reduction in batch sizes. An improvement, but not enough to expose the idle time inherent in almost any plant and consequently the system didn't really change. In '86 came the drastic change which exposed the idle time of the plant. It wasn't easy to establish these facts—it took almost half an hour—but now Les and Jim are outdoing each other in describing the huge impact and difference in attitude that this last step had on the floor. Stories are now surfacing like having to put a lock on the material warehouse in order to prevent the "stealing" of material to keep workers busy.

Still a little bit confused that a two step process can be described as a continuous one, I'm asking whether the change in early '86 was the last one. "Yes" comes the answer and Jim with a broad smile says, "Why? That's the next question?" Everybody laughs. Jim tries to show what can be done next, basing his approach on what Bob explained to him during the lunch break and then asks us to verify whether or not he understood it correctly.

Here I make a huge mistake. I didn't continue with the Socratic method that will enable the management of this plant to reach the really important conclusion that they have changed the system only once and that they are now in '87 in the same situation as they were prior to '86. The same situation from the point of view of the attitude toward change and that they haven't implemented at all a process of ongoing improvement focused on the constraints. Rather than proceeding in this direction, we plunge for the next two hours into an explanation of how they can dramatically improve their plant. The Aristotelian method of giving the answer and the reasoning behind the answer is as effective as ever—which means not effective at all. Except for irritating the plant management it doesn't achieve anything. The last two hours could have been devoted to provoke management to deduce the next improvement steps in the system itself instead has been wasted while putting the management in a defensive position. I kick myself for this error and vow, once again, not to repeat it.

Nevertheless we depart as good friends. In the car heading to the airport I'm trying to summarize with Bob what we learned. It looks like there are two major problems that prevent the plant from moving along a process of ongoing improvement. One is certainly lack of information, but the second one, which is probably an even larger obstacle—because it prevents the plant from seeking that information—is the attitude toward change. In the McHenry Plant a drastic external shock caused the plant management to change the system itself. The positive results that stemmed from this single, one-time action were enough to improve them to the extent that the external pressure disappeared. It looks as if the plant is not ready to change the system again in spite of the hazards facing it if it won't do so. In this sense it certainly is in a stagnation mode today and if the market picks up rapidly it could fall very quickly into the deterioration mode.

The external blow was enough to open the gate for a system change. Was this single change and the positive results that followed enough to slam the gates from further system changes? Will they open again without another punch in the nose? We examine carefully whether or not the "internal Jonah"™ program which we recently launched, will answer both concerns. As much as we can determine it looks like a good and sufficient answer, but we're not absolutely confident since there isn't enough experience yet.

Lost in our thoughts we continue on to O'Hare. When we reach the airport it turns out that a Flying Tiger 747 had a fire on takeoff and has been blocking one of the runways since early in the day. O'Hare is more a zoo than usual.

™ Internal Jonah is a trademark of the Avraham Y. Goldratt Institute.

MODINE MANUFACTURING COMPANY • RINGWOOD ROAD, P O BOX 458, MC HENRY, ILLINOIS 60050 • PHONE 815/653 2841

September 22, 1987

Mr. Robert Fox
Avraham Y. Goldratt Institute
57 Trumbull Street
New Haven, Ct. 06510

Dear Bob:

I just finished reading Eli's story about his visit to our plant on August 21, 1987. I have nothing to edit, but would like to make a few comments.

While it is obvious that Eli was disappointed with what he experienced at our plant, he makes no mention of the fact that we expressed the same disappointment. We know full well that our efforts toward further improvement in our existing production area have been stagnant, because of our plants' concentrated efforts in bringing a new multimillion dollar production process on line. We expressed our concerns regarding the difficulty for a small plant with limited resources to introduce three new product lines utilizing new heat transfer technology within one years time. While I feel the facts in your article are accurate, they give the impression that we spent the last year sitting on our asses doing nothing. I feel this is an unfair representation of our plant and the people who work here.

Maybe you and Eli were somewhat taken aback because our efforts had been focused on other issues over the past year other than on continued improvement in our existing Alfuse production area. If you were, I apologize, but remind you that it is my job to focus this plants' efforts on the areas I feel are important to our future. In our case, particularly due to our environmental situation, I opted to focus on our new process.

In summary, I feel you focused on a very narrow area of what is occurring at our plant and painted a rather unpleasant picture with predictions of upcoming disaster. We on the otherhand are trying our best to keep our arms around a much larger more complex entity which I feel will secure the future of our plant.

All of us here greatly enjoyed your visit and appreciate the time you spent with us.

Sincerely,

James R. Rulseh
Plant Manager

MODINE

MODINE MANUFACTURING COMPANY • RINGWOOD ROAD, P O BOX 462, MC HENRY, ILLINOIS 60050 • PHONE: 815/653-3841

October 4, 1986

Dr. E. Goldratt
Creative Output, Inc.
60 Commerce Park
Millford, Ct. 06460

Dear Dr. Goldratt:

It has been some time, but I wanted to take a few moments to thank you for the stimulating presentation you gave to Modine Manufacturing Company management in Racine, Wisconsin during late July of this year. Your presentation, plus your dinner conversation the evening before, reinforced my belief that your ideas are critical to our future.

After reading THE GOAL in late 1985, and implementing many of the concepts, all of us at the McHenry, Illinois plant of Modine Manufacturing Company believe we are on the track to a better future. Outlined below is what the last year has brought us.

Work in process inventory has fallen by nearly 70% overall. Accordingly, our average manufacturing lead time from raw material to packaging (shipment), of our heat exchangers has dropped from 12.7 days to 3.0 days. Many products are started and finished within a two shift period. This allows us to react to short term customer schedule changes with minimal "heroics".

Batch sizes for 80% of our heat exchangers have been reduced from one week's quantity, or more, down to one day's quantity. Batch sizes of press made parts have dropped by 38% and will be reduced by another 40% very soon.

During our dinner conversation in July to you told me to check our absenteeism figures for the plant. You felt, by reducing work in process inventory we will notice a 10% drop in absenteeism. Well, on this point I am happy to say you were mistaken. For the past six month period, our absenteeism has dropped by over 20% over any other six month period. Our current absenteeism rate is the lowest level in our plant's 25 year history.

Total inventory turns have increased from 7.5 to 9.2 over the last twelve months. While we know this is not overly impressive, we are taking steps to reduce our raw material inventory with improvements to our MRP system.

This past year has been a real awakening for us as we shed ourselves of many old "givens" and "policies".

While I am doubtful that this plant will be exposed to the entire OPT system, the use of your teachings will continue to benefit us now and in the future.

Thank you (and Alex), for the inspiration.

Trying to stay in The Race,

James R Rulseh

James R. Rulseh
Plant Manager
Modine Mfg. Co.
McHenry, Illinois

Chapter 2

LAYING THE FOUNDATION

1. Stating Precisely a Problem

How do we effectively manage an organization? We used to call a very difficult and important question a sixty-four thousand dollar one. This description for our problem is a gross understatement—even by British standards. In the previous chapter, we elaborated on the magnitude of this problem. We even discouraged ourselves by exposing three major obstacles to an effective solution. It looks like all this was done by following the explicit phrase which promises: "state precisely a problem and you are half-way toward solving it."

At this stage it doesn't look as though we are half-way to anywhere. Still, lets not dismiss such a likable phrase so lightly. Too many times we have all experienced its validity—even though in most cases only in hindsight. "State precisely a problem. . ." what does it mean? In our case, what can be more precise than stating how do we effectively manage an organization? If we feel that this statement is too concise to clarify the problem, then certainly this sense doesn't apply to the previous lengthy chapter. It looks as if we have beaten this statement to death and still have no clear idea of where to find a solution.

> *It should be emphasized that this "optima" is really nothing but another name for "tolerable compromise."*

This situation is very common and probably stems from the lack of a detailed procedure for presenting a problem. State precisely a problem..., in my vocabulary translates to the absolute need for presenting the problem as a conflict between at least two requirements. A general presentation should state that we would like to accomplish some objective, which we will denote by the letter A. In order to accomplish it, we find out that at least two requirements, B and C must be filled. Assume that we logically derive the fact that in order to fulfill B we must have D (or we must have more of D), but in order to fulfill C we must not have D (or we must have less of D). We have a conflict.

In schematic form it looks like this:

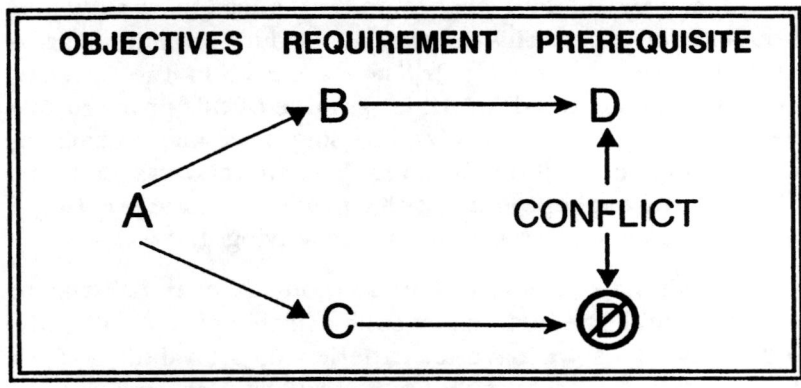

Let's try to formulate our problem using this nomenclature. The objective A might be something like "better performance of the entire organization." Organizations employing more than a few dozen people would certainly conclude that one of the requirements would be to "have a large span of control," which we'll denote by B. From B we can logically derive—as we have done in the previous article—the need to "extensively use a pyramid structure," which we will denote by D. In order to achieve A, the organization needs "to operate without internal distortion"—requirement C. However in order to fulfill requirement C we have logically concluded—after quite a long and careful debate—the need to "suppress the use of the pyramid structure," which is the opposite of D.

In a schematic form it will look like this:

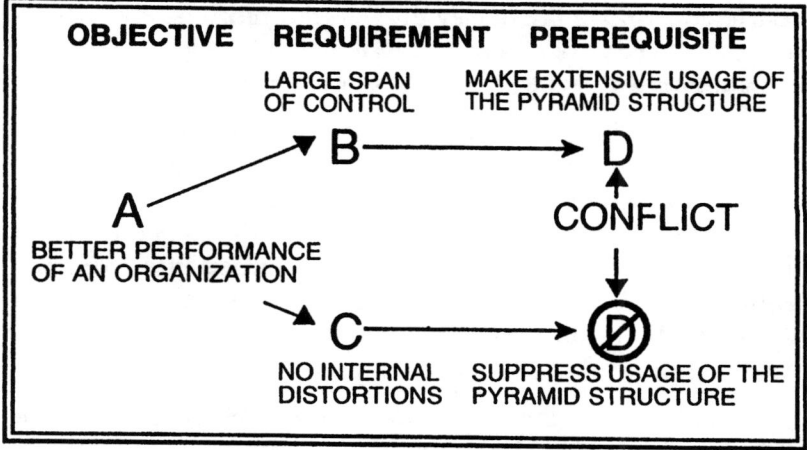

2. First and Second Degree Solutions

When confronted with this type of dilemma, the usual tendency is to reduce the conflict by relaxing the requirements. The endless shifting of most large organizations between centralization and de-centralization; more or less autonomy for the various operating levels; continually adding and trimming of personnel; instituting, changing and cancelling dotted line reporting; all are attempts to find a tolerable compromise between the requirements that cause our conflict. The search for an "optimum" solution is a constant on-going one. It should be emphasized that this "optimum" is really nothing but another name for "tolerable compromise." We give a little bit of B, we give a little bit of C and we search for the proper amounts that we should give of each so that the damage to A is minimal. If we try to present even day-to-day problems, such as buying a new house or dealing with a rebellious teenager, in this way we find ourselves searching almost immediately for an acceptable compromise between the requirements.

What should be very clear is that if the requirements are real, any relaxation in them, by definition, reduces our ability to satisfy the objective. Confronting an existing problem in this way makes us realize that our ability to reach the objective is more restricted than we previously perceived. Unfortunately, most of us are in the habit of accepting this line of thinking as a given and are satisfied with achieving some tolerable compromise.

A very different and much more promising avenue is opened up when we realize that there is at least one underlying assumption behind each of the arrows in our diagram. These assumptions, which we accept too often as "facts of life," are in many cases either erroneous or can be turned into irrelevant assumptions for our particular case. If an assumption can be shown to be invalid, its corresponding arrow will no longer exist.

Let's clarify this with an example. Suppose that the objective A is to "reach the top of Mt. Everest." Requirement B appears in our diagram as: "participants must be expert mountain climbers." It looks logical, but the connection between A and B is based on the unstated assumption, that we intend to reach the top of Mt. Everest by climbing it. Since the objective is not to climb Mt. Everest but to reach its top, we can easily challenge this assumption. If, for example, we decide that it is feasible to reach the top by using a helicopter, then the arrow connecting the objective to the expert climber requirement no longer exists. Eliminate even one arrow (it does not matter which one) from our diagram and the conflict simply vanishes. The problem is not just solved, it evaporates. Whenever we are successful in addressing the problem in this way, the objective is not compromised at all. In most cases eliminating an arrow leads us to a new perception of the situation. This new perception significantly increases our ability to satisfy the objective over and above what we previously perceived possible. We call such solutions "second degree solutions."[1] All technical and scientific breakthroughs belong to this family of solutions. But these breakthroughs are sporadic and all too rare. Our challenge is to make them routine and commonplace. How can we systematically find such solutions?

> *"the objectives of local areas are in conflict with the objective of the global organization."*

Surprisingly it's not too difficult. What is really required is to refuse to take the seemingly easy way out and compromise between the requirements. A better way is to try and verbalize the assumption underlying each of the arrows in the diagram. In order to force these assumptions to the surface, we must make extensive use of the question WHY. We must ask WHY with the innocence of a small child, otherwise the most "vulnerable" assumptions, those that we unquestioningly accept as facts of life, will not surface. Once the assumptions are verbalized, we must not hesitate to challenge them.

Since we are going to use this technique extensively throughout this book, let's give it a name. I call it (jokingly) "The Theorem of Evaporating Clouds."[2] The theorem states that "for any problem a second degree solution exists." This totally unsubstantiated theorem provides the missing link in the process. The first step in the process of finding second degree solutions is annoying and not as simple as might be thought—to present the problem in the diagram format. The second step, of exposing and verbalizing the assumptions behind the various arrows, (remember there are five arrows in the smallest diagram) is sometimes more demanding. The third step is the most

---

[1] This phrase is taken from a remarkable book entitled "Change" written by Paul Watzlawick, Ph.D., John Weakland, Ch.E. and Richard Risch, MD.
[2] This phrase has been taken from "Illusions" written by Richard Bach (the author of "Jonathan Livingston Seagull"). I've just assumed that a problem can be lyrically referred to as a cloud.

difficult one—to challenge the assumptions to the point that one of them is exposed as invalid. At this difficult stage faith in our theorem provides the necessary determination to continue our effort—to not give up and revert to compromising the requirements.

3 Just a Motto or a Warning?

In the preceding chapter the underlying assumptions of the arrows connecting the requirements to the conflicting prerequisites were discussed at length. The requirement to "have a large span of control" leads to the prerequisite of "extensive use of the pyramid structure" only if we accept the assumption that the direct span of control of an individual is limited to a relatively small number of people. Thus to achieve a large span of control a repetition of this basic unit is needed, leading directly to the need for a hierarchical pyramid. This assumption can be challenged but, due to its widespread usage, any solution that will emerge from this avenue (even if it is successful) will require such a drastic reorganization that our solution, for most organizations, will probably be impractical to use in the near future. Thus the conclusion we reached was "...the most promising ways to look for improvements are within the framework of a hierarchical pyramid and not outside it." Thus we made a conscious decision to focus our challenge on another arrow in our diagram.

The second requirement is to build the organization in such a way that internal distortions do not occur. We discovered that the pyramid structure generates internal distortions, causing us to conclude that its usage should be suppressed. Once again our deduction is based on a seemingly acceptable assumption. The assumption is that intermediate management levels will distort evaluations and interpretations because of their local rather than global points of view. The essence of this assumption can be verbalized as "the total of local optima is not the optimum of the total." I have used this phrase as the motto of my theory for years and found that everybody agrees whole-heartedly with its inherent truths. Nevertheless this is the assumption that I would like us now to challenge. We are not questioning if this phrase is valid for our current organizations—which is certainly the case. The real question is—should it be valid? Is it possible to institute changes in our organization that would cause this assumption to be false?

What we need to do is to examine the assumption more closely. "The total of local optima. . ." optima has a meaning only in respect to some objectives that we are trying to maximize (or minimize). In other words, our assumption has a meaning only if we assume the existence of some local unspoken objectives. ". . .is not the optimum of the total," another optimum, this time the optimum of the total organization. This means that we assume another unspoken objective—the objective of the global organization. Now we are at a stage where we can rewrite our assumption using slightly different words. Our assumption simply states: "the objectives of local areas are in conflict with the objective of the global organization." If we accept this statement as a given we accept an inherent conflict. If we view it as a warning, it suggests that we should reformulate the objectives of the local areas. The conflict exists because we a-priori assume that it exists—a self-fulfilling prophecy.

To get out of this trap we can replace this assumption with a guideline that does not state the existing (unsatisfactory) situation, but the essence of the improved situation that we are seeking. "The objective of a local area is to contribute positively to the objective of the entire organization." Now it is obvious what should be done next. We have to first determine the objective of the entire organization. We have to define its goal. Once this is done we have to clarify what is really meant by "contribute positively." In doing so we will have to define measurements and formulate rules for local areas. But before we immerse ourselves in this tremendous task, let's take a detour just to ease our minds about another concern.

4. Can We Now Deal With the Information Problem?

We now demand that a local area conduct its activities in a way that "contributes positively" to the good of the organization. It seems that such a demand is likely to be met only if the management of a local area has extensive knowledge and understanding of all the other areas. Is it possible to ensure that each area will have current knowledge and understanding of all other areas? This requirement is truly frightening. It borders on the underlying reasons for the limited span of control of an individual. Can it be that we have managed to disqualify one requirement just to find ourselves in the grip of another one? Before we go too far, we should remember that the knowledge one area needs about other areas is only the knowledge necessary to conduct its local actions so that they will "contribute positively" to the overall goal. If this information is quite limited and easy to obtain we might have solved our problem. How can we determine this before we clarify what is meant by "contribute positively"?

The last two sentences that we used to specify our problem have manifested our fear of the information problem. We don't want to spend a lot of time and effort constructing measurements and rules just to find ourselves at the end, stuck with a seemingly well constructed solution that cannot be put into practice due to the information problem. We can accept the fact that the management of one area does not need to know all the detailed information about other areas in order to effectively manage their own territory. However, in order to avoid traditional local optimas, they must know quite a bit about other areas. The information obstacle we keep running up against looks real and we can't continue to put it off merely by saying that we are going to deal with it later. So let's examine what information is absolutely necessary for a local manager to make a local decision that will be compatible with the global picture. It doesn't take long to recognize that information of this type exists. The information concerning the organization's limitations is what is vital to local managers. Otherwise they might innocently violate a global limitation when executing a local decision. Such an occurrence will certainly cause a local manager to do

Certainly the first step is to precisely define the term "constraint," otherwise everything will creep into that category.

the opposite of "contributing positively" to the objective of the entire organization.

We can conclude that it is vital that information about the organization's limitations be distributed to all management levels of the pyramid. To generalize this conclusion we might include under the organization's limitations, all the organization's constraints. It's perceived that we have plenty of constraints and, moreover, most managers are under the impression that the constraints are changing rapidly. One plant manager told me that he feels as though he is in a swimming pool filled with ping-pong balls and is trying to keep all of them under water at the same time.

If it is true that we need to spread information about the organization's current constraints to all managers; and if it is true that most organizations contain many constraints; and if it is true that these constraints are changing rapidly; then we are in a real jam. Let's approach this problem systematically. Certainly the first step is to precisely define the term "constraint," otherwise everything will creep into that category. Let me suggest a broad definition: "a system's constraint is anything that limits the system from achieving higher performance versus its goal." This looks general enough, but a more thorough review of the definition reveals that it suffers from a typical problem. This definition uses terms that we have not yet defined.

It appears that "system" is the first new word we must define, but this is not the case. In this context it is used as a

> *"The goal of Western industrial and service organizations is to make more money now as well as in the future."*

synonym for the word organization. I chose this particular word since I suspect that the Theory of Constraints is general enough to encompass not just organizations but is probably also valid for systems that are not organizations. The two terms in the definition of a constraint that bother me are the word "goal" and the words "higher performance." Before we can use the word "constraint" we must define the goal of the system. Moreover the term "higher performance" indicates that we are assuming that measurements are already defined, otherwise we cannot talk in terms of higher or lower performance.

Once again, we reach the stage where any further logical discussion cannot occur unless we define the goal and the measurements. They are the foundation of any systematic approach to our problem. I suspect that any attempt to run away by starting from another angle, as we just did, will after a few steps, bring us back to this same point. To ease the minds of anxious readers on two issues that were just raised, the next chapter will be devoted to proving that any system can contain only a very limited number of constraints, and in one of the following chapters I will show that a system's constraints change very infrequently.

5 Determining the Goal

In determining the goal of the organization the first question to ask is not what should the goal be, but who is entitled to determine the goal. Viewed from this perspective it is quite obvious that the people that should have the power to determine the goal of an organization are the owners of that organization. For Western industrial and service companies, the owners are the shareholders. While the owners are entitled to determine the organization's goal, anybody who has the power to ruin or severely damage the organization should have "influence" in the determination of the goal. Otherwise the organization may cease to exist or its performance versus its goal will be severely degraded. Thus the goal should be at least tolerable to any powerful group (powerful in the above sense) and it might be necessary to impose some limitations on the goal that the owners establish. This is the way, at this stage, that the constructive and destructive power of vendors, customers and the work force should come into play—not in determining the goal itself, but by imposing additional necessary conditions.

> *As for not-for-profit organizations, any attempt to formalize quantifiable measurements are bound to fail, until they agree on a suitable unit of measure for their goal.*

Once we agree that the shareholders should dictate the system's goal it is quite easy to state the goal of Western industrial and service organizations. A lengthy discussion can be found in the books *The Goal*[3] and *The Race*[4] so I will not repeat it here. For our purposes it is sufficient to state the final conclusions: "The goal of Western industrial and service organizations is to make more money now as well as in the future." Other types of organizations will have different goals. The goal of a hospital, a city or an army will certainly (hopefully) not be to make money. The biggest obstacle in determining the goals of these organizations is the realization that a goal and a measurable unit of that goal must be determined concurrently. Otherwise the goal will remain just a phrase or at best will be interpreted intuitively in too many different ways. In industrial and service organizations we don't have this problem. The

---

[3]*The Goal* by Goldratt and Cox
[4]*The Race* by Goldratt and Fox

measurement unit of their goal is simply the unit of money. Throughout this book I will use the term dollar and I ask understanding of those readers from countries with different currencies.

6 The Insufficiency of Bottom Line Measurements

Now to the tricky subject of measurement. For profit-making organizations, it looks as though we have a ready-made set of measurements in their financial statements. The profit-and-loss statement provides the net profit measurement. The balance sheet provides both return on investment and return on shareholders equity measurements and the cash flow statement provides the cash measurement. Do we really need all three measurements? It seems logical. The first one—net profit—is an absolute measurement. An absolute measurement is necessary, but by itself is certainly not enough. We need a relative measurement as well—like return on investment. Cash is sometimes extremely important, as companies that run out of cash discover to their dismay. Nonetheless I would like to point out that cash is not a measurement, but a necessary condition. To clarify this, let me quote a well-known statement: "If you have enough cash, cash is not important at all. If you don't have enough cash, nothing else is important." Cash is thus a boundary condition—a line that your organization should not cross. This is exactly the definition of a necessary condition.

In judging the performance of an organization we intuitively weigh the relative importance of net profit and return on investment to reach a conclusion. If we could formulate this intuitive judgment, we would establish a relationship between these two measurements. Such a numerical connection could then be used to eliminate one of the measurements (they will not be independent but will be dependent through that connection) leaving us with just one measurement. Until we can convert this intuition into a formula, we will have to continue using these two measurements while keeping an eye on the goal.

The last two paragraphs should not be interpreted as support for the way our financial statements currently calculate net profit, return on investment and cash. On the contrary, how can we accept a cash flow statement that considers inventory as part of cash? Try paying your workers with inventory. Or consider the dichotomy concerning inventory. Today most corporate managers consider inventory a liability. Nevertheless the balance sheet categorizes it under assets, which is the exact opposite.

As for not-for-profit organizations, any attempt to formalize quantifiable measurements are bound to fail, until they agree on a suitable unit of measure for their goal. Nevertheless it should be noted that the necessary condition of cash is as valid for non-profit organizations as it is for profit-making ones. Dollars play a major role even if the goal is not "to make money."

Now back to constraints. It seems that we have finally defined the goal and the measurements—at least for Western industrial and service organizations—and thus we can start to use the term "constraint." Unfortunately the situation is not quite so simple, as is clear for the readers of *The Goal* and *The Race*. The measurements that we were looking for were not just a set of measurements that can be used to judge the goal, but we were seeking measurements that can judge the impact of constraints on the goal.

Let's clarify this last point, since it is not widely recognized that for the same entity we might have more than one valid set of measurements. Each set may be perfectly capable of judging the desired entity, nevertheless these sets can differ dramatically in their ability to expose the various parameters that are responsible for the final performance. In our definition of the word constraint we alluded to the existence of a set of measurements that can judge the impact of a constraint on the performance of the system. A constraint, in many cases, is something having a local nature—lack of sufficient market for a particular product, a restricting technology, lack of capacity of a particular resource, etc. The two financial measurements—

> *We must now bring suggested alternatives and not just end a vicious attack by non-committal words like, "more research in this problem area is urgently needed."*

net profit and return on investment—even though a valid set for measuring the goal of making money, are woefully impotent to judge the impact of something of a local nature on the performance versus the goal.

The impotence of the financial statements to guide local decisions and thus the need to use "financial management" procedures was discussed at length in both *The Goal* and *The Race*. Here I would like to touch on the conceptual problems, assuming that enough examples of the fallacy of "cost" based financial management are already well known. For those interested in an historical overview of how those—on the surface—erroneous procedures have evolved, I would recommend Kaplan and Johnson's book "Relevance Lost, The Rise and Fall of Management Accounting."

7 The Hazards of the Current Attacks on Cost Accounting

Today it has become almost a fad to attack cost accounting. I see two major hazards in the way these attacks are currently made. First, is the careless manner in which we conduct this rather needed reappraisal. We're not distinguishing enough between attacking wrong procedures and attacking the subject itself. Financial accounting today is under a vicious attack, a movement that may lead some to the conclusion that internal financial control is damaging. I must emphasize that, in my opinion, even distorted, inadequate financial procedures are better than no financial measurements at all. The anarchy that would result from the lack of any numerical measurement would cause much more damage than wrong procedures that are moderated, as they are today, by solid management intuition.

The early warnings that this problem is upon us, are already here. In most companies, under the correct flag of improving quality, the amount of waste, money and mental energy drain that is resulting from lack of measurement is staggering. Phrases like "Quality is job one" — that stem from a realization of the inadequacy of traditional measurements to evaluate the true impact of quality—are intuitively useful in moving quality efforts forward. At the same time they give shelter to so many unneeded investments and expenses. Certainly at this stage—unlike in the initial stages—the additional net gain is negative.

> *Yes, the more direct labor becomes less important, the more it becomes more important.*

The situation has deteriorated so much, I believe, that even critiques of management accounting by professionals should be accompanied by some reasonable concrete suggestion or alternative. The days when it was allowable to just expose the problem are over. We must now bring suggested alternatives and not just end a vicious attack by non-committal words like, "more research in this problem area is urgently needed."

The second hazard in the current attacks on cost accounting lies in the popular way of exposing the invalidity of the current financial management procedures. These partial, shallow attacks do not expose the real underlying, root problem and thus misdirect the needed efforts to find a valid replacement. The two most popular arguments that are used today by most professionals are:

1. The invalidity of direct labor as a base for cost allocation

2. The inability to quantify many important factors

8. It's Not the Base, it's the Concept of Allocation That is Wrong

Let's view these two arguments in some detail. In an organization we have many types of expenditures. Some expenditures, like for material and direct labor, are easy to allocate to the products produced, but many others are too general in nature and do not lend themselves easily to association with any particular product. A few examples are: the salary of a foreman in charge of a department where several different products are manufactured; or the salaries of top management and their secretaries; or computer department expenditures; or even the interest that we pay for money borrowed and used for many different purposes. The degree to which we are troubled by this problem is revealed in the names that we call these general expenditures. We refer to them as overhead, or even burden, as if we don't feel comfortable in admitting that they are as necessary as direct labor to profitably run a business. We use a technique, developed at the beginning of this century, to allocate all these general expenditures to specific products in proportion to some other expenditures that are readily allocatable. The most popular method is to allocate general expenditures based on the amount of direct labor. Often we do this allocation in several steps. First we allocate the department overhead to the various products produced in that department using the time the workers invested in processing these products. Then we allocate the plant overhead according to the resulting departments numbers, and finally corporate overheads are allocated in the same fashion.

In the beginning of the century, when this procedure became popular, most industries were very labor intensive operations. The overhead factors at that time, ranged between 1.1 to 1.4. Overhead was a small correction to the main expenditures for material and labor. But we didn't stand still, advances in technology drastically reduced the amount of direct labor, while at the same time increased the more general expenditures. The net result was a dramatic growth in the overhead factors—the factors which represent the ratio between the general expenditures and direct labor expenses. For example if in the seventies factory overhead rates already reached the range of 2.5 to 4 for most industries, in the eighties they have grown to the 5 to 8 range.

An interesting consequence of this technique of allocating costs is that, as direct labor becomes a smaller and smaller part of our expenses (for most industries direct labor represents less than the 10% of total expenses) it nevertheless becomes more and more important. Yes, the more direct labor becomes less important, the more it becomes more important. How is such a paradox possible? Suppose that we improve the production of a certain part and shrink the process time per unit by two minutes. At the beginning of the century when our overhead factor was let's say 1.3, we put on the scoreboard the equivalent of $2 \times 1.3 = 2.6$ minutes saved per unit because of this improvement. Now when the overhead factor is let's say 7, we get the impression that the same improvement is much more beneficial since the score card shows the equivalent of $2 \times 7 = 14$ minutes saved per unit. Funny? Not really if we remember that by deceiving ourselves in this way we direct our efforts away from our real goal. To take this problem to the extreme we just need to be reminded that we are heading toward total automation. What are we going to do then—multiply by infinity?!

This severe deficiency in our technique of cost allocation should definitely be highlighted. Unfortunately the lessons learned here are leading us to a search for the solutions in a direction that can only deepen our hole. Today there are attempts to shift the allocation base from direct labor hours to something more significant and less erodible, like maintenance or machine hours. This superficial and complicated attempt does not even address the real problems. The first of which is: is there a direct one-to-one link between the allocatable cost and the overhead cost, a link in the sense that if one grows by 10% then the other must grow by the same proportion? If not,

> *We are painfully beginning to realize that intangible and unimportant are not synonyms.*

this allocation game just serves to confuse us into making irrational decisions. The second problem is: do we really need to know the product cost in order to make decisions? Don't we really need to know just the bottom line contribution of the sale of a specific product sold at a price dictated by the market? If it appears that I've asked the same question twice using different nomenclature, maybe it's because "product cost" has become so much a part of our vocabulary that we no longer even recognize that it is just a technique that was developed to answer a real life question. As will be shown in the next chapters there isn't any connection between "product cost"—no matter what the allocation technique—and the contribution to the bottom line.

9. Cost is Blind to the Impact on Sales

The second management accounting problem, the one that many professionals are highlighting, is the fact that many important business parameters cannot be quantified by the existing cost procedures. The business impact of better due-date performance, shorter quoted delivery lead times, and the speed at which new designs or engineering modifications are introduced into the market are well recognized as main parameters that can determine the success or failure of a company. Nevertheless improvements in these parameters, when mentioned on an appropriation request for new equipment, will be listed under the heading of intangible. The most startling example—quality—was mentioned above. Even though for years we have had procedures for quantifying the cost saving in material and labor from improved quality, it has become more apparent lately that when we damage a product we don't just lose material and labor, we damage our market. The dichotomy between the abysmal cost savings shown by existing cost procedures, and management's intuitive understanding of the absolute need to improve quality in order to survive, finally yielded to the cry to increase quality at all costs. We are painfully beginning to realize that intangible and unimportant are not synonyms. Declaring an entity as intangible just means that we haven't developed a cost procedure that is able to quantify the impact of that entity.

Once again the problem is very real but the direction proposed for solution is very mistaken. We are told that more cost procedures have to be developed to allow us to explore these remaining "white" holes. A close examination reveals the fallacy of this direction. All the "intangibles" have one thing in common. They significantly impact our ability to compete in the market, or in other words our future sales. "Cost," by definition, focuses on the operating expense side of the equation, where future and even current sales are foreign words to the "cost" world. No wonder that an entity is declared an orphan, or intangible, when its impact is through sales rather than through expenses. But those who care about profits are aware that the bottom line is effected by sales even more than by expenses. The answer must lie in looking for measurements that focus not only on expenses but also on how these other parameters impact the goal of making money.

10. The Cost Concept is Based on an Erroneous Assumption

Nonetheless can we still somehow modify cost to serve us better? My answer to the question is an absolute no. Any research in this direction will be an additional waste of time because the basic assumption of the cost concept is erroneous. The cost concept is based on the assumption that "we can measure the impact of a local area (or local decision) on the bottom line, by measuring how much money this area (or decision) absorbs or releases." This assumption holds only if we accept that the importance of all things in an organization are in proportion to the operating expense spent on them. Daily life teaches us the opposite. Take for example a case where we run out of a specific material. The damage to the system might be out of proportion to the cost of this material. Or compare the influence on the bottom line of a breakdown of a bottleneck machine to a similar breakdown at a non-constraint machine. The impact is without any relation to the salaries of the workers running them. The mere fact that we intuitively accept the existence of constraints and non-constraints in an organization indicates that we acknowledge the invalidity of the basic assumption of the cost concept.

We should look for a solution not by modifying and extending the cost concept but by looking, without any inertia, for a set of measurements that can measure the impact of something local on the global goal. The next chapter will concentrate on answering the two questions that were raised in this chapter. What should the measurements be and do we really have only a manageable number of constraints in any organization (the information problem)?

Apologia

*Apologia**

OR

IN THE MOVE TOWARD THE THIRD STAGE

Everyone who has spent some time in an organization has probably asked himself whether managing an organization is a science or does it border more on the side of an art? The more time one spends in an organization and the more a person climbs toward the top of the pyramid, the more he seems inclined to believe that managing an organization is more of an art than an accurate science. The art of managing people. The art of reaching intuitive decisions when hard facts are not available. The art of often managing in spite of the existence of numbers that others, less experienced, think are hard facts.

It is almost a consensus today that since we are dealing with so many unknowns in an organization that this field will never be a science. The unpredictable reaction of the market, the unknown actions of our direct and indirect competitors, the changing reliability of our vendors—not to mention the constant stream of internal "surprises"—all combine to defeat any attempt to approach the subject in a "scientific" way. Some—and they certainly are not a small group—even claim that since organizations comprise human beings whose reactions cannot be scientifically predicted, it is an absurdity to hope that the subject of managing an organization can be turned into a science.

---

* The name, not coincidentally, is taken from the famous dialogue of Socrates

Is this really so? I believe that any attempt to answer this question must first establish what is meant by "science". Does the word science carry with it the premise of having a precise answer for every situation? Is it a collection of well established procedures? Or is it the glorified and somewhat mysterious notion of "finding the secrets of nature"? Not surprisingly, science—for most people—is a blend of all of the above. This muddled view stems from the fact that the various sciences did not spring up as fully developed subjects. Rather each science has gone through three quite distinct and radically different stages of development. In each stage every science completely changes its perspective, nomenclature and even its intrinsic premise, much like a caterpillar turning into a worm in its evolution to becoming a butterfly.

The three distinct stages that every science has gone through are: classification, correlation and cause-and-effect. Let's clarify these stages through some examples. Probably one of the most ancient sciences known to man is astronomy. The first stage—classification—begins in prehistory. Several classifications of the stars were developed according to their location in the heavens. The most popular one was invented by the ancient Greeks. They segmented the sky into twelve sectors called the signs of the zodiac and classified the stars according to these sectors. Within this broad classification they invented an elaborate subclassification, coloring the night sky with their vivid imaginations and succeeding to etch above us most of their stormy mythology. Some stars they observed "refused" to stay in one sector, so they classified these wandering stars in a class of their own—the plants. This mammoth effort had its own practical use. It created a common terminology and today it still has some use in navigation, even though we must admit that its principal use is in horoscopes.

> *The three distinct stages that every science has gone through are: classification, correlation and cause-and-effect.*

The second stage started with Ptolemy in Alexandria about two thousand years ago. This wise man postulated the first known correlation on this subject. The planets move along a circle, whose center moves along another circle, whose center is the earth. This correlation has been improved upon by others, who have more precisely pinpointed the radii of the circles and even added more circles to an already quite complicated model. These efforts certainly bore fruits. They enabled us to predict eclipses and to forecast the position of the planets in tomorrow's skies.

The correlation stage is not a stand-still stage. It has its turbulences and fierce debates. Copernicus aroused a somewhat sleepy community by his daring suggestion that a much more powerful correlation would be achieved if we put the sun as the center of the planet's orbits. Kepler created another turbulence by suggesting a correlation based on elliptical orbits rather than the almost holy circular ones. It should be noted that in the correlation stage, even though it is based on careful observations and often involves substantial mathematical computations, the question WHY is not asked at all. Rather the question HOW is the center of interest.

The man who moved this subject into the cause-and-effect stage is known to everybody—Sir Isaac Newton. This man was the first to insist on asking the question WHY. He had the courage to ask it not only about remote planets but about seemingly mundane day-to-day events. Why do apples fall down rather than flying in all directions? How easy it is to shrug off such a trivial question by the impertinent answer—"that is the way it is." Newton didn't, instead he assumed a cause for this phenomenon. He assumed the gravitational law. He suggested that if we assume that any two bodies attract each other in proportion to their masses and in reciprocal proportion to the distance between them squared, then we can logically explain many effects in nature. Because of his assumption (the gravitational law), three of Kepler's correlations were explained for the first time and eight more were exposed as just coincidences that had not been thoroughly checked. With Newton's assumption of a cause the word *explain* appears on stage. It is a foreign word to the classification and correlation worlds where the only "proof" is in the pudding. Try it, it works.

Not surprisingly, the cause-and-effect stage opened a whole new dimension. We are no longer just observers tracking what already exists in nature. We can now predict the orbit of satellites that we ourselves add to space. Past experience is no longer the only tool. Logical derivations based on existing assumed causes can predict the outcome of entirely new situations.

It's worthwhile to note that before Newton, astronomy was not considered a science. As a matter of fact the name used at that time is the best indication—astrology. Even Kepler was an astrologer (and mathematician) and had to supply his king with weekly horoscopes. Only when the third stage is reached, only when cause-and-effect is established and logical deductions/explanations are suddenly mandatory, do we fully recognize that a subject matter is a science.

Let's examine another subject—diseases. The first stage—classification—is mentioned as far back as the Old Testament. When certain symptoms are present—put a quarantine on the house, when other symptoms exist—isolate the person, and with yet other symptoms—don't worry about them, they won't spread because of contact with the person. Diseases were classified not only by their symptoms but also by their ability to infect others. This stage was certainly very helpful. It served to localize diseases and prevent them from spreading. The second stage—correlation—was achieved only in the modern world. Edward Jenner found that if serum is transferred from an infected cow to a human being, this human being would not be infected by small-pox.

But the most important stage—the one that is by far more powerful because it enables us to create things in nature—is the stage of cause-and-effect.

Immunization had been found. We were no longer

limited to just preventing the spread of the disease. In one specific case we even prevented and eventually eliminated it. But once again the question WHY was not asked. The only proof was "try and see." No wonder that it took over seventy years before Jenner's methods were generally accepted.

The man who moved us into the cause-and-effect stage was Louis Pasteur. He said: let's assume that those tiny things that Leeuwenhoek found under his microscope more than a hundred years before, those things we call germs, are the cause of diseases—and bingo microbiology sprang to life. Bingo, of course, means many years of hard work for each disease. By having a cause-and-effect we could now create immunizations for a very broad spectrum of diseases. Yes, not just find immunizations, but actually create immunizations, even for those diseases where such immunization is not created spontaneously in nature.

We can go over each subject that is regarded as a science, whether it is chemistry, genetics or spectroscopy, and the pattern is the same. The first step was always classification. There are often some practical applications from this stage but the major contribution is usually to create the basic terminology of the subject. The second step—correlation—is usually much more rewarding. It supplies us with procedures that are powerful enough to make some practical predictions about the future. Mendeleev's table and Mendel's genetic rules are examples of this important stage. But the most important stage—the one that is by far more powerful because it enables us to create things in nature—is the stage of cause-and-effect. Only at this stage is there a widely accepted recognition that the subject is actually a science. Only then does the question WHY bring into the picture the demand for a logical explanation.

Today there are quite a few mature sciences that have been in the third stage of cause-and-effect for many years. The debate of what is a science is basically behind us. There is a consensus among scientists that science is not the search for truths or the search for the secrets of nature. We are much more pragmatic than that. The widely accepted approach is to define science as the search for a minimum number of assumptions that will enable us to explain, by direct logical deduction, the maximum number of natural phenomena.

These assumptions—like the gravitational law—can never be proven. Even when they can explain an infinite number of phenomena this does not make them true. It simply makes them valid. They can still be disproved. One phenomena that cannot be explained makes the assumption false, but in doing so it does not detract from its validity. It simply puts the boundaries on the circumstances where the assumption is valid and exposes the opportunity to find another assumption that is even more valid. Science does not concern itself with truths but with validity. That's the reason why everything in science is open for constant checks and challenges.

Accepting this general view of science, let's turn our attention to the field of organizations. Certainly we see many phenomena in organizations. It would be quite ridiculous to consider these phenomena, that we witness every day in any organization, as fiction. They are no doubt a part of nature. But if all these organizational phenomena are phenomena of nature, which of the existing sciences deals with them? Certainly not physics, chemistry or biology. It looks as if this is an area waiting for a science to be developed.

If we narrow our focus to a subset of the subject of managing organizations, the logistical arena, we can easily trace the three stages. The first one crystalized in the last thirty years. We refer to it under the generic name of MRP (Manufacturing Resource Planning). It is now evident that the real power of MRP is in its contribution to our data bases and terminology and much less to its original intent—shop floor scheduling. Bills of material, routings, inventory files, work-in-process files, order files—all are nomenclatures brought

> *Common sense is the highest praise for a logical derivation, for a very clear explanation.*

by MRP. Viewed from this perspective it's quite clear that MRP is actually the first stage—classification. We have classified our data, putting it into clearly defined categories. We have created the basic language of the subject and tremendously improved communications.

The West invested considerable money, time and resources in the classification stage. On the other side of the globe, the Japanese moved almost directly into the second stage—correlation. One man was the major force behind it—Dr. Taichi Ohno. He started his career as a foreman and recently retired as the Executive Vice President of Production for all of Toyota. He is the inventor of the Toyota Production System and the Kanban approach. He is the inventor of the powerful correlations that we call Just-In-Time. Correlations like: if products are not needed downstream—as indicated by the lack of Kanban cards—it is better for the company that the workers stay idle or, cut the batch sizes of parts even if the cost of setup skyrockets. I received the best proof that the question WHY was not asked at all from Dr. Ohno himself. He told me in our meeting several years ago in Chicago, "My system does not make sense at all, but by God it's working". The best sign of the correlation stage—the only proof is in the pudding.

Have we evolved already into the third stage, the cause-and-effect stage? My answer is, definitely yes. Most of *The Goal*[1] readers claim that this book contains just common sense. Common sense is the highest praise for a logical derivation, for a very clear explanation. But explanations and logical derivations are the terminology of the cause-and-effect stage. In *The Goal* only one assumption is postulated. The assumption that we can measure the goal of an organization by Throughput, Inventory and Operating Expenses. Everything else is derived logically from that assumption.

The Theory of Constraints Journal is intended to expand this cause-and-effect logic to cover other aspects of an organization—from marketing, to design, to investment, to distribution, and so on. This is the main task of the first article

---

[1] *The Goal* by Goldratt and Cox

in every issue. The task of the second article in each issue is quite different. The purpose of this article is certainly not to give real life testimonials that the Theory works. Who would be helped by such testimonials? The people that have already been persuaded by *The Goal* do not need them, they have their own real life proof. Those who were not moved by the common sense logic in *The Goal* will certainly find it easy to demonstrate that their situations are different and that these ideas will not work in their environment. No, the purpose of the "Visit" articles is quite different. What is not well appreciated is that the cause-and-effect stage brings with it some significant ramifications that we have to adjust to. It involves a different approach to untieing a subject. It also gives us the ability to change the system in which we operate, but in doing so it obsoletes for awhile our intuition on how to operate in this new environment. In addition, and not less important, it demands a much more pragmatic approach to newly created "sacred cows." The second article's task is to deal with all these subjects. Let's elaborate on these points.

First, how do we usually approach a subject today. The first step is typically—let's get familiarized with the subject. We are thrown into the mammoth task of assembling information. We try to collect as much relevant data as possible. Sometimes it takes a while to identify what is actually relevant. Often times it's quite frustrating to discover how difficult it is to get reliable data. But usually, determination, effort and time enable us to put our arms around an impressive collection of relevant pieces of information. Now what?

Our usual tendency is to start arranging things. To put some order into the pile of information that we worked so hard to assemble. This is not a trivial task and certainly it takes time and effort. In most cases there is more than one alternative way to systematically arrange the data. It's not at all easy to choose between the various possibilities and too frequently we decide to switch in mid-stream between one systematic approach and another, throwing the entire effort into one big mess. The most frustrating part occurs toward the end when we are always stuck with some pieces of information that do not fit neatly into our system. We twist and bend, invent some exception rules and in the end it is all organized. What have we actually achieved? Classification!

Many times we call the above task a "survey." But it is customary to finish surveys with findings. Many of these "findings" turn out to be just statistics that we verbalize or present in a graphic form. This statistic, that "finding," is a direct result of our classification and sub-classification efforts. But let's not treat these statistics lightly. In many cases they are quite an eye opener. Nevertheless, most of us will feel uneasy in finishing such a mammoth job with just statistics. We are eager to get more concrete things out of our work. To accomplish this we usually screen the statistics looking for patterns and common trends between the various graphs and tables. We are looking for correlations. Usually we find some, but everyone who has been involved in such an effort knows that there are two problems with these correlations. The first is that even when we find quite a clear-cut correlation we are still haunted by the suspicion that it might be a coincidence. The only way to get some verification is to perform an experiment. To deliberately change one variable and to closely monitor another to find out whether or not it changes according to the prediction indicated by the correlation.

The second and more serious problem is that we don't understand why the correlation exists and are always haunted by the possibility that the correlation involves more variables than what we have identified or that we haven't identified the known variables narrowly enough. Numerous examples of the first case are well known. Unfortunately the second case is more common and carries with it a larger problem. If a variable was neglected in a correlation, it will not take long until it emerges or we decide to declare the correlation invalid. Unfortunately, this is not the case if the variables were

This correlation was broadcast as "Inventory is a liability."

not defined narrowly enough. Most experiments will prove the validity of the correlation, but its implementation will involve a lot of wasted effort.

A classic example of this problem is the correlation between a company's level of inventory and its performance. The surveys taken in the late seventies and early eighties indicated that the Japanese carried substantially less inventories than their Western counterparts. It also was very clear that the overall performance of these Japanese companies was superior to ours. This correlation was broadcast as "Inventory is a liability."

It is hard to overestimate the impact that this correlation had on Western industry. A frantic race to reduce inventories started. We are now in the midst of this race even though our financial statements have not yet caught up. They still penalize—in the short run—every company that manages to substantially reduce its inventory. The amazing thing is that this widespread effort has occurred without most participants having a clear picture of why it is important to reduce inventory. We still hear the usual explanation of investments tied up in inventories, carrying costs and interest cost. These cannot be valid explanations since the level of these factors has not changed significantly from ten years ago when inventory was still considered an asset.

The disturbing thing about this movement is that we have not distinguished which portions of inventory are really responsible for the improved performance. A very close scrutiny, as can be found in *The Race*[2], reveals that the reduction in the work-in-process and finished goods portions of the inventory is the prime reason for improvement in a company's performance. Raw material inventory reductions are shown to have a relatively small impact. Nevertheless, due to lack of this understanding many companies are paying their dues to the current crusade by leaning on their vendors, in order to reduce their raw materials inventories. In general most correlations are extremely helpful. The inherent limitation of any correlation

---

[2] *The Race* by Goldratt and Fox

is due to the lack of understanding of the cause-and-effect relationships between the variables connected by the correlation.

As we can see, the current approach of assembling information as the first step in approaching a subject leads us down the classification path, which may eventually evolve into fruitful correlations. Unfortunately this path fails to trigger the cause-and-effect stage. In order to appreciate this, let's examine how a researcher in one of the established sciences operates. When such a person becomes aware of a new effect, the last thing that he desires at this stage is more information. One effect is enough. The burden now is on the scientist's shoulders. Now he needs to think, not to look for more data. To think, to speculate, even if in thin air. To hypothesize a plausible cause for this effect. What might be causing the existence of this effect? When such a cause is finally speculated the real task begins. The scientist must now struggle with a much more challenging question. Suppose that the speculated cause is valid, what is another effect in reality that this cause *must* explain? The other predicted effect must be different in nature from the original, otherwise the speculated cause is regarded as just an empty phrase. The researcher must search then to see if this effect actually exists. Once a predicted effect is actually found (and in the established sciences it might involve years of experimentation) only then does the speculated cause gain the name of theory. If the predicted effect is not found, it is an indication that the speculated cause is wrong and the scientist must now search for another plausible cause.

Kepler had in his possession all the voluminous and surprisingly precise measurements that Tycho Brahe and his group gathered over several decades. By analyzing this data Kepler succeeded, after a mammoth mathematical effort of more than thirty years, to produce some correct

We should strive to reveal the fundamental causes, so that a root treatment can be applied, rather than just treating the leaves— the symptoms.

correlations and some more mistaken correlations. Newton, on the other hand, started by examining one effect—why an apple falls down. He speculated the gravitational law as a plausible cause and derived from its existence a totally different effect—the orbits of the planets around the moon. Correlations do not trigger the cause-and-effect stage. At most they shorten the time required to check the existence of some predicted effects.

This process of speculating a cause for a given effect and then predicting another effect stemming from the same cause is usually referred to as effect-cause-effect. Many times the process does not end there. An effort is often made to try and predict more types of effects from the same assumed cause. The more types of effects predicted—and of course verified—the more "powerful" is the theory. Theory in science—unlike in the common language—must be practical, otherwise it is not a theory but just an empty scholastic speculation.

Every verified, predicted effect throws additional light on the cause. Oftentimes this process results in the cause itself being regarded as an effect thus triggering the question of what is its cause. In such a way, a logical tree that explains many vastly different effects can grow from a single (or very few) basic assumptions. This technique is extremely helpful in trying to find the root cause of a problematic situation. We should strive to reveal the fundamental causes, so that a root treatment can be applied, rather than just treating the leaves—the symptoms. I myself usually elect to stop the process of finding a cause for a cause, when I reach a cause which is psychological and not physical in nature.

We believe that real life examples of applying this way of thinking to analyze a company—the "Visit" articles—will be very helpful in moving from the classification-correlation approach to the cause-and-effect stage. But, as mentioned above, this is not the only reason for publishing the "Visit" articles. The second reason is intertwined with the basic nature of how the conclusions of a cause-and-effect theory need to be applied. These conclusions, in many cases, involve a change in the basic assumption on which our current systems are based.

Change a basic assumption and you have changed the system itself. We are so accustomed to changing within the system, that most of us are unaware of how we need to act when we change the system itself.

Let's not fool ourselves—most of our correct actions are not guided by some logical deductions but by our intuition. Nobody knows exactly how we acquire intuition, but it is quite clear that intuition does not grow in thin air. It evolves from experience. When the system itself is changed, our intuition temporarily becomes obsolete until we gain it back from our *new* experience. How do we know that such an event occurs when the system itself changes. It is not by realizing that our intuition is no longer valid—only a person with immense internal honesty can reach such a conclusion. The best sign is that we have just experienced a drastic improvement in the system's performance that came as a direct and rapid result of changing a fundamental assumption. In such situations we have to be very careful to reexamine all aspects of the new system. To rethink logically what must be the ramifications. If we don't do this, if we don't rely on extensive usage of logic—since for some period intuition is obsolete—what can shield us against the outcome? Do we want to rely only on extensive prayers?

These "visits" are supposed to highlight and show how to logically derive such outcomes. Outcomes that if we are prepared for them, are usually very beneficial. But if they come as a surprise, they might throw the entire system into chaos. Remember, cause-and-effect gives us the ability to change our current reality, but we must then be ready to adjust our actions in accordance with this new reality.

The third reason for these articles, and in our eyes the most important one, is to fight the tendency of the correlation stage to create new sacred cows. As we said earlier,

> *Consequently change must be understood as the norm, not as the exception.*

the only proof available in the correlation stage is—it works. Thus, correlations that have passed for some period, the test of reality, are accepted as truths. They will be constantly used, even when the situation changes and they are no longer valid. One of the most startling examples is the use of cost procedures. Conditions have changed dramatically from theinvention of these procedures at the beginning of the century, causing these procedures not only to be obsolete, but in many cases to be very damaging. Nevertheless, in spite of overwhelming evidence thrown in our faces by reality, it has been only in this decade that we, as a group, have had the courage to declare these cost procedures invalid sacred cows and recognize that a basic change is needed quickly. Even when a correlation is still valid, it acts as an immense blockage to efforts to find a better way.

This concept of "that's the way we have always done it" or "don't rock the boat" is almost the antithesis of the cause-and-effect stage. In this stage everything is open to scrutiny, everything must be under constant change. This is the case in any mature science. This should be the case here. The only thing that we can be sure of, is that there certainly are better answers. We must constantly look for them and never fall into the trap of "don't rock the boat." Under cause-and-effect we constantly change our reality. Consequently change must be understood as the norm, not as the exception. Truths are no longer the target, only validity exists, and always there is a better way.

These three things: the effect-cause-effect way of thinking, the need to explore logically all ramifications and the constant search for better ways, are what we want to radiate in these "Visit" articles. Those were the things that guided us in writing the visit to Modine—The McHenry Plant[3]. Frankly, I thought that we had done a quite decent job. So you can imagine my surprise to find out that about half the readers interpreted the article as a criticism of Jim Rulseh and his people. Some even claimed that it was a vicious criticism. Let me explain why I couldn't understand these interpretations. In my eyes—and I'm

---

[3] The Theory of Constraints Journal by Goldratt and Fox, Volume 1, Number 1

always very tightfisted with praises—Jim is one of the best plant managers that I've ever met. He is definitely gifted, determined and above all a doer. I thought that was exactly how I described and portrayed Jim. I also thought that I had described and praised in detail the plant's achievement.

When I became aware of this reaction I went and checked with some of the readers who thought I was criticizing Jim. Yes, they all understood very well the magnitude and importance of what was achieved at the McHenry plant. As a matter of fact, most of them claimed that was exactly the reason why they thought I was unfair. I must admit that it took me quite a while to understand what seems to be an illogical connection.

The only explanation that I could find is that when someone highlights open opportunities that stem from another's achievement, it is interpreted as criticizing the achiever himself. For a scientist such approach is indigestible; like criticizing Galileo—the first modern physicist—because he did not invent Newton's rules. Or, like thinking that Einstein with his general relativity (which replaces fundamentally the gravitational law) reduces Newton's phenomenal achievement. I view this as illogical, but it probably exists. Since it probably exists, it must be taken into account.

I don't believe that a goal justifies the means. I don't believe in hurting people, certainly not if they deserve the opposite. Thus I deeply regret writing this article, not because of its content, but because of its style. I owe Jim and his people an apology, but I don't believe in empty apologies. Yes, when you do things you are bound to make mistakes. The only way to avoid them is not to do anything, which is the biggest mistake. But making a mistake and repeating a mistake are two different things. I believe that not repeating the same mistake is the only valid apology. As a result we scrapped the following visit article and we are struggling hard to find the appropriate way to write such real life visits. To write them in a way that will not hurt people and at the same time bring this important knowledge. Correctly writing the next visit's articles will be my apology to Jim and his people.

This task has turned out to be more complicated than we thought, leading to a delay in the Journal publication, so now we owe the Journal's readers an apology for delaying the mailing of the second issue. It looks as if we have finally found an acceptable style to write the visits, so we hope that such a delay will not be without benefit.

Chapter 3

THE FUNDAMENTAL MEASUREMENTS

1. The Intuitive Choice

Tell me how you measure me and I'll tell you how I'll behave. It's no wonder, with the growing recognition that current measurements are inappropriate, that most companies are struggling to find a better answer. These attempts range from exotic ways of changing the base for cost allocations, to the other end of the spectrum, constructing an exhaustive list of non-financial measurements. How should we methodically approach this problem? I believe that whenever we reach a point where we doubt the foundation of a subject—when we can no longer accept something that has guided our actions for decades—then the only effective way is to go back to the root of the subject. We need to start with the innocence of a child, as if we haven't any preconceived knowledge of the subject. If we don't do it in this way, we run the almost certain risk of extrapolating from the past and allowing, unconsciously, an erroneous unchallenged assumption to creep in and cripple our new solution.

Where to start is obvious. We already agree on the most fundamental entity of our for-profit-organization, it's goal. The goal of our organization is to make more money now as well as in the future. Why don't we think of our organization as a "money-making machine"? This way of looking on the essence of our company provides us a fresh point of view, which makes it difficult for the current detailed cost procedures to impact our analysis. If we have to choose between several "money-making machines", how do we determine which one to choose? What are the factors that we should consider in making such a choice? It is quite obvious that one of the more important elements to look for,

Why don't we consider our organization as a "money-making machine?" is the rate at which the machine generates money. We certainly will consider a machine that generates money at a fast rate, as superior to a slower rated one. Thus, this quality—the rate at which money is generated—is one of the most important measurements.' What else are we going to consider when choosing such a machine?

Looked at from this point of view, the question seems almost trivial. The two other most important considerations are; the amount of money captured in the belly of the machine—money that we cannot use (which of course includes the money paid to purchase the machine)—and the amount of money that we will have to spend continuously in order to turn the wheels of the machine. Let's examine it again. If we have already made up our mind that we want such a machine—we already decided that the goal is to make money—then these three measurements are the only ones that jump into our mind.

What about the reliability of the machine, how frequently does it break down? Isn't that an important measurement as well? Machine breakdowns will influence the rate at which the machine generates money—the more breakdowns, the lower the rate. Also more breakdowns might increase the money that we have to spend on maintenance. In other words, it might increase the amount of money we have to spend continuously in order to turn the wheels of the machine. Thus we see that reliability of the machine is not an additional measurement, but just a contributor to the measurements that we have already found.

What about the life span of the machine? Is it an additional measurement? The answer is no. We just have to remind ourselves that the stated goal includes the words "now as well as in the future." Thus the three measurements that we have just found, measure not only the current situation, but also the future capabilities as well. A short life span will mean a very low rate of generating money in the future. Once again this is not a new measure, but a contributor to the measurements we have already found. As we check even further we are hard pressed to come up with an additional measurement which adds anything to the above set.

But what is sales-per-period if not... the rate of generating money?

2 | The Intuitive Measurements in Current Use

Such a strong intuitive conclusion should be widely used in reality. It's hard to conceive that by looking at a situation from one angle we can immediately get an intuitive definitive answer and yet, when we look from another angle, that we could totally ignore that answer. So it is reasonable to expect that we will be able to find some evidence that these measurements are currently used in some fashion. These three measurements—the rate of generating money, the money captured, and the money spent to move the wheels—are certainly not the traditional bottom line measurements. They are not the profit and loss statement or the balance sheet. Likewise, these three measurements are not our cost based procedures. We see that they don't have a place in our formal system, but do they exist as part of the informal system?

In all for-profit organizations that I know of, one of the prime concerns is their rate of sales. It may be expressed as sales per month, per quarter, or per any other quite arbitrary period. Everywhere, top managers track it closely. There will be numerous detailed charts and even explanations for every dent in these charts. It is quite obvious that sales per period is a major measurement. But what is sales-per-period if not a variation of our first measurement—the rate of generating money?

What about the other two measurements? We find that they too exist as major measurements in every plant. Who does not closely track the amount of inventory that the organization holds? Who does not monitor in detail the total expense of the organization? Inventory is just some of the money captured in the belly of our money-making machine, while, operating expense is the

> *Throughput ... cannot possibly be associated with a re-allocation of money within the system.*

money that we have to pour in constantly in order to turn its wheels. We see that these measurements are used intuitively today on a very wide scale. It looks as if these measurements have passed any conceivable test of validity, so why won't we use them formally? Why won't we construct our formal system according to these three measurements?

The first step in any attempt to build a formal system based on these three measurements is to define them precisely. I'll use the definitions that have been published in *The Goal* and in *The Race*.

> THROUGHPUT: The rate at which the system generates money through sales.
>
> INVENTORY: All the money the system invests in purchasing things the system intends to sell.
>
> OPERATING EXPENSE: All the money the system spends in turning Inventory into Throughput.

3 Throughput

These definitions are just a more precise expression of the three measurements mentioned above. Nevertheless some nuances need further clarification. Let's start with Throughput, the first definition. In this definition I included the words "through sales". A more precise definition would not include these words, since if the system generates money by earning interest at a bank, or for that matter in any other conceivable way, it is certainly Throughput. The words "through sales", were added to the definition of Throughput, since so many production people think that if they produced something it's Throughput. This is not the case. If you have produced something and haven't sold it, it's not Throughput, it's still Inventory.

The need to add these two words was further amplified since production is interpreted as Throughput, not only by production people, but also by our financial people. If, for example, a company increases its finished goods stocks, the financial statements currently interpret a portion of this increase as additional profits.

> *Throughput is thus, sales minus all the money paid per item to entities which are external to the system.*

In any event, Throughput must be interpreted as money entering from outside the system being measured (like through sales) and cannot possibly be associated with a re-allocation of money within the system.

In many instances, a sale is registered when goods are sent to a client, even if the client has the unconditional right to send the goods back and get a full refund. This situation is very common in consumer goods industries. Industries like cosmetics, food, detergents and books. This practice leads to the tendency to over-use techniques like "promotions" in order to boost the current quarter's financial results, and too often sacrificing the actual performance of the system. In such environments, I would strongly recommend that Throughput be recorded only when the final consumer has purchased the goods. Not only would we get a much clearer and more true to life picture, but many bad practices would be suppressed. A more rigorous analysis of this situation will be given in one of the future chapters, by analyzing in detail the consumer goods environment according to the Theory of Constraints.

How shall we attach a number to Throughput? The most convenient way is not to try and find the mathematical expression of rate, but rather to measure the average rate at a convenient period of time—a week, month, etc. Throughput in that period will be the sales made in the period minus the purchased materials that went into these sales. It should be emphasized that Throughput is not sales, it's money generated by the system. Since purchased materials were not money generated by the system (it's money generated by the vendors) we must view this money

> *this definition disregards altogether added value as part of the inventory evaluation*

as just flowing through our system, not being generated by it. Thus, Throughput is: sales minus the purchased materials used in the specific items sold.

Adopting this interpretation for "money generated by the system", we will be hard-pressed not to recognize that money paid to outside sub-contractors is the same as money paid for materials. Both are money flowing through our system and not money generated by our system. In this same category I would also put royalties that are paid to an outside patent holder—royalties that are paid per item sold. Likewise commissions on specific items sold, when these commissions are paid to sales people who are not part of the organization (eg. agents).

Throughput is thus, sales minus all the money paid per item to entities which are external to the system. If these monies are not paid per item—like one time up-front royalties or salesperson's salary—they should be viewed as part of the system and thus will find their impact in the other measurements. The up-front royalties will be Inventory and the internal salesperson's salary will be Operating Expense. If money cannot be easily identified with a specific item sold, this is the best indication that the system has purchased a capability that should be regarded as part of the system itself.

4 Inventory

When we turn our attention to the definition of Inventory, it is quite obvious that this definition differs quite significantly from the traditional way of evaluating inventories. Certainly it is not the First-In, First-Out or Last-In, First-Out method. As a matter of fact, this definition disregards altogether added value as part of the inventory value. According to our definition even a finished goods item will be valued only according to the price paid for the materials that were used in it. Our definition does not take into account any value added by the system itself, not even the direct labor used to produce the products.

Why such a drastic departure from convention; a departure that will force us to record inventory differently than we do for external purposes? To fully understand why, it is best to go back and examine the concepts underlying our current methods of evaluating inventory. Using these concepts, if we want to measure the net profit that the system has generated in a given period, we do it by measuring the sales of that period less the expenses incurred during that period. The tendency is always to try and make as much net profit as possible, thus it is quite tempting to "play" the numbers in order to improve the end result.

> *Since lately most corporations have started to view inventory as a liability, it is more than a little inconsistent to record inventory as an asset.*

A logical avenue in this effort is to question whether all the expenses incurred during the period were for that period's sales or whether a part of them were incurred for sales of a future period. If we succeed in finding such expenses we are still hard pressed to reduce them from the current sales unless we can find a way to camouflage these expenses as investments. One obvious way is to attach, or allocate at least some of the expenses to work-in-process and finished goods inventories. Through this allocation mechanism we can regard manufacturing-related-expenses as part of the plant investment in inventory. This procedure is very cumbersome and time-consuming and the only purpose is to enable us to move expenses from one period to the other. The justification is two-fold. The first is that we have to do this task anyhow, in order to determine a product's cost. The second is that we must get a clear idea of the last period's profit in order to better manage our company in the next period. It is quite ironic that the end result is exactly the opposite of these well meant intentions.

The mechanism of cost allocation as a base for product

> *Certainly that will be everyone's opinion. Everybody, that is, except our current financial statements.*

pricing is coming under increasingly intense scrutiny. There is now almost a consensus that the current allocation mechanism is misleading in fixing product prices. This means that all this time consuming effort, of allocating expenses to inventory, is done solely for the purpose of inventory valuation. As for the argument that we should allocate expenses to inventory in order to get a more accurate figure for the last period's net profit, this is also currently perceived as a totally false argument. For quite a long time auditors have been feeling more than a little uneasy about inventory profits—profits generated by increasing work-in-process and finished goods inventory. Since lately most corporations have started to view inventory as a liability, it is more than a little inconsistent to record inventory as an asset. Moreover, to consider inventory in a way that treats an increase of work-in-process or finished goods inventory as contributing positively to the net profit, is becoming more and more indigestible to top management.

5 The Damage Caused By Current Inventory Valuations

Let's review it is some more detail. Most corporations are demanding that their plants reduce inventory. But what happens to a plant manager who has done a very nice job of reducing inventories. Let's look at an example. Suppose that a plant manager succeeds in reducing his finished goods inventory to one-half of its previous level, without jeopardizing sales or customer service and without incurring even one additional cent in operating expense. An excellent performance! Certainly that will be everyone's opinion. Everybody, that is, except our current financial statements.

The ending finished goods inventory of the plant will be half of the starting inventory. The difference will be interpreted as additional expenses incurred during the period. These expenses will traditionally be only partially compensated by the reduction in expenses for purchases of raw material. The entire difference between the value of the finished goods reduction and the value of purchased material in them (the value added) will reduce this period's net profit. This gives the impression that the plant has performed very poorly, most likely showing up as a considerable loss. Let's not forget that most plant managers are evaluated primarily on their P & L results. Who wants to achieve a real improvement and then find himself in a position where he has to justify and explain?

> *this decline will be exposed two or three quarters earlier on our new chart*

The full fallacy of the approach of using inventory to allocate expenses incurred in one period, to yet another period, in order to calculate net profit more precisely, is revealed when we examine the net profit of a company for several time periods. Take the profit and loss statements of any company and plot the net profit (loss) as a function of time. Usually you'll get a zigzag curve with mountains and valleys. Now strip the value added from the profit and loss numbers—strip "inventory profits" (losses). In order to see the resulting phenomena a, very easily done, rough cut calculation is sufficient. You can most likely get a good estimate of what percent of the "cost of goods sold" is purchased material. Usually this ratio is somewhere between 30% and 60%. The profit and loss statement will probably also provide a breakdown of the distribution of inventory between the categories of raw material (including purchased parts), work-in-process (including finished parts storage), and finished goods. The value added in the raw material will be zero while the finished goods bear the full brunt of the value added allocation. If for example, raw material on the average composes 40% of the product cost, the remaining 60% is just value added. As for work-in-process inventory, assume that the value added represents about 30% of this inventory's value—a good midpoint between raw materials and finished goods. Now let's reevaluate the inventories that appear in our P & L statement, without the value added.

For example, suppose that the distribution of inventory in our plant is 30% raw material, 30% work-in-process and 40% finished goods, and altogether totals $10 million. Under our proposed inventory valuation scheme (raw material content only) the total inventory value is only $6.7 million. We can see that $3.3 million of the inventory is value added since the value added to the finished goods is $2.4 million [$10 million (total inventory) x 0.4 (the finished goods portion) x 0.6 (the finished goods added value percentage)] and the added value in work-in-process is $0.9 million ($10 million x 0.3 x 0.3). This type of calculation, which by no means has to be precise for our purposes, can be done very quickly. In order to do it, the beginning and ending inventories appearing on every P & L statement need to be recalculated using this approach. Then the difference (plus or minus) between the new numbers for ending and beginning inventories should be subtracted from that period's net profit number. We can now plot the new profit (loss) numbers on the previous graph.

In almost all cases the new graph is just a shift to the left of the previous picture by about two or three quarters. In other words, if a particular quarter shows a decline in profit versus a constant increase in the previous three quarters this decline will be exposed two or three quarters earlier on our new chart— where the added value was stripped from inventory. The reasons for this phenomena are quite obvious. In a down turn, where sales are dropping, we use the excess capacity to generate more inventory. In our current method of inventory valuation and net profit calculation, this will compensate for a significant portion of the lost sales. This approach thus overstates the net profit that was actually achieved. When the market rises again, we sell from our inventory (which is hopefully not obsolete by then), but we record only the difference between the "cost" (including value added) and the selling price, thus understating net profit. By going through these calculations we can see how this mechanism, of converting operating expenses into investment, obliterates the actual picture and many times gives misleading information on the current trend of a business. We end up achieving the exact opposite of what we wanted—the way that we compute net profit for the current period misguides our actions for the next period. Moreover, as long as we have reason to believe that we should strive to reduce inventories, any company that still uses added value as part of its internal profit and loss statement just sends mixed and confusing signals down to the troops.

> *Everything in our system is for sale... the best indication is the fact that we include machines and buildings on the balance sheet.*

6 Different Internal and External Reporting

In my opinion, the best and most straightforward way to deal with this devastating phenomena of "inventory profits" is simply to eliminate all value added from inventory. In this way any change in inventory is compensated by the change in money paid for materials and the difference truly reflects the change in the investment made by our organization. No penalty is imposed on a plant that reduces its work-in-process and/or its finished goods. This plant will enjoy the savings in operating expense from reduction in the various expenses comprising the carrying cost categories. It will also be in a much better position to reap the benefits stemming from the positive impact of reduced inventories on its competitive position in the market (see *The Race* Pages 34-67).

Today external forces, like the IRS and Wall Street, demand that inventories on the financial statements be calculated using the value added approach, especially if this is an industry practice. It is more than naive to expect that this requirement can be changed in the very near future. But this requirement should not stop us. We can continue to report to the external world in one way, while for internal purposes we judge the performance of P & L centers using a more sensible method. Most professionals recommend today that we distinguish between the financial statement that we have to submit externally and the financial statements that we prepare to give top managers a clearer picture of their company's situation. The additional work involved in compiling the internal reports is negligible. All the data has been assembled anyway and it is just a matter of changing one or two steps in the procedure for calculating the numbers. Some companies are already using this straightforward method for internal purposes and many more are sure to follow.

The raw material and purchased part inventories, that are collected in various forms by our systems, are only one part of the money captured in the belly of our money-making-machine. Another portion includes all other investments—machines and buildings alike. Does the suggested definition of inventory—"all the money the system invests in purchasing things the system intends to sell,"—lend itself to such interpretation? An immediate reaction is that we do not intend to sell the system's machines and building and thus they are excluded by this inventory definition. This is a superficial interpretation. Everything in our system is for sale, that's what our shareholders are doing when they trade their shares. The best indication is the fact that we include machines and buildings as assets on the balance sheet. If they are not for sale, there is no justification for this classification.

This immediately raises the question of the value that we should be attaching to a piece of equipment, that was purchased several years ago for a certain use . Should we attach the original purchase price or the current value (which is estimated by the original price minus depreciation). Maybe an easy way to reach a decisive answer is by analyzing some other items. How should we treat the money that we pay for lubricating oil needed for our machines? When the oil is purchased it certainly should be recorded as Inventory. As we consume it we should transfer it to Operating Expense (money the system spends in turning Inventory into Throughput) and subtract it from Inventory. What about materials that are scrapped? When we buy the material, it should be recorded as Inventory, but the minute that it is scrapped, it should be moved into the category of Operating Expense. These two examples make the answer for the value that we should attach to a machine, quite obvious. If we want to be consistent we should look on our machines as being gradually scrapped with time. The depreciation should thus be treated exactly as is done today. It should be reduced from Inventory (assets) and moved to the Operating Expense category.

> *Any expense that does not contribute to converting Inventory into Throughput is a waste and as such should be trimmed.*

7 Operating Expense

Operating Expense is just our old friend "cost". Nevertheless I strongly recommend that we do not use the term "cost" for awhile. Cost today, is a word used too loosely. It has three totally different meanings. The first one is as a synonym for "price", whether it is the price of a material or a machine. The second is a synonym for Operating Expense. Thus the usage of the word "cost" contributes to the confusion between money spent (Operating Expense) and money invested (purchase price). But the most devastating connotation of the word "cost" is its third meaning—that of "product cost", an imaginary entity that exists only as long as we use the misleading allocation mechanism. Until this phantom is erased from our thinking, continued usage of the word "cost" will just lengthen the period of confusion.

Our definition of Operating Expense does not distinguish between the expense of the salary of a direct worker and that of the Chief Engineer. Both are conceptually doing the same task. They assist in turning Inventory into Throughput. Likewise, a salesperson's job is certainly to convert inventories into sales. Why do we insist on a totally superficial distinction between these payments to employees doing the same task unless it is for the purpose of converting expenses into investment.

> *control is... where things are versus where they were supposed to be, and who is responsible for any deviation.*

A reverse definition of Operating Expenses provides us with an excellent definition for "waste". Any expense that does not contribute to converting Inventory into Throughput is a waste and as such should be trimmed. Don't be too short sighted in using this definition. Effective promotional activities, for example, certainly contribute to converting Inventories into Throughput.

As a matter of fact these three measurements—Throughput, Inventory and Operating Expense—are perfectly capable of measuring the goal of making money, eliminating the need to use Net Profit (NP) and Return on Investment (ROI). But since we are accustomed to Net Profit and ROI and have developed the intuition or "feel" for them (like we have a "feel" for centimeters or inches), it would be counterproductive not to continue to use them, especially when the conversion between T,I,OE, and NP,ROI is so straightforward.

Net profit is just Throughput minus Operating Expense:

$$NP = T - OE$$

Return-On-Investment is just Throughput minus Operating Expense divided by Inventory:

$$ROI = (T-OE)/I$$

It is worthwhile to notice that we are currently using as measurements other combinations of T,I,OE. For example one of the most used non-financial measurements is inventory turns. Inventory turns is expressed readily by the ratio between Throughput and Inventory. Likewise the ratio between Throughput and Operating Expense is nothing but our old friend "Productivity".

$$\text{Inventory Turns} = T/I \qquad \text{Productivity} = T/OE$$

8 Control Measurements

This mechanism will necessitate the introduction of the "plant-department" alongside the actual departments in the plant.

In addition to measurements which judge the performance of an entire system (T,I,OE and NP, ROI) we also need control measurements; measurements that can be used to monitor subsystems as well as complete systems. First let's clarify what is meant by the word "control". This word is badly used today. For instance, today when we refer to "inventory control" we mean, assembling data that will tell us where inventory is located and at what stage of processing it is. The real meaning of control is having the knowledge of where things are versus where they were supposed to be, and who is responsible for any deviation. Any other interpretation is, in my eyes, just an attempt to avoid the issue. Using the proper control measures, very good control can be achieved even for subsystems that interact not only with the external world but also with other subsystems of the same organization. The three control measurements are Throughput-Dollar-Days, Inventory-Dollar-Days and Local-Operating-Expense.

Local-Operating-Expense is the operating expense over which the local area has full control. This definition would not require any further clarification if it weren't for the syndrome of expense allocation. One of the most important things that we have to take into account when we compose control measurements, is to be very careful not to assign any expense to an area that does not have responsibility or power to change this number. A good example is—assigning 6% of the divisional computer center to the operating expenses of a plant. The plant does not have any responsibility for the divisional computer center, and thus—even though it is a user of the computer—should not carry the burden of these expenses, when we deal with the plant's control measurements.

> *Missed due dates is certainly a deviation of the first type; things that we were supposed to do and haven't done*

Mechanically we should assign to a subsystem, all the expenses which are controlled solely by that subsystem. For example, we should assign to a department the salary and fringe benefits of all the employees working in that department. There is no point in distinguishing between the direct workers, the foreman, and fully dedicated process and maintenance engineers who work in that department. Likewise we should be very careful not to assign to this department some percentage of the materials management personnel, shared with other departments, and certainly not some part of the administrative staff of the plant. This mechanism will necessitate the introduction of the "plant-department" alongside the actual departments in the plant. To this plant-department, we will assign all expenses which are not solely under the responsibility of any individual department. Likewise we will have to create the "divisional-department" and so on. This Local-Operating-Expense measurement is very easy to compute since all the relevant data exists and since it's logical and fair. Furthermore our experience shows that it does not encounter any resistance.

The other two measurements—Throughput-Dollar-Days and Inventory-Dollar-Days can be fully explained only after the concept and procedure of Buffer—Management is introduced. Thus at this stage a rough concept will be described, with a full discussion postponed to the appropriate chapter. These control measurements should measure *deviation from plan*. There are two types of deviations. The first one is; things that were supposed to be done and nevertheless were not done. The second is; things that were not supposed to be done but nevertheless were done. The first type of deviation already attracts the attention of all management and occupies a significant portion of their time. Expediters in the plant deal mainly with minimizing the damage caused by these deviations—things that are behind schedule. Nevertheless it is very rare to find a numeric measurement for this type of deviation. This is exactly the task of the Throughput-Dollar-Days control measurement. The situation is even worse when we deal with the second type of deviation. Not only do we find that no measurement exists to help control this type of deviation, but the existing measurements—like local worker's efficiency or process variance—encourage rather than suppress, doing things that should not be done.

The intuitive feeling that the answer involves both the unit of money and the unit of time is very strong everywhere.

9 Throughput-Dollar-Days

Let's first clarify what is meant by Throughput-Dollar-Days through a specific example. Due date performance is currently a very important non-financial measurement. This measurement deals with quantifying the magnitude of the deviation of the plant from its promised commitments to clients. Many plants measure it, using the number of orders missed, others use the number of units that were not shipped on time. Even a superficial examination of such situations would cause an objective observer to raise an eyebrow. It seems logical that when such units of measure are used, the difference between the size of the orders would be relatively small, or that the difference between the selling price of the units sold would be almost negligible. But this is certainly not the case. In most situations, the spread between the size of the orders is at least one order of magnitude and the selling prices of the units differs by a similar amount. Moreover, the time delay in the shipment is generally not factored in and thus an order that is delayed one day, carries the same weight as an order that is sent two weeks after the promised date.

Missed due dates is certainly a deviation of the first type—things that we were supposed to do and haven't done—and thus

Throughput-Dollar-Days should measure it at any given point in time. Using this control measure, a unit such as a plant or a division can measure its due date performance by assigning to every missed order, a value equal to its selling price multiplied by the number of days the shipment is already late. A summation on all the missed orders will give the unit an objective measurement of its level of performance, at any given point in time. This measurement forces a plant to concentrate on the very late orders—not just because of the level of complaints from the customers—but also because an order which is late by ten days has a measurement impact that is ten fold larger than an order that is one day late (provided of course that both orders have the same sales price).

This measurement of Throughput-Dollar-Days is not restricted to measuring just a plant's deviation. It can also be very effectively used internally, to measure the delivery performance of every production department, work center and even the performance of functions like engineering and accounting. In order to carry it to this extent, we must have a very good understanding of the required internal "sales dates", which can be achieved only through the mechanism of Buffer Management. In every case the effect is the same. We acquire a very logical, almost intuitively obvious measurement. On top of this, each unit measured, has the incentive to achieve a perfect score of zero Throughput-Dollar-Days.

10 Inventory-Dollar-Days

Inventory-Dollar-Days measures deviations of the second type—things that we should not do but were done nevertheless. Once again I'll try to demonstrate the concept by using an example of an entire plant. Let's review, for example, the finished goods inventories held by a plant. When plant management is asked how much finished goods inventories the plant holds, they usually respond in one of two different ways. They might give a dollar value or a time value—an answer like we hold $10 million or we have about 4 weeks inventory. The intuitive feeling, that the answer involves both the unit of money and the unit of time, is very strong everywhere.

Let's review whats generally constitutes this answer of $10 million, or about four weeks. Usually it means that some products that are needed are totally missing from finished goods inventory. In addition, out of the $10 million about $1 million is due to be shipped in the next two days. Another $1.5 million is due to be shipped during the coming week and so on. The following table is a typical representation of such situation.

> *Looking on inventory as a liability, rather than an asset, actually means that we regard inventory as a loan made to the plant.*

Dollars:	2.5	1.5	1.5	1.5	1	1	1	= $10 million
Days Until Sold:	2	5	10	20	40	100	300	= 4 week average

As a matter of fact the last million are probably obsolete products that should be written off, but for the time being we refrain from taking the bite. So let's assume that some day (in about 300 days) we'll sell them.

If the plant is directed to reduce inventory, it will naturally concentrate on reducing the levels that it carries for the near term sales. This is where the majority of the dollars is concentrated, seven out of the ten million. The dilemma of the plant manager is that he/she knows that a substantial cut in these inventories will, very likely, jeopardize customer service, turning life into an even bigger hell than it already is. As a matter of fact, we force the plant manager to deal with the wrong issue. The corporate emphasis to reduce inventories comes through the quite new appreciation of inventory as a liability. Looking on inventory as a liability, rather than an asset, actually means that we regard inventory as a loan made to the plant. Money was loaned to the plant which has bought material with it. We expect the money returned, in the form of sales. But what is the unit of measure of a loan? On what basis do we repay a bank for a loan? We do not just consider the sum borrowed, but must deal also with the time the loan is held by the borrower. The unit of measure of a loan is not dollars but dollar times days.

Viewed from this angle we'd better add another line to the description of the plant's finished goods inventory; the line of dollar-days, which actually expresses where the investment is captured. Multiplying the first two lines of our table produces the following result:

| Dollar x Days: | 5 | 7.5 | 15 | 30 | 40 | 100 | 300 | = 497.5 million |

It is now quite apparent that the plant should concentrate on reducing (and certainly not recreating) those inventories that are in the plant's possession for an extended period. The reduction of these inventories is certainly not in conflict with customer service. These inventories are mainly a result of things that should not have been done but were done nevertheless (probably in the attempt to increase local efficiencies, reduce variances or to cover up for a drop in sales in some previous period).

In order to establish the Inventory-Dollar-Day control measurement, we first have to define the buffer appropriate to this specific case. In order to do this let's first define the concept of Customer-Tolerance-Time. This is the time from when a client places an order, until he expects delivery of the order. Customer-Tolerance-Time might differ quite dramatically from product to product. For example, when the product is a jumbo jet, the airlines have a Customer-Tolerance-Time which exceeds three years. But, when the product is a piece of soap our Customer-Tolerance-Time is not much longer than two minutes. Let's further define Product-Lead-Time as the elapsed time to produce the product without giving it any special priority versus other products, and also considering the fact that the most active person residing in our plant is named Murphy.

If our Customer-Tolerance-Time is longer than the Product-Lead-Time for all products, then we do not need to hold any finished goods inventories. If the Customer-Tolerance-Time is zero (i.e., we must ship immediately upon receipt of an order), we should hold inventories to cover what can be expected to be ordered within the next interval—an interval equal to the Product-Lead-Time (plus a little bit of paranoia is appropriate). For all products we should hold finished goods inventory to cover the expected demand in the interval equal to the Product-Lead-Time minus the Customer-Tolerance-Time. These intervals are part of the plan and any inventories in excess of the plan are simply a result of things that we should not do but are doing nevertheless.

In our example, let's assume that this interval is the same for all products and equal to 20 days. This will mean that the plant should be assigned a value of $380 million Inventory-Dollar-Days. Like with the Throughput-Dollar-Days (TDD), here again the plant should strive to reduce it to zero. Inventory-Dollar-Days, is similar to Throughput-Dollar-Days in another aspect. Once Buffer management is applied, the Inventory-Dollar-Days can be used at any level and for any function in the plant. Every unit can be measured by the three control measurements running from the corporate level to the smallest units that we desire to measure.

At this stage the Fundamental Measurements are defined. In the next chapter we will have to start, at last, to deal with the constraints of our system.

A Visit

WHEN QUOTED LEAD TIMES ARE THE PROBLEM

"In manufacturing we have people who are getting much better at dealing with their constraints. Al has done a lot of work. Tom, one of our plant managers has made some physical changes on the floor that really made a nice, big difference. More than once we have broken bottlenecks and now we can ship things we were not going to ship before." Bert—the company's president—takes a deep breath and turning to Chris, his V.P. of Operations, remarks, "We have quite a few Alex Rogo's in your area. In my opinion the problem is no longer in manufacturing!"

Chris, leaning back in his chair answers slowly, not looking at anybody in particular, as if voicing his internal thoughts. "At this stage I would say that we don't have any more bottlenecks—we broke them all. I would estimate that we have cut our work-in-process inventory to about one half of its historical level. But in the last six months we haven't reduced it by more than 10%, maybe 20% at the most. I'm afraid that we are once again stagnating."

It's a little bit unusual. To visit a company that achieves a 50% reduction in work-in-process, and still pushes forward, is not so surprising. But to call an additional 10% improvement, stagnation—that is unusual. Accurate but unusual.

"I can't agree that we should be satisfied with the current performance of manufacturing," Chris continues. "For example, the gap between our computer systems and the reality on the shop floor is widening. Al, can't you do something about it?"

"Come on, Chris," Al the Director of Materials replies, "the situation is not so bad. My people do release all material's schedule promptly. What can I do if sometimes we have to release partial orders because Engineering slips their schedule? Overall, I don't think that our systems are much worse than the rest of our industry. The accuracy of our data is quite good, even though I would like to get a little bit more cooperation from your production people in this area. You must admit that the timeliness of reporting transactions on the floor can be substantially improved."

"Al, we have discussed it more than once," Chris sighs. "How can we insist on prompt reporting of each transaction, when the updated report is available only once a week? The superintendents and foremen are already complaining that the hassle to feed the computer is too much. If you want better and faster data from the floor, you need to provide updated feedback reports within a day, not a week."

"Our system simply can't do it. The computer is so loaded that it's a miracle that you get the response we are currently giving. You know that almost every weekend my people have to stay to guarantee that everything will be ready on Monday morning. If you need faster response, and I agree on that point one hundred percent, we must go to an online system." Al shifts his eyes to Bert. "That means a new, larger, computer and a new state-of-the-art system."

Bert is not impressed at all. "I know that we can pour more money into computers, but the fact is that manufacturing has improved dramatically without investing anything in computers. No, I maintain that the problem is no longer in production. It is on the preparation side of the house. J.P., your area must improve!"

"I know that we can pour more money into computers, but the fact is that manufacturing has improved dramatically without investing anything in computers."

This company is in the business of bidding on furnishing new facilities, such as supplying the furniture for a new laboratory or an auditorium. In this business everything is made to order and the engineering and paperwork functions needed to design and specify the furniture are a big part of the organization. J.P. is in charge of the "preparation" activities and it's apparent that he has been under the gun for quite some time.

"Bert, I don't have to tell you that preparing the drawings is not a trivial task. We must have more modern technology if we want to change things around here. Our CAD systems are simply not good enough. We must provide our people with new systems. I gave you my estimates of the cost involved. It will take us quite some time to train our people properly to use these new systems. Every postponement in the decision just delays further when we can improve. If you decide today, we can improve our side by more than 30% in less than 12 months. I know that the payback is a little bit more than two years, but if we have to do it, let's do it."

"More computers, more technology, more investments, that cannot be the only answer!" Bert starts to explode. "The technology we use today is infinitely better than what we used even ten years ago, but I haven't noticed a comparable improvement in the results. I doubt if today we are responding much faster than ten years ago."

"The bids are much more complicated," J.P. murmurs under his breath.

Chris and Al nod their heads in approval.

"I'm not so convinced," Bert replies. And then, turning to me he says, "You see Jonah, it seems that we cannot even agree on where our constraints are."

I shift uneasily in my chair. It's quite tempting to agree with Bert and to dive into the subject matter, to try and sort out the maze. But it's obvious that this conversation, or a variation of it, has taken place more than once in the past. Thus, it seems reasonable to expect that an intuitive, underlying agreement of the problem, has already been very well established. The best way to proceed is to expose this unverbalized agreement.

Leaving things at the intuition level makes communication almost impossible.

"No Bert, I cannot say that

I see it," I start. "To tell the truth, I have the feeling of someone who enters a movie an hour after it has started. I'm still trying to figure out what's going on. Somehow I have the impression that while you don't agree on the tactics, at the same time, the strategy is agreed on to the extent that you already take it for granted."

They all smile and Chris says, "It's very comfortable to hear that we all agree on something, but unfortunately I don't think that your impression is correct."

I wait for the laughs to calm down and facing Bert, I ask, "What is the biggest business problem facing your company now?"

Bert answers immediately, "We don't win enough bids."

J.P. nods and adds, "Competition is more fierce than ever."

I shift my eyes to Chris and in reply he says, "No doubt. As I said, we have broken all our bottlenecks in production. We can easily handle more orders." After a short while a broad smile spreads across his face and winking his right eye he says, "We do agree on something. You are right. We do agree on the most important thing—on our biggest business problem."

The tension has left the room. I puff on my cigar waiting for Bert to pick up the conversation, which he does. "Touche. But this agreement doesn't preclude us from violently disagreeing on where the constraint is now."

I don't answer, but it doesn't take long until J.P. supplies the answer. "But we do agree on the major constraint. We just said that our current major constraint is the market."

"Yes, of course," says Bert impatiently. "What we actually don't agree on, is how to elevate it."

A hum of agreement is in the room.

Verbalizing what we know intuitively, is a foundation on which we can build our next steps. Leaving things at the intuition level makes communication almost impossible. Thus when a team effort to find a solution is made, it is almost essential not to leave important steps unverbalized. I'm trying to be very careful not to fall into that trap myself. In the conversation they didn't even speculate about the reasons for insufficient sales, indicating that that is another thing that is totally agreed upon among them.

"I have the impression that you agree on an additional thing," I say. "What is the major stumbling block to getting more sales? Is it price, quality or something else?"

Bert answers confidently—"It's not price or quality. It is certainly our too long quoted delivery lead times. You see Jonah, our clients are almost always pressed for time. Maybe it's because furnishing a new facility is the last step in completing it. So if we quote 20 weeks from receipt of order until everything is mounted at the client site, it's always too long. And if a competitor is quoting 10 weeks, he will get the order. Yes, there is a lot of cheating going around, but I insist on quoting reliable estimates. As a matter of fact, we have a very good reputation for delivering when promised. We get quite a few orders because of our reputation. Many times, when a competitor slips significantly on his promised date, the order is transferred to us. No, I will not allow false quotes."

"Nevertheless many times we have to climb up the walls to meet the promise date," Al throws a remark into the room.

"That's the understatement of the year," Chris adds with a tortured expression on his face.

I look at J.P.

"Yes, this is a fair assessment. Our prices are good. We have very high quality products. We have good designs. The problem is definitely in our long quoted lead times. In many cases, too many cases, the competition is quoting as low as half the time. To reduce our estimates, is to squeeze the system even more and you see it's impossible. It's already tight as it is. We must use better and

He had already proven to himself that drastic lead time reduction can be achieved without improving the individual processes.

faster technology if we want to reduce the quoted times and still be reliable."

"Here we go again," says Bert.

I do a quick assessment in my mind. The core of the disagreement between Bert and J.P. is quite obvious. They simply differ in their basic assumptions. J.P.'s assumption is that if his people will do their jobs more quickly, the company will be able to quote shorter lead times. Bert's intuition leads him to assume that the current long quoted lead times are unrelated to the speed at which each individual job is done, but related to the synchronization between the jobs.

Chris's disagreement must stem from a different source. He had already proven to himself that drastic lead time reduction can be achieved without improving the individual processes. What is it? Can it be that manufacturing is still the biggest contributor to lead time or is it just part of the political power struggle? Something does not click since Chris didn't ask for any new investments. And what about Chris's remark on the widening gap between the floor and the computer system? Al succeeded, probably unintentionally, in diverting him, but something important must lie under Chris's remark. I've too much respect for management intuition to ignore it. Questions! Questions!

How to peer into it? I decide to continue in the most obvious way. If they claim that their quoted lead times are the major cause of their marketing constraint, let's dig into this subject.

"When the client is pressed for time, we can even offer it for free and it will not help us to get the order."

"Bert, you all say that the long quoted lead times preclude you from winning enough bids. Can you give me a rough breakdown of the components of this lead time? What are the activities, and estimates of their duration, that you take into account before quoting a delivery date to a prospect?"

"It differs from bid to bid," Bert starts slowly, searching for a way to clarify this complex situation to an outsider who does not "live" his business. "There are very small orders and also very large and complicated bids. Let's take, for example, an average bid, something in the range of $100 to $300 thousand. A typical breakdown will be something like four weeks for the design, then there's approval. . . .J.P. this is your area. Can you help me?"

"Certainly," J.P. says. "As a matter of fact I have some statistics here on the various bids. You wanted bids between $100 and $300 thousand. . .just a minute." Quickly he sifts through a pile of papers that he has brought with him. After a very short while he raises his head. "Here is a breakdown of quotes for laboratories in the range of $100 to $250 thousand. It takes one week to process the order, five weeks to draw the project, two weeks to approve the drawings with the customer, one week to enter the corrections to the drawings and then two weeks to prepare it for release to manufacturing. Then add ten weeks for manufacturing plus one week in shipping and five weeks for installation."

"Thank you," says Bert and turning to me he continues, "add it all up and you get. . .26 weeks. The competition is quoting about 20 weeks, which means that we promise to ship our first truck when our competitor is promising to complete the entire order. When the client is pressed for time, we can even offer it for free and it will not help us to get the order."

I nod my head to indicate that the severity of the problem is well understood, waiting for Chris to jump in, which he doesn't. That puzzles me. The numbers certainly support Chris's position that manufacturing is still the major area to focus on. From the 26 weeks quoted, 16 weeks are needed after all the preparation is completed. Why doesn't Chris take this opportunity to clearly demonstrate his point?

Conversation has stopped and everybody is looking at me.

> *. . . each person, when asked to evaluate the time it will take to complete a task, will instinctively add a safety factor.*

Maybe on-site-construction, or as they call it 'installation,' does not report to Chris. If this is the case, then he is responsible for just 10 weeks out of the 26. This seems a remote possibility since Chris's title, "Vice President of Operations" indicates that he is responsible for more than just manufacturing. Besides, if another person was responsible for installation, it is reasonable to expect that Bert would have invited him to this meeting. Since I cannot find any other plausible explanation, I turn to Chris. "Who is responsible for the on-site-construction?" I ask.

"Me," comes the answer.

Now what? I wonder. Can it be that Chris does not believe in these numbers and thus hesitates to use them as a base for his position? This might be the answer. Certainly there is not a direct communication between Chris's production people and the people who prepare the quotes for the bids. They report to J.P.. From my experience I've learned that each person, when asked to evaluate the time it will take to complete a task, will instinctively add a safety factor. If the process involves a series of people, each will add an additional safety and the end result will be vastly exaggerated. This phenomena takes on grotesque proportions when the people involved don't trust each other. In this case the people in marketing and product engineering don't exactly trust the production people, and thus will tend to protect themselves, against future complaints from clients, by inflating the time estimates.

So it is reasonable to assume that Chris does not agree at all with the numbers that J.P. has quoted. But how to verify it? I cannot take a straightforward approach and simply ask Chris if he does not agree with the numbers. At Chris's and J.P.'s levels, they are very careful not to get into an open confrontation in front of their boss. A direct question will just put Chris in a very embarrassing situation and the only thing that will result, is a very vague "political" statement.

If my hypothesis is right, the recent reduction in production lead time, will not be fully reflected in the estimates currently used in the quotations. The same overprotective mechanism will guarantee it. The next (now) obvious question is, "What did you use as an estimate for the production lead time of such an order two years ago?"

"About 12 weeks," J.P. answers.

Bingo! The quoted production lead times have gone down by only 2 weeks even though the actual production lead time dropped by much more. I make a fast calculation in my head. The work-in-process inventories were cut by more than 50%. The level of work-in-process is proportional to production lead times (see *The Race* pages 64-65). The current production lead time is probably less than 6 weeks, not 10 weeks.

The dichotomy does not escape Bert. "Wait a minute," he says, "the actual reduction in manufacturing is much more than two weeks. Chris, what is your estimate?"

"I would say that in the last year, manufacturing has cut at least five weeks," Chris replies. "Everybody knows that we have made major strides in this area."

J.P. raises his hand. "Sorry fellows. My people must rely on the numbers that are supplied by the computer. According to what is reported, the production lead time has dropped by only two weeks."

In response Chris immediately turns to Al. "You see what happens when we have such a crooked production planning system? I've told you a hundred times that the gap between our computer system and the reality on the floor is intolerable!"

Al looks totally puzzled. "But these numbers don't have anything to do with the production planning system. They are derived directly from the completion dates reported by the production people. It is impossible that such a gross error is generated by the computer."

"It's a fact," Chris states, but even he looks unconvinced.

"I don't care what the

> *"I would estimate that about 80% of top management time is absorbed in fire fighting."*

— 31 —

damn computer says," Bert cuts into the argument. "Everybody knows that the production lead time has been cut by more than just two weeks. J.P., your people must update their numbers. It's essential. This overcaution is costing us the entire business."

J.P. doesn't look too enthusiastic.

"The minute that we start to ignore hard numbers and start to rely on things that everybody knows, there is no way to predict where it will end. Bert, I agree that something is wrong, and maybe very wrong. But the fact is that the hard numbers indicate only two weeks reduction and even now we sometimes have difficulties completing an installation on time."

He has a point, but I'm totally unsatisfied with the president's response.

"J.P., it is still obvious that something is wrong. Will you please look into it in depth?" Bert presses.

"Yes, of course," is the expected answer, but it's apparent that nothing will actually be done.

* * * * *

"Do you have difficulties in completing every order?" I ask Chris.

"No, no," he replies. "Lately we finish some orders even ahead of the promised date and most are met without exceptional hassle. But those that we have difficulties with are enough to make you old."

"What percentage of the orders do you have difficulties with?"

> "...but if these are the things that absorb most of management's time, I wonder if it pays."

"Oh, not many, thank God. But there is always at least one. And they are draining everybody's time. For example, just now, we have a serious emergency. It's a last minute change that has caused us to work overtime in one of our shops, for the last two days. A special truck delivery had to be arranged and the entire construction schedule is disrupted. I envision that I'll probably have to go to the site personally, to straighten things out."

"It's constant fire fighting," Bert contributes his share. "I would estimate that about 80% of top management time is absorbed in fire fighting."

Everybody nods his head in full agreement.

"You mentioned that the current problem order was due to a last minute change," I ask.

"Which the client has handsomely paid for," J.P. remarks.

"Yes, I assume so," I continue. "Would you say, Chris, that last minute changes are the cause for the vast majority of these problem orders?"

"Yes, definitely," Chris answers in a very confident tone. "If it wasn't for these last minute changes, and sometimes the changes come after the last minute, there is no problem at all. I can categorically state that in the last year we haven't had any problems with any order that didn't involve last minute changes."

A very thoughtful expression is now on Bert's face. After a short while he turns to J.P.

"The clients are paying very handsomely for these changes. I wonder if it is really the case."

"We are charging more than twice the usual rate for changes. If that is not a nice price, what is?"

"Yes, we charge twice as much," Bert continues in a thoughtful tone, "but if these are the things that absorb most of management's time, I wonder if it pays." After a short while he continues, "And if due to these changes, we are under

"So, as our quoted lead times are longer, we simply give more time for the client to change his mind."

the impression that our lead time estimates are not conservative enough...I wonder how many bids we have lost due to this probably false impression."

"Even if we want to stop it, we can't," J.P., reading what Bert is alluding to, hurries to state. "We cannot stop a client from making changes and we simply cannot charge more without creating an outrage. As long as the client doesn't feel that it is absolutely too late, he feels free to make changes. And we, as a reputable company, must respond."

"Yes, I see what you mean," sighs Bert.

After a short while I ask, "What do you think makes a client feel that it is too late?"

Everyone looks at me as if I have asked an improper question. But J.P. answers, "When it's obvious that it's too late."

I feel a little bit stupid, but I keep on looking steadily at J.P. until he adds, "Like when all the pieces are already on the client's site and construction has started."

"Hey, that is not necessarily the case," Chris jumps in. "Take, for example, this current problem order. We definitely received the change after the last truck was sent."

"It might be the case. But most probably the client initiated the change at least two weeks before," J.P. answers.

"I see," says Bert. "So, as our quoted lead times are longer, we simply give more time for the client to change his mind. Which causes last minute changes. Which gives us the impression that our quoted lead times are not long enough. Which prevents us from cutting them, even if the reality is that our production lead time has been shortened dramatically. How did we allow such a vicious cycle?"

It is quite obvious that he feels good. I don't.

"Come to think about it," Al adds oil to the fire, "in all

cases where we are not hit by last minute surprises, the actual construction is finished well ahead of time."

"Yes," Chris contributes his share. "The big allowance for construction time was never due to the actual time of construction, but in order to enable us to ship the last pieces that were always missing. After we broke all our bottlenecks this situation improved dramatically."

"What is your estimate for construction time?" Bert asks.

"For the type of bid that we are discussing, it certainly is below three weeks," Chris replies.

That's my impression," is Al's back up.

"So I see," Bert speaks, looking at nobody in particular. "We exaggerate our production estimates by about 4 weeks and then two more weeks in construction. Here are the six weeks we are missing."

He looks at J.P.

But before Bert can summarize, J.P. jumps in, "We should check this new assumption about the shrinkage of construction time." He emphasizes the words "new assumption" to the extent that it's clear that his opinion on this subject is vastly different. "I believe it's possible to separate the orders that do not contain any last minute changes, and then check the reported construction time. If there are no unforeseen problems, I think that we can dig out the facts in less than a month."

"I don't see why we have to wait a month for something that we already know," Bert starts to lose his patience. "This business has started to lose money because we don't win enough bids. The times that we could afford this overcaution are over. We must move and move fast. J.P. I don't want any postponement in the implementation of what we just found. The lead times, quoted in the bids, must be cut immediately."

"Jonah, you don't look very happy. What's the matter?

"If that's what you want," comes the very reluctant answer.

Bert is not too happy with J.P.'s response and so, after a short silence, he continues, "Competition is more fierce than ever, those were your words, J.P. We must move aggressively in order to keep pace. I'm sure that you understand. Sometimes we have to take chances."

"As long as we all understand that it is taking a chance," J.P. says. "Yes, I understand your decision and you can count on me to take all the necessary steps immediately."

"Thank you," says Bert. He looks around with a determined expression on his face.

It is quite obvious that he feels good. I don't.

* * * * *

The three of them are chatting about something, using the local jargon that is characteristic of each plant, so I stand up to pour myself a cup of coffee. I wonder why it is that we are so satisfied with finding solutions for immediate problems and are so reluctant to expose the causes. It's not the first time that I've witnessed it, and unfortunately, it's won't be the last time.

Bert stands up and joins me.

"Jonah, you don't look very happy. What's the matter? Aren't you satisfied with what we achieved this morning?"

"Oh yes," I answer. "But we cannot ignore the fact that some questions have been left unanswered."

> "We have an MRP computer system. We bought a commercial package and modified it considerably to fit our particular needs."

"Which questions?" asks Bert, certainly interested.

"There are several. For example, why do the numbers indicate that production lead times have been reduced by just two weeks?"

"Hey, that's computer stuff. I'm certain that the reduction is at least five weeks. Probably more."

It's clear that in his mind this problem is a triviality. "And Chris's complaint about the widening gap between systems and the shop floor?" I continue.

"Jonah, don't worry. It's just the same computer stuff," Bert answers confidently.

"Maybe," I say, "Nevertheless, passing on erroneous information might be hazardous."

"Yes, I agree," says Bert, but he doesn't seem to be too concerned. "Any other open questions?" he asks.

"Nothing, except for clarifying the root cause for the disagreements among you."

"What disagreements?" he asks in a much more interested tone.

"If I'm not mistaken, you claimed this morning that the problems have shifted to the preparation side of the house. We didn't touch on this subject at all."

"Yes, that's true."

"And besides, J.P. and Al are quite convinced that they can improve only if additional investments are approved. Let's remember that even if this reduction in the quoted lead times can be implemented without problems, it will just put you on par with your competitor. I assume that they will continue to improve their performance and thus you still have to face this demand for more investments."

"You are absolutely right, Jonah," he says. "Why don't we return to the table and continue our discussion."

I pour myself another cup

"But if we take a week for each level, how did you actually reduce your work-in-process?"

and we all sit down.

"Al, can I ask you some technical questions," I start. "How do you plan the material release?"

"We have an MRP computer system. We bought a commercial package and modified it considerably to fit our particular needs."

"Can you be a little bit more specific?" I slowly light my cigar to indicate that we have all the time in the world.

"It's actually very simple," Al continues, "as long as we don't dive into the tiny, nitty gritty, of course. Once the information is coded by J.P.'s people, you know the bill of materials and the routings, we explode down the requirements from the specified shipping dates. Our bill of material is quite deep. It ranges from 6 to up to 11 levels, so we net the requirements against the stocks at each level and..."

I raise my eyebrows in surprise. I was under the impression that they build just to order, so what stocks is he talking about?

Al, noticing my surprise, hurries to clarify the issue. "There are many standard finished products and certainly many standard components. These we manufacture to forecast. So there is a need to net at each level. Besides at almost every level we use standard purchased components that we hold in stock."

"What are the lead times you are using in your MRP data base?" I ask.

"The usual. One week for each level," comes the reply.

Bert, who looked somewhat bored during the discussion of these technical details, cannot hold back his surprise.

"What? A week for each stage of assembly? Have I heard you right?"

Chris comes to Al's aid. "It's not intended to reflect the actual assembly time, Bert. It's the traditional number that we have used for years to allow all the components to be gathered together. You know the problem of assembly. All fifty parts that are needed to be assembled are there, except for one."

"Oh," says Bert. "But if we take a week for each level, how did you actually reduce your work-in-process?"

"We don't release to the floor according to the timing of the computer. We just use the quantities it specifies," Chris answers with a broad smile. And, turning to me he continues, "We have learned something from *The Goal*. We are using the painting area as the 'Herbie'. It's not a real bottleneck any more, we have improved it so much, that we operate it only 2 shifts 5 days a week, instead of running constantly on weekends, as in the past. But at our current level of manning, it's definitely a 'Herbie'."

Turning back to Bert he continues, "Today my superintendents delay the release of material by more than a month and time the release according to the rate of the paint shop. It's working very well. It also gives us a nice protection against delays in the release of the last drawing for an order. It was a big problem before."

"Yes, I've noticed that you don't complain about it any more," says Bert.

It's obvious that he is deep in thought. You can almost hear the wheels clicking in his head.

After a short while he continues, "So that is the reason why J.P.'s numbers indicated that the production lead times have been reduced by only two weeks. Most of the lead time reduction was used to increase the time gap between preparation and manufacturing, rather than reduce the delivery time." He pauses and then slowly he asks, "Chris, to time the release of all the work must be a lot of manual effort. How do you handle it?"

"That is exactly what I'm complaining about. We have to work with old computer lists and spend a great deal of time

"So, we will be able to make the same mistakes faster and on a bigger scale."

basically monitoring everything manually," Chris replies in a voice that indicates, "at last somebody understands."

Bert turns to face Al. "Why shouldn't the computer do these calculations?"

Al, with a miserable expression on his face answers, "I've explained it to Chris more than once. Our systems simply are not capable of doing it."

"And the new online systems that you are so inclined to purchase. Can they do it?" presses Bert.

Now Al looks really miserable, and with a twisted grin he says, "I really didn't check into it thoroughly, because I actually don't know what to check. But I suspect that they are not much different than what we already have, except for speed and online capabilities, of course."

"So, we will be able to make the same mistakes faster and on a bigger scale," Bert concludes sardonically. After a minute or two Bert starts again. "We must do something about it. We can't leave all the benefit of the lead time improvement in manufacturing, it's on the wrong side of the process. We must use it to shorten the overall lead time, rather than just to increase the protection between preparation and production. Jonah, can you help me?"

I puff on my cigar for a short while and then say, "You don't need me to tell you the answer. Your people know how to do it."

"But we don't," says Al almost desperately.

"Al," I say. "Am I right in assuming that your people are doing this manual work for the production superintendents?"

> *"And try not to fall into the trap of considering the process time in calculating the overall lead time."*

"Yes, you are right," answers Chris instead. "The cooperation between the production and the material people is very good."

"Good," I echo. "Al, will you try to describe the sequence of this manual work."

"Chris, I'll need some help."

"Certainly, Al. I doubt if I know enough, but let's give it a try."

"Okay," Al starts. "The first step is very clear. The scheduler and the assembly superintendents decide on the schedule of our 'Herbie', the paint shop."

"Yes," adds Chris. "We have created a nice, big wooden chart on the wall for this purpose."

"Jonah, how can we mechanize this first step," says Al. "I've been racking my brain for quite some time, but it's clearly beyond me."

"Can't our current MRP software do it?" asks Bert.

"No. And it's not just our MRP," answers Al, "but any MRP. You see Bert, one of the basic assumptions of MRP is infinite capacity, which in other words means internal constraints do not exist. If they do exist, as in our case and probably many other cases, then you are on your own!"

"That's not entirely accurate," Chris remarks. "You are supposed to handle these internal capacity constraints through changing the dates and quantities required at the upper levels—the final products. This is actually what is meant by the 'Master Schedule'. As a matter of fact that is exactly what we do in the second step of our manual procedures. Based on the schedule that we construct for the paint shop, we update our truck shipping schedule. This is simply a detailed procedure to create a Master Schedule, nothing more."

"Yes, I guess you're right," replies Al. "But I still don't know how to mechanize it."

"Why should you?" asks Chris. "This is not a time consuming step. Moreover, the superintendents like to do it themselves. It gives them the

"Don't forget that MRP assumes that the transfer batch is equal to the process batch."

feeling that they are in charge." After a short while he continues. "As a matter of fact, I want this critical step to be under their control, I myself will feel much better. No, Al, this is not the problem. The vast majority of the manual work and all the stupid mistakes, are in the next step where we determine the timing of the release of the thousands of components."

Al thinks for a minute or two. Everybody is silent, letting him self-digest this.

Finally he says, "I guess that this can be done by our current system, even though I will have to hammer out the details." And then, turning to me, he asks, "I understand that I will have to incorporate the buffer time into the MRP lead time. But this will increase the overall lead time." And, without waiting for an answer, he concludes, "I guess I will have to study the mechanism of Drum-Buffer-Rope again. It's already apparent that I'll have to erase most of the lead times that now are specified for the various levels."

"You are right," I say. "And try not to fall into the trap of considering the process time in calculating the overall lead time."

"Why?" asks Al. "I thought this would give us more precise answers than we get today."

"Don't forget that MRP assumes that the transfer batch is equal to the process batch. It might considerably distort the release," I add.

"What do you mean by those terms?" asks Chris.

"It's okay," says Al. "I'll explain it to you later. But, Jonah, how can we neglect the actual process time?"

> "...but this is your instruction."
> "Mine?!" explodes Bert.

"The buffers must be much larger than the process time of a single unit. I assume that today you are using weeks for the time buffers. What is the actual process time, on the average, for a single unit going through the shop?"

"No more than two hours at the most," answers Chris.

"I see," says Al. "But it is still very hard to swallow. To ignore all process times! Hmmm—I'll have to think about it."

Bert wasn't listening at all to the last part of the conversation. He is deep in thought. Chris looks a little bit puzzled, while J.P. is definitely bored.

But then Bert starts again, "If we cut the time allotted to manufacturing then we will not be able to tolerate any slippage in the release of the drawings. Today, we don't have this problem since manufacturing is using most of their shorter lead times to give more leeway to preparation. They release the material much later than scheduled. J.P., I knew that your area must improve."

J.P. is no longer bored and a tense expression now forms on his face when Bert continues. "We must look in more detail into your area."

"What do you mean exactly?" asks J.P., still surprised by the sharp shift in the conversation.

"Do your people release the complete details of the order to manufacturing all at once, or are there almost always some drawings that are released much later?"

"You know the situation," answers J.P.. "There are always, for some reason or another, some problem details that take longer to complete."

"Yes," says Bert. "And there is more than enough time allotted to complete them as well."

"Not with the existing CAD system."

"Here we go again," Bert says in a quite low tone. And then looking at the statistics that he holds in his hand continues, "What is this two weeks to get the approval from the client? If he is pressed for time we

"Have you viewed The Goal *in a more generic way? As a story about completing a task using a number of different resources?"*

— 43 —

certainly can ask him to approve it in two days. Especially when most of the approval is done piecemeal anyhow, during the four weeks that it takes us to do the drawings."

"Yes, that is right," says J.P., "but this is your instruction."

"Mine?!" explodes Bert.

"Yes. You remember. Three years ago, when we had the debate with Olson and we had to replace a lot of furniture because some signatures were missing. You instructed us to allow two weeks for this stage and to make sure that every drawing is signed by the client."

"Yes, I do remember. But it was different then. Our problem at that time was capacity, not orders."

Bert looks angry and confused.

"Bert," J.P. speaks in a pacifying tone, "we were stressing the need for quoting reliable lead times. I don't see any problem of putting only two days for approval in our bids and adding a small section that clearly states that any delay in client approval, will delay the completion of the installation by the same number of days."

"Thank you," says Bert, "I appreciate it." But then after a short while he continues, "Can't we squeeze more time from the preparation?"

"Not with our current technology," answers J.P. in a rigid tone, careful not to show his impatience. "All my people are working all the time. I simply cannot see how we can squeeze anything more out, without giving them better tools."

...it is not a gift, it's just a skill honed by practicing some very specific techniques...

Bert looks at me seeking help. "J.P.," I start. "Would you say that on the desk of your engineers we will find only the work that they are currently engaged in, or an additional job or two?"

"Since so many times a job is stuck due to some details that have to be clarified with someone else, we are very careful to supply everyone with more than one job. This is the only way that we can make everyone efficient. I would guess that on the desk of each of my people you will find at least two or three jobs."

J.P. looks quite satisfied with his answer, and he is surprised that Bert isn't.

"J.P., have you tried to look at the situation from the point of view of the jobs?" asks Bert.

"What do you mean," is J.P.'s puzzled response.

"If on each table there are two or three jobs," Bert tries to clarify, "then each job is waiting to be processed more time than it is actually processed."

"Try it on me once again. I don't see your point."

Bert looks at him in the attempt to find a better way to explain but at last he asks, "Have you read *The Goal?*"

"Yes, about two years ago," replies J.P. "But it's about manufacturing. What does it have to do with our preparation efforts which are mainly engineering and paper work?"

Bert shows that a president must know the art of patience.

"Have you viewed *The Goal* in a more generic way? As a story about completing a task using a number of different resources?"

"To tell the truth, no," answers J.P.. "I'll have to read it again."

"Why won't you do it and then we will discuss the situation further," Bert concludes. He starts to rise from his chair. "It was certainly a very fruitful day."

* * * * *

As Bert accompanies me to the lobby, he continues to speak about the events of the day. Finally, when we are at the front door he asks, "Jonah, are you satisfied with what we accomplished?"

"Yes, definitely," I answer. "Provided that you are aware that the most important question is still open."

"What do you mean?"

"Why did you need me to trigger the discussion? Why didn't you do it on your own?"

"Come on, Jonah," Bert bursts into laughter. "I don't fool myself. If it wasn't for your pointed questions we would still be debating this thing and going in circles as we have done for the last six months."

"Yes, I see. But why couldn't you do the same on your own?"

Bert puts his big hand on my shoulder, "Not everyone is as gifted as you are, Jonah."

I turn to face him. "Bert, it is not a gift, it's just a skill honed by practicing some very specific techniques, like cause-and-effect reasoning to find the root cause problems and the 'evaporating clouds' technique to come up with those 'common sense' solutions." (See Issue 2 of the Theory of Constraints Journal). "My recommendation is that you invest some time learning and mastering them."

"Is it possible?" Bert asks in a totally unconvinced tone.

"Yes, it definitely is!" I answer.

Chapter 4

THE IMPORTANCE OF A SYSTEM'S CONSTRAINTS

1 | How Medium-Range Decisions are Made

In medium-range decisions and, of course, in short-range ones, the financial statements are exposed as totally impotent. Nevertheless, such decisions are routinely made in every plant. How are they made? An objective examination reveals that the decisions themselves are usually reached intuitively, and then communicated through a formal cost procedure.

Pretend, for example, that you are in charge of a production department, and you know, intuitively, that another machine must be bought. So you go to your boss and say, "We must purchase this machine." If you feel strongly about it, you will probably add another "we must" in a very decisive tone. But when your boss asks, "Why do we need to buy this additional machine?" your only answer will be "because I feel it." As long as the decision is intuitive, this is the only available answer. It is quite obvious that intuition is not a basis for communication.

Many times your boss is quite close to you and has learned to trust your judgement, so he will agree with your request. But an appropriation request has to be prepared to get higher level approval for the purchase. In this case, an informal

> *... that intuition is not a basis for communication.*

connection will not help. Did you ever try to submit an appropriation request for the purchase of new equipment and write, as the formal reason, something like "I feel it?"

How are such approvals actually obtained? You will probably first estimate the cost savings per part that will result from purchasing the new machine. Then, to find the total savings per year, you will estimate the number of parts that you can run through this machine. This cost savings number will be compared to the price of the machine to establish the return on investment period. Usually, if the end result is a pay back that is more than two years, a re-evaluation will be done to drive the payback period below the sacred two-year level. Incidentally, this threshold is used by almost every company for individual pieces of equipment, while a substantially larger number is used for investment in an entire plant or a product line.

We can see clearly, at least in this type of situation, that even though the decision was made intuitively, the formal communication is based on a cost procedure—in this case, a cost-saving procedure. Let's review another situation, one where a cost procedure comes first and the intuition-based decision is second in the sequence of events. Suppose a client of yours says, "I'm impressed with your products and I want you to ship me 1,000 units on such and such a date." Then, immediately after you state that there are no problems, he adds, "but at this price!" We all know that it is the market, and not our companies, that determines selling prices. What is your decision? Should you accept the order?

Usually, you (or the accounting department) will then go through a cost procedure. You will calculate the cost of the raw materials and purchased parts that are needed for a single unit. Then you'll make a very careful estimation of the labor time per unit and extend it by the appropriate rate. On top of this, the overhead will be added, usually by multiplying the direct-labor portion by the overhead fudge-factor established last year. As a result, you'll have the "product cost." You will compare the product cost to the price offered and hope that the difference is larger than the profit margin you seek. What happens if it's smaller? No, the decision is not necessarily to refuse the order. Many times you'll recognize you don't have enough work in the plant. Your intuition will then cause you to override the cost recommendation and accept the order.

> *Cost procedures are the main formal way to communicate medium-range decisions.*

2 The Two Financial Worlds

Cost procedures (all of them involving cost accounting) are the main formal way to *communicate* medium-range decisions, even though in crucial situations the decisive factor in *reaching* a decision is intuition. Because of the impotence of the financial statements as a guide in local decision making, and the virtual sovereignty of cost procedures for communicating the reasons for local decisions, we have been brought to the current situation where there is almost a consensus that more than one financial method is needed:

- One method—the financial statements—for the purpose of judging the performance of the system as a whole

- The second method—the various cost procedures—for the purpose of judging the impact of a local decision or a local area on the system's overall performance

It looks a little bit strange that we need two almost disconnected methods to judge what is, intuitively, one system for us. Do we really need to separate between measuring the performance of a system and measuring the impact of a component on the performance of the system? If so, why is it that the connection between these two methods (a connection that *must* be there) is not clear to us?

> *It looks a little bit strange that we need two almost disconnected methods to judge what is, intuitively, one system for us.*

The fundamental measurements—Throughput, Inventory, and Operating Expense—that were proposed in the previous journal, cast a long shadow of doubt on the need for more than one financial method. If we take two measurements that clearly represent the existing segmentation (between judging the performance of the system and the impact of a component on the performance), they will be Net Profit and Productivity. One measure is taken from the "macro" representation of the financial statement world, while the other belongs to the more "micro" representation of the component level—the cost procedure world. Nevertheless, if we try to express these two vastly different measurements of Net Profit and Productivity using the operational measurements, we'll find out that Net Profit is just the difference between Throughput and Operating Expenses (NP = T − OE), while Productivity is the ratio between them (Productivity = T/OE). It looks like the operational measurements (T, I, and OE) merge the two worlds into one. If this is really the case, where does cost accounting enter into the picture?

To answer this question, we'll have to explore in greater depth why (and not just how) cost accounting was invented. As we said before, Net Profit is the difference between the Throughput and the Operating Expense. The Throughput of a given system is the Throughput achieved through the sale of one type of product, plus the Throughput achieved through the sale of another type of product, and so on. Thus, the Throughput of the system is the summation of the Throughputs of all the various products. In a more formal way, it can be written as $T = \Sigma_i T_i$, where i encompasses all the types of products that were sold during a given period.

The formalized way of handling Operating Expenses is slightly different. The Operating Expenses of the system are those that the system spent on one category of expense (like labor) plus those spent on a second category of expense (like interest paid to the bank), and so on. In a formal way, it can be written as $OE = \Sigma_j OE_j$, where j encompasses all the categories of expenses incurred during the same period.

> *It looks like the operational measurements merge the two worlds into one.*

In summary, the formal presentation of Net Profit will be: $NP = \Sigma_i T_i - \Sigma_j OE_j$ (where i refers to product type and j refers to expense category). It should be noted that, in such a presentation, there is no meaning to the phrase "the profit of a product."

3 Why Cost Allocation Was Invented

What is the inherent difficulty that prevents the use of this formula for making local decisions? The problem lies in the difficulty of answering questions like:

- What is the impact of increasing the Throughput of one product on the Throughput of others or on any of the Operating Expense categories?

- What is the impact of trimming the expense of one Operating Expense category on other expenses and on the Throughput of the various products?

In order to answer this type of question, which is exactly what is required in order to make any local decision, a very clever—almost ingenious—approximation was proposed at the beginning of this century. At that time, the two main expense categories were Material (which according to our definitions is not an expense, but rather a conversion of investment from one category-Cash, into another-Material Inventory) and Labor. All other categories of expense, taken together, were almost negligible compared to either one of those two. So the following approximation was proposed: Why should we talk in terms of categories

> **What is the impact of increasing the Throughput of one product on the Throughput of others...?**

of expenses, when it is *almost* as accurate to talk in terms of expenses associated with making a product? As a result, the following nomenclature was suggested:

Net Profit $\approx \Sigma_i NP_i = \Sigma_i (T-OE)_i$ (where i refers to product type).

Using this approximation, the Net Profit of the system is just a summation of the Net Profit generated by each of the types of products the system sold. These various Net Profits are, in turn, the summation, for all products, of the difference between the sale of a particular product minus the Operating Expenses caused by the decision to produce that particular product. What was achieved by this approximation was staggering. It enabled us to segment the system into many non-interactive pieces, dissecting the ties between the various products. Decisions regarding one product could now be made without the need to check the impact of such decisions on other products. It became possible to make local decisions relatively easily.

It can be argued that, as long as it's impossible to add or subtract resources in infinitesimal increments, this approximation is not always valid. Nonetheless, it is quite clear that in the environment where it was first suggested, (an environment where the quantities produced of each product were very large compared to the number of workers employed and where the other expenses were basically negligible), it was a very valid and powerful approximation.

[The Theory of Constraints will argue with this last statement, claiming that, even under the above conditions, the approximation is valid only for the "productive capacity" and not for the non-negligible "protective capacity" and, thus, even at the beginning of the century this approximation was not valid. But since these terms have not yet been defined, any in-depth discussion must be postponed to a later chapter.]

4. Other Terms That Must Go

All it has done is replace a small i by a small j...

Let's review the above approximation a little further. All it has done is replace a small i by a small j, namely: $\Sigma_i T_i - \Sigma_j OE_j \approx \Sigma_i (T - OE)_i$, (where i refers to product type and j to expense category).

What is OE_i (Operating Expense due to product i)? It doesn't take long to realize that it's the costs (Operating Expenses) that we *allocate* to a product. Here is our old friend—cost allocation. We reached the conclusion in the previous article that the cost allocation mechanism has to be replaced, which implies that we must discard the above approximation. Thus, we will have to go back and find another answer to overcome the difficulty of using the explicit formula of Net Profit for local decisions.

But, before doing that, it is worthwhile to explore the nomenclature that this approximation has brought with it. It should be stressed that this allocation mechanism, which was introduced in order to facilitate judging local decisions, has brought with it a new nomenclature. This nomenclature is valid and useful only as long as we accept the validity of the approximation. Once we no longer accept the approximation, then we should immediately abandon the nomenclature. We have to be careful not to fall into the habit of continuing to use it once we decide to replace the allocation mechanism.

One term that will have to be discarded is obvious: OE_i (where i refers to product type) does not exist. It is just a bad approximation. We are accustomed to referring to this entity not just as "cost allocated to product i," but also by its short version, the "cost of product i." Can we accept that the term "product cost" has to be discarded?

But that is not all. How have we referred to the expression T-OE? This is the "product profit margin." Will we ever get used to living in a world where the terms "product margin" or "profit of a product" no longer exist? Based on my experience, the transition

> *Can we accept that the term "product cost" has to be discarded?*

is not going to be short or easy. These terms have already become part of our reality and it will be hard to recognize that they are not real, but just the brain child of our mind —mathematical expressions which are no longer valid.

I will go even further and recommend that, for the time being, we totally abolish the word "cost" from our terminology. The most devastating words are ones that have multiple meanings, where one of these meanings is misleading. The legitimacy of other valid meanings makes it quite difficult to pinpoint when the word is used erroneously. This leads to mis-communication and confused reasoning.

Since the word "cost" has three totally different meanings, it definitely belongs in the above category. One use is "cost" as a synonym for Operating Expenses, as in the phrase "the cost of running an organization." The second use is "cost" to mean "price," as in "the cost of purchasing a particular machine or the cost of a particular raw material." The danger, of course, is in using the third meaning of the word "cost," the artificial connotation of "product cost."

Since we currently have popular synonyms for Operating Expense and Price, it makes sense to abandon the use of the word "cost" altogether, and shorten the time to convert from the erroneous allocation approximation.

It's worthwhile to note that, while the allocation mechanism was introduced to bypass the difficulty in the Net Profit formula, little attention was given directly to Return On Investment. Written explicitly, this formula would be: $ROI = (T - OE)/I = (\Sigma_i T_i - \Sigma_j OE_j)/(\Sigma_k I_k)$ where k encompasses all categories of Investment.

One of the major categories of investment is material inventory. The negligence—or the difficulty—of relating k to i, (the investment required by a particular product), has brought us to the current situation, where usually little attention, if any, is given to the impact of a decision on the change in Material Inventory that the system has to carry. Even in decisions where it represents the major change in the investment (like buying new equipment to capture additional market) it's usually not considered at all!

> *...usually little attention, if any, is given to the impact of a decision on the change in Material Inventory that the system has to carry.*

5 Substitute For "Cost Allocation"

Going back and reviewing our ability to make local decisions based on the explicit expression of Net Profit, it doesn't look so difficult at first glance. Suppose, for example, that we want to consider trimming a product from our portfolio. Conventionally we will have to calculate the dollar value of its material content. Then we will measure, as accurately as possible, the direct labor minutes that are needed to process one unit. We will have some problems deciding how to handle the time required to set up the machine, but we'll overcome them by fixing some standard batches. I don't want to think about how to handle cases where the set-up time is heavily dependent not just on the product in question but also on the type (or family) of the product that the machine has just finished processing. You probably don't want to think about it either. But we'll manage by choosing some approximate average set-up time. Then we will multiply the overhead factor that was generated in the last period or over several periods, (depending on what is the customary procedure in the company), by our measured/estimated direct labor effort per unit. This result, together with the material, will finally give us the "cost" of producing a unit of our product—OE_i.

If we want to be very sophisticated, we will use different overhead factors for the different work centers used to process our product...but enough is enough. Once we have the "product

> *So we trim that product as well, the merry-go-round continues, and soon we close the plant.*

cost," we'll compare it to the product price to determine whether the difference is large enough relative to the "cost." We have some standard "percent margin" that we would like to achieve for each of our products. If the margin is large, we will call this product a star and, certainly, will not consider dropping it. If the margin is negative, or even small, we have a dog on our hands. The temptation to trim it is very big.

We won't always trim it. We do remember (sometimes) that trimming a product doesn't always lead to an actual cut in expenses. Even if we can lay off some people, it is very hard to fire machines or management. As a result, our overhead factor will increase. It might be a small increase, but it will raise the "cost" of all the remaining products. Often, in the past, managements were not aware of this impact or they chose to ignore it, and experienced the infamous "domino-effect." One product is dropped because of the above reason and the "cost" of the other products goes up. One of the other products reaches a level where its "cost" is too high compared to its selling price. So we trim that product as well, the merry-go-round continues, and soon we close the plant.

If we had used the explicit formula of Net Profit directly, the reasoning would have been totally different. By trimming the above product, we would know how much the Throughput is reduced. It's simply the result of the selling price minus the material price per unit multiplied by the number of units that we currently sell. What we have to consider now is the impact of trimming that product on the Operating Expenses. How many people will we be able to lay off (not just in production but also in sales, engineering and administration)? We want names. It's impossible to lay off three minutes of a worker. If we are just going to transfer them to another department, then we would like to know how much the Throughput can be expected to increase there. Just moving people from one department to another does not reduce the Operating Expense.

If the resulting reduction in Operating Expense is larger then the reduction in Throughput, trimming the product will definitely increase the Net Profit of the company. If it's smaller, it will certainly reduce the Net Profit, even though our artificial "cost" calculation says the opposite.

> *...it will certainly reduce the Net Profit, even though our artificial "cost" calculation says the opposite.*

It should be noted that sometimes when we examine the possibility of trimming one product, the result comes out as negative. When we consider another one, we again get a negative answer. But when we consider both together, the result is positive. This phenomenon is simply due to the fact that each product alone didn't release a full person while trimming both of them together did.

The comparison of these two procedures based on the quality of the answers derived and the cumbersomeness of one procedure versus the simplicity of the other certainly raises the question: Why did we even start to use cost accounting procedures? The answer lies in more complicated situations. Suppose we would like to examine the possibility of increasing the Throughput of one product and would like to know if there is an impact on the Throughput of other products or on the various categories of expenses. When do we have such an impact? . . . only if the increase of the Throughput of this particular product requires the use of something that we don't have enough of—a constraint. In such a case, any increase of one product will reduce the Throughput of other products or increase Operating Expense (and Investment) because we must add more of the constraint.

A similar situation will arise when we want to trim some category of Operating Expense. We must evaluate the impact of

> *We see that tradeoffs exist only when we are dealing with situations where the constraints of a system are impacted.*

such an action on the Throughput of our products. A negative impact will exist only if, by trimming, we cause something to be unable to support the current volume. In other words, we create a constraint.

We see that tradeoffs exist only when we are dealing with situations where the constraints of a system are impacted. Thus, if we understand the cause and effect relationship of constraints and the operational measurements, we'll be able to use, in all cases, the explicit formulas of Net Profit and ROI. We will not replace cost accounting with something new, but exactly the opposite. Once we understand the role of the constraint, we will be able to replace the many cost procedures used for all local decisions and for all local areas by NP and ROI ... Quite an advantage!

But, before we do this, we will have to find out how many constraints a system can tolerate. If the number is big, it will probably be beyond our power to juggle many balls in the air. In the next article it will be proven that this is never the case, and the number of constraints in any system is definitely manageable.

Visit

(Fictional Visit-Real Plants)

LOOKING BEYOND THE FIRST STAGE; JUST IN TIME

"It will be sent no later than tomorrow morning. You can count on it."

The voice on the other side loses some of its sharpness, but it's clear that he's still very dissatisfied. After three or four more frustrating minutes, I manage to break in. "Come on, Joe, don't tell me that you too don't have some problems meeting your delivery promises."

Judging from the harsh response, it's clear that the last comment was a mistake. So hurriedly I rush into a conventional, well practiced excuse. "Give us a break. I don't think you can complain about the excellent service that we've given you this last year...Yes, yes, I know that is why you increased your business with us. But you know how it goes, sometimes Murphy attacks more than usual and now he's launched a full scale assault. Exactly when we took a machine down for maintenance, the other two quit. A whole shipment of raw material was bad and we had to return it, and on top of that my master scheduler became ill.

> *What has happened lately? How can we put it back on track?*

It's like a madhouse. So please don't add to it. I'm certain that in a week or two we'll overcome this nasty situation and everything will get back to normal."

Even that doesn't help. Finally I succeed in pacifying Joe by promising top priority on his past due orders plus swearing on my mother's grave that all shipments will be promptly delivered from now on. I hang up the phone with a sigh. Lately this type of conversation has become much too frequent. I seriously contemplate adding the qualification of chief pacifier to my job description. What has happened lately? How can we put it back on track? But first things first. I ask my secretary to locate Phil—the production manager—to tell him that another client has joined the top of the priority list. It is starting to become crowded up there.

It doesn't take long before Phil is standing in my office. He is demonstrating his unparalleled ability to string together an impressive list of four-letter words.

"We simply don't have a choice." I try to calm him down. "We have to squeeze this customer in as well. You see, Phil, I wouldn't ask you to do it unless I was under the impression that otherwise we are certain to lose them. As a matter of fact, Joe was so mad on the phone that he actually threatened to give the business to HDP. You wouldn't want that to happen, right?"

Phil nervously wipes his forehead and mutters back. "Yes, I see your point, but that is exactly what you said yesterday and the day before yesterday. Gregg, we can't make everyone top priority. The shop is already full of 'red-hot' and 'do-it-now' jobs. I hate to do it, but I must ask you to authorize an additional increase in overtime. It's apparent that we'll have to put almost the entire shop on weekend shifts once again. I wonder how the people will respond. This will be the fourth weekend in a row."

"I can't recall the last time that we used so much overtime in a month."

"Hey, not so fast." I jump in. "We're already way over budget. Tell you what. For tonight, take all the overtime you need to ship what I've already promised. As for the weekend, let's discuss it tomorrow. I want to consult with Charlie first."

Charlie is our Director of Finance and I want to explore the ramifications of this extensive use of overtime on the monthly report that we have to submit to the division. Charlie usually has a few things up his sleeve that enable us to improve our reporting. I hate it. I thought we had gotten out of these mumbo-jumbo reporting tricks, but it looks as if we're thrown into it again.

Phil doesn't look too happy and in his frank manner says, "Do you really believe that the numbers game will help us to ship on time?" Turning to walk out, he continues, "But if you want to discuss it tomorrow, let's discuss it tomorrow. That's fair enough with me."

I contemplate calling Charlie into my office but then decide against it. He probably will need his numbers so, rather than causing him to go back and forth, I stand up and walk to his office.

Charlie looks young, almost boyish, compared to his thirty-five years. His looks can fool you. Not only is he very shrewd, he is also very experienced. He knows all the accounting tricks and probably has invented a few of his own.

When I enter, he raises his eyes from his papers and says, "I was just about to drop into your office."

"Yes," I reply. "This overtime situation is really getting out of hand."

"That's not what I had in mind," said Charlie. "But tell me."

"Charlie, by how much are we over budget on overtime?" I ask while I'm settling myself on the big leather couch that Charlie insists on having in his office.

"Not by much," comes the surprising answer. "If you would like to see the exact numbers I can very easily get them for you, but my estimate is that we will not go over bud-

Charlie and his cookie jar...Always count on a good accountant to have his private reserves.

get by more than 3 or 4%."

"How come?" I ask in a voice that probably shows my surprise. "I can't recall the last time that we used so much overtime in a month. Even in the chaotic days of two years ago I don't think we exceeded this month."

"Yes," says Charlie in his precise, calm voice. "We are now operating at a rate where 34.6% of all hours used are from overtime. It's certainly unparalleled, but that's ok."

"What do you mean, it's ok?" I respond, raising my voice and trying unsuccessfully to escape the grips of Charlie's deep couch.

"Why are you surprised?" says Charlie. "Two months ago when we adjusted the budget to accommodate for the sudden increase in sales volume, I automatically adjusted the overtime budget. If you recall, you didn't allow for any direct labor increase."

"Certainly. What is the sense in hiring new people whenever sales blip? You know that it takes more than six months to train any new employee," I reply in a harsh tone.

"Well it certainly doesn't look like a blip. It's about time we admit that it's a real expansion in sales volume," Charlie responds.

"Yes," I say. "You are definitely right."

"Anyhow," Charlie continues, "We are now sitting on a very comfortable overtime budget, even though I must say that we are eating into it faster than I anticipated. Still we are in good shape, especially when we consider the reserve of last month."

> *What do you think the division's opinion of us will be if we change our budget up and down like a roller coaster?*

Charlie and his cookie jar... Always count on a good accountant to have his private reserves.

"How long do you think we can continue in this maddening way before it will show up on our report?" I inquire.

"For at least another month or maybe even two," answers Charlie.

"Oh," I say. "But long before that our work force will rebel. They are already bitching and moaning. It will be impossible to ask them to give up all their free time just because we are hardly coping with the demand. But this is not your headache, Charlie. It's good to know that at least I don't have to worry about complying with the budget," I say, and stand up to return to my office.

"Gregg, as long as you are here. . ." Charlie starts and then I remember. "Yes, Charlie, you wanted to see me about something else."

"It's not exactly something else," says Charlie. "It is just the other side of the same coin that you were talking about."

I sink back into the couch and with a not too enthusiastic voice say, "Ok, Charlie, let's hear it." A thought flashes through my mind. Why is it that whenever you think that you've gotten rid of one problem it turns out that it is just an introduction to the real blow? But what Charlie says is even worse than my expectations.

"Gregg, I'm afraid that we have to resubmit our budget. We must scale it down significantly."

"But we just submitted a new optimistic budget less than two months ago," I explode. "I told you we were too hasty. We should have waited. What do you think the division's opinion of us will be if we change our budget up and down like a roller coaster? No, Charlie, even if it's needed we can't afford to do it."

"Gregg, I'm afraid that we can't afford *not* to do it."

I'm struggling to stand up and walk out as Charlie says, "Gregg, dismissing it will not help. We must hammer it out."

I finally succeed in standing up. Pacing up and down in his too small office, I throw quick, sharp retorts at Charlie.

"I told you that we shouldn't have submitted a new forecast."

I pace and take a 180 degree turn. "Yes, I know I was afraid that this is just a blip in sales."

Pace. . .turn. "Why did it take so long for our clients to react. . ."

Pace. . .turn.

". . .to our substantially improved performance and then. . ."

Pace...turn.

"...it was like an avalanche?"

I stop pacing, face Charlie and say, "I know that up there they hate good surprises almost as much as they hate bad ones. We had to increase our forecast."

Resuming my pacing, I throw a cheap shot at Charlie. "Couldn't you hide the profit for a little bit longer?"

Pace...turn.

"I guess not. Sorry. I guess we didn't really have any choice." And then, turning to him, "But what are you complaining about? The last two months were record months in terms of net profit and you are still sitting on hefty reserves."

Charlie opens his mouth to answer but, before he does, I raise my hand and resume my pacing. "Yup. I guess I know what is bothering you. Almost all of this month's orders went into the backlog. Our shipping schedule is sliding rapidly and we have once again resurrected that almost forgotten but nasty "past due" category. I see what you mean. You are afraid that next month we will miss the budget."

"Gregg, I'm not afraid of next month. I'm afraid of this month." Charlie succeeds in throwing in a sentence.

"Ok, ok, let's discuss it."

"Can I ask you a favor?" he says with a grin. "Can you please sit down? Your up and down pacing disturbs my concentration."

"No, Charlie." I pull rank. "The pacing helps mine. As a matter of fact, let's move to my office. I need more space."

"Oh well," Charlie smiles back.

> *"I don't think I ever heard a summary of such good events given in a more mournful tone. What is bugging you?"*

Relaxing behind my table, holding a fresh cup of coffee in my hand, I signal to Charlie to start. "The current budget," Charlie says in his logical, almost frigid, factual tone, "was submitted based on two assumptions. The first one was that we were entering a new phase of increased sales due to our remarkably improved performance. Our JIT implementation really paid off. Our new high levels of due-date performance, quality and the fact that we reduced our lead time from five weeks to one place us in a category all our own. Gregg, it's not accurate to say that we were hasty in making a new forecast. I don't have to tell you the breadth of the in-depth checking that we did with all our major clients. No, we didn't rush into it blindfolded and certainly we were very careful not to be overly optimistic. As a matter of fact, reality proved that we were a little bit too cautious. Sales have continued to rise at the rate of over 22% a month for each of the last three months. Unparalleled. And, this I have to stress, we achieved at a time when our market, as a whole, was basically flat. We are eating rapidly into our competitors' market share. I guess we shouldn't be too surprised. This is our reward for being exceptionally good."

I smile at Charlie and say, "I don't think I ever heard a summary of such good events given in a more mournful tone. What is bugging you?"

"The second assumption."

"What second assumption?" I ask.

"The second assumption underlying our forecast—the one we never verbalized and took basically for granted—the assumption that we can maintain our excellent performance while sales continue to pick up. I don't have to tell you, Gregg, that what has happened in the last two months, and more so in the last two weeks, is more than just an indication that we are simply not up to it."

I twist uneasily in my chair. Not that what Charlie is saying is new to me. I am already losing sleep over it. But Charlie is about to force me to see the impact that the intensified rate of daily fires has on the global picture. I should have done it myself but didn't. Not that I haven't thought about it,

". . . the assumption that we can maintain our excellent performance while sales continue to pick up."

but somehow I avoided the issue, trying to fool myself that our difficulties were just temporary and we could fight our way through them with brute force. "Ok, Charlie," I say. "Lay it on me. Don't spare anything."

"Gregg, you know that lately our customers are very unhappy with us."

"You don't have to tell me that. I'm the one standing in the front line getting all the crap."

"Yes, I know. But have you seen the figures behind their complaints?"

"What exactly do you mean, Charlie?"

"Just a minute. Let me get them for you," and he walks out, just to reappear in a minute, holding a bunch of papers in his hand. "Look at this graph, for example," and he places one of his colored computer diagrams in front of me. "Our percent of shipments on time for the last two years. Here is the historical percentage level," and he points to the left of the diagram. "Oscillating basically in the low seventies. Here is where we seriously decided to implement JIT."

I love this period. Within three months we brought our due-date performance up to the high nineties. As a matter of fact, throughout all of last year there wasn't a single month where we slid below 98%. But now Charlie points to the right side of the diagram.

"Gregg, you see, we are talking a nose dive. Last month we dipped below 95% and the last two weeks are already at 85%. This is certainly not due to any lack of effort on our part. Look at this diagram," and he lays out the overtime profile for the same period. "Our overtime, which was historically at the level of 10%-15% a month, dropped to almost nothing last year but now it is skyrocketing. A perfect correlation," Charlie

> *Now they won't tolerate anything below a 90% due date performance. They have become accustomed to relying on us.*

points out.

I lean back in my chair digesting this new-old information. Charlie keeps quiet. Finally I say, "Oh well. But we are still much, much better than before."

"Not so fast," says Charlie. "In the past, when we had a 70% shipping performance, that is what our clients expected from us. But in the last year we spoiled them. Now they won't tolerate anything below a 90% due date performance. They have become accustomed to relying on us. That's probably one of the major reasons why they increased their orders. I suspect they now feel betrayed. Gregg, are you aware that two of our major customers have already threatened to withhold payment?"

Charlie, I think to myself, this is just the tip of the iceberg. You should have to sit by this phone to realize that the situation is even worse. I'm afraid that they are contemplating not just delaying payments, but also canceling orders. I think that Charlie is right. Once you improve significantly, it doesn't take long before your clients adjust their level of expectation upward. Then you simply can't afford to slide back.

Charlie breaks into my thoughts. "And it's not just due date performance. Look at the quality chart," and he places another diagram in front of my nose. "Remember, we agreed to measure quality not by measuring units of scrap or rework, but by simply counting the number of client complaints. Look at what has happened lately."

"Wow!" The line is about to go off the chart. "Charlie, I don't believe it! I don't believe that our quality is worse now than it was two years ago."

"I didn't think so either," says Charlie. "But certainly the numbers talk. My only explanation is that our clients are much less tolerant today. They don't hesitate to shout and complain, even about problems that they ignored in the past. It's basically just another indication of the same phenomenon. Gregg, I

> *All those furious telephone calls caused me to panic. Could I have resisted it? Should I have just ignored them? I guess not.*

think we should start to anticipate that, unless we immediately get back on track, we are probably facing a huge drop in sales. I'm afraid that sales will drop, but I am not sure to what level."

His words are like an echo of the thoughts passing through my mind, but nevertheless I try to brighten the atmosphere. "But, Charlie, at least our lead times have not deteriorated. This should give us a very good springboard for more business."

"Don't be so sure," says Charlie. "Look at this."

I swiftly scan the new diagram. "But this is our work-in-process level."

"Yes," says Charlie. "And since today we don't release anything into the plant that is not needed, it is exactly proportional to our average production lead time."

"Yes, you are right, but how did it happen?" I stare at a diagram that shows a 35% increase in work-in-process inventory. It must be a result of the extensive expediting. Deviate from JIT and you'll pay for it—a thought flashes through my mind. But I was the one who instructed people to deviate. Why have I done such a stupid thing? All those furious telephone calls caused my to panic. Could I have resisted it? Should I have just ignored them? I guess not. Something much deeper must have happened. It's not the expediting that forces us off the track. I don't think that I had any choice but to expedite. Have we reached the limits of JIT? I'm certainly not going to sort it out on the spot, so I shift my attention back to Charlie.

"I see why you are so concerned about next month," I say, pointing to the diagrams that by now are covering the table's top. "But if I'm not mistaken, you've voiced a concern about this month. That I don't understand at all. This month's orders are still very high."

> *"I think that the events of the last two months are sufficient to cause a logical person to have second thoughts. Don't you?"*

"Higher than the forecast," Charlie says. "But have you looked at shipments lately? If we continue at the current rate we'll be 14% below target."

"I see what you are saying, Charlie. You mean that we will once again be thrown into the end-of-the-month syndrome. In the past we were very good at shipping more than half the month's sales in the last week. We just have to do the same now. We still have a whole week to go."

"Gregg, I'm not so optimistic. I'm under the impression that you are already running the plant in the highest gear. Where are you going to get the inventory? In the past we had so much inventory stuck all over the place that, at the end of the month, we could just concentrate on everything that was near completion and push it out. But now, even with the recent increase, our work-in-process is so low that we simply don't have anything to push out."

He is absolutely right. We don't have any more of these huge piles that were, in a way, our reserves. Our JIT mode of operation helped us to get rid of them.

"We certainly could use some Just-In-Case inventory now," says Charlie, as if continuing my thought.

I smile at him. "Yes, if we had a crystal ball that would have told us when to build it."

"But we had," comes Charlie's surprising response. "We knew that sales were picking up. Why didn't we build finished goods inventory?"

"What? Are you seriously suggesting that we drop JIT and start once again to build Just-In-Case? If I'm not mistaken, it was only a few months ago that you told me that you finally believed in JIT. What happened?"

"I think that the events of the last two months are sufficient to cause a logical person to have second thoughts. Don't you?"

That really gets to me. I stand up to pour myself another cup of coffee when Charlie says, "No pacing again, please."

I don't even smile. Why am I so hurt? Maybe because Charlie has verbalized my hidden doubts. "Charlie, I know that you weren't a big supporter of JIT before we started it. But you yourself told me more than once that JIT drastically changed your attitude toward inventory. Knowing you, you didn't reach this conclusion without deep thought. Are you going to tell me that a few weeks of difficulties are enough to cause you to start to waver?"

"Gregg, if you will stop pacing and sit down, I promise to try and explain my thoughts the best I can."

"It's a deal."

"You see, Gregg, originally I was unimpressed with the JIT advocates. I didn't need them to point out to me that inventory costs money. I've been involved more than once in corporate efforts to pinpoint the actual cost of carrying the inventory. Certainly I didn't have to learn the value of cash flow from them. How much money is captured in inventory? I could have told you that even if you woke me in the middle of the night. The new zealots who preach that inventory is evil just clash with my logical nature. When corporate started to press for inventory reduction, it didn't come as a new thing. I know inventory levels are important, but I interpreted the new emphasis by me as another fashion. Sometimes we push for market share, other times for return on investment and this time it was for less inventory. To tell you the truth, I hated the song and dance that went with it. 'Inventory is evil', the target should be zero inventory'. How can anyone take those statements seriously? Do you really believe that we can produce and ship goods with zero inventory? Ridiculous! Now I'm going to reveal to you something more private—you know that we financial people love to hold reserves just so we can bail out a plant manager when he gets in deep trouble for the short term. What you probably don't know is that one of our major avenues is the inventory game. The overhead absorption mechanism gives us a lot of room to adjust the numbers. Now you can appreciate why, in order to comply with corporate instructions, I helped Mason put the squeeze on our vendors. We had too much raw material and purchased parts

> *The overhead absorption mechanism gives us a lot of room to adjust the numbers.*

anyhow. Reducing them will satisfy corporate but will not jeopardize our overhead absorption. We just transfer investment in inventory into cash. On the other hand, reducing our finished goods and our work-in-process would have a devastating impact on our bottom line. As you recall, I didn't have to stand in Mason's way when he preached JIT. Phil was doing it for me in a much more persuasive way."

"I see all that, Charlie, but when we decided to implement JIT on the shop floor, I don't recall you resisting. You were surprisingly cooperative."

"I'm happy that you asked me this question now and not two weeks ago," Charlie smiled. "Lately I've re-read all the material dumped on us and have given it a lot of thought. Do you recall what triggered you to get off the fence and lead the implementation?"

I smiled back at Charlie. "Yes, of course. I still remember the morning that I came in all charged up waving a copy of *The Goal.*"

"I was infatuated by that book too. It was the first logical, non-emotional explanation I'd seen. But there was more in it for me. It made me more convinced that as we attack and break our bottlenecks, the unavoidable result will be that we will eat into our past due. I calculated that this would give us a short-term increase in throughput that would be more than sufficient to cover the one-time impact of the accompanying inventory reduction. As it happened, my calculations were on the nose. Do you want me to show it to you?"

"No, not now. Keep on talking. I'm fascinated, but you haven't told me yet how JIT changed your attitude about inventory."

"Right, Gregg. That came much later. But first let me show you some other numbers." Once again, he disappears from my office. I knew that we should

"Here I've calculated the impact that cutting batch sizes had on improving utilization of constraints."

— 25 —

have held the meeting in his office. This time it takes a little bit longer until he shows up.

"Sorry, I had to dig them out of last year's file, where I put them just last week. Look here." I stare at three pages full of numbers.

"What are all these supposed to mean?" I ask.

"Don't you see?" He points to one of the sheets. "Here I've calculated the impact that cutting batch sizes had on improving utilization of constraints or what we thought were our constraints."

Before he starts to dive into the explanation, I raise my hand. "Charlie, spare me the details. Just give me the bottom line."

"Ok," he says a little bit sadly. "Here you can see how I've calculated the impact of choking the release."

"Choking the release?" I repeat.

"Yes, you know. . .releasing what is needed and not releasing material just to supply work to our workers."

"Oh yeah. But what have you calculated?"

"The impact that this action had on the constraints. See, just these two actions were sufficient to break them. All the other steps that Phil is so proud of were just gravy. The two actions that Mason was zealously preaching, more that a year before, were sufficient. They alone were enough to have gotten us the same results. Maybe a little bit slower. Maybe with more pain and hassle. Anyhow, in retrospect, it's clear that we didn't have any bottlenecks. The machines that appeared to be bottlenecks were a result of our true constraints— our batch size policy and the worker efficiency syndrome. I guess we are not the only ones in this situation. Mason was conceptually right, even though I doubt if he understands deeply why."

> *My attitude toward inventory changed when the side effects started to become apparent.*

"Very interesting, but you still haven't answered my question."

"Yes, yes, I'm coming to it. My attitude toward inventory changed when the side effects started to become apparent. You see, I was expecting a drop in inventory and an increase in our throughput. But the other things that came, basically for free, were the big surprise. Things like improving our delivery performance. Remember how hard it was to maintain a slightly above 70% on-time delivery performance? All that expediting. Then, as a side effect of the JIT implementation, we found ourselves approaching 100%. If someone had told me that it was possible to achieve such high levels in our plant, frankly I would have laughed in his face."

"Or the overtime—it was so hard to keep under 20%. Then we implemented JIT and, whoops, overtime—basically on its own—fell to almost zero. And the quality improvement. Don't tell me *about* statistical process control. Yes, that helped. But my numbers show that the big improvement happened simultaneously with the inventory drop. That was before we adopted the SPC techniques. But the most staggering effect, at least in my eyes, is our ability to react to fast change. To react to urgent customer orders within 5 days became a matter of routine. Basically without special effort."

"Could you imagine all this two years ago? Yes, we all now expect it. We all understand why it happened. But, for me, it was the real understanding of what stood behind a sentence like 'Inventory is evil'. I can frankly and wholeheartedly say that JIT changed my perception of inventory from an asset, as I used to call it on our balance sheet, to a liability. An entity that caused us so much expediting grief, hampered our delivery performance, damaged our quality, forced us to use extensive overtime and in general caused us to move with the inertia of a dinosaur, such an entity is certainly a liability."

"So now you should be at peace with yourself."

"Not at all, Gregg. Don't

> *We are back to the bad symptoms even though we adhere as much as we can to the JIT philosophy.*

you see that all those bad effects are coming back in spite of the fact that we are using small batches and we release JIT?"

"I'm starting to see your point, Charlie. Our due dates are regressing rapidly, our overtime is skyrocketing, our quality is deteriorating. We are back to the bad symptoms even though we adhere as much as we can to the JIT philosophy. How can it be? Do you have any idea?"

"I can't even call it an idea but, you see, inventory can't be all bad. We can't produce without inventory and, more than that, right now we if we did have some Just-In-Case inventory it would be a big help. No doubt about it. I'm afraid that JIT is a little bit too zealous. Reducing inventory was certainly right, but some level of inventory is not only good, but absolutely necessary. What is the desired level? I don't know. But I'm starting to have the sneaking suspicion that this last increase in sales, which I fully admit is a positive result of our JIT implementation, probably raised the required level of inventory. And my fear is that the bad symptoms of having too much inventory are almost identical to the bad symptoms of having too little."

I'm impressed with this guy. What he says makes a lot of sense. "Charlie, is what you are saying that we should reexamine what we understood from JIT?"

"Something like that," comes the answer.

"Ok," I say. "The best definition of JIT is claimed to be 'elimination of waste—any waste'. We can certainly agree on that."

To my surprise, Charlie starts to become a little bit disgusted. "Gregg," he says, "I'm just a bean counter. For me something makes sense only if it is defined precisely, preferably measured by a number. What do you mean by eliminating waste? Can you define for my simple mind what you mean by 'waste'?"

According to our definition, you and I don't add any value to the product.

"No problem," I say diving

quickly into the knowledge that I've recently gained from so many books and seminars. "Waste is anything that does not add value to the product."

"Gregg, be serious." Charlie is almost on the verge of giving up. "The only meaning of 'giving value to the product' is defined by us—the accountants. According to our definition, you and I don't add any value to the product and, for that matter, Mason and all his staff are also classified as burden. Are you seriously suggesting that all our work is a waste? Do you recommend that we fire ourselves?"

Looking at his gloomy face I burst into laughter. "Charlie, you are something! Certainly you've persuaded me to do my homework. I have an idea. Since it looks like we have to make most of the plant work this weekend anyhow, why don't we do the same thing that we demand from our workers? Why don't *we* also spend the weekend here trying to figure out a method that will put us back on track—what do you think?"

"A great idea. What I suggest is that we invite Mason as well. He has more knowledge of JIT that both of us and, besides, a Director of Materials should contribute his share."

"Then I will invite Phil as well. Nine o'clock Saturday suit you?"

"Fine with me."

We haven't solved a thing, but at least we are out of the "throwing punches" mode. Somehow I feel much better even though I shiver remembering the amount of material that I have to skim through before the weekend.

We don't start at nine as planned. It's almost eleven before we begin and, within a few minutes, Mason is raving at what he interprets as a suggestion to abandon JIT. "So we drain the lake to some extent and the rocks are surfacing. Is

...shuffling priorities as if this whole damn plant were just a deck of cards...

that a reason to bring back the water? We should take out the rocks, not cover them again with inventory. That's what we agreed, that's what I thought, until now, we were determined to do. These small difficulties shouldn't distract us from doing what is right."

"Some small difficulties," Phil barely controls his temper. "That's what you call this madhouse? I'm sweating trying to ship the stuff out and your people, yes your people, are running around like chickens without heads, shuffling priorities as if this whole damn plant were just a deck of cards."

"What do you expect? If your people can't produce on time we have to adjust the priorities. Remember, the clients must be satisfied and it's not that the clients are changing their due dates, even though they do to some extent. Your people are simply lagging behind. Don't blame me for shuffling the priorities. You are bringing that on yourself."

"What?!! Me?!! You dare to say that my people are lazy?" The veins on Phil's forehead are about to burst.

"Whoa, whoa," I jump in. "This is not exactly the time for finger pointing. We are here to drag the wagon out of the mud, not to dig it deeper with such fights."

Phil and Mason still look as if they are going to be at each other's throats in a second. "Phil!" I say, but it doesn't help. He still looks at Mason. "Phil!" I have to repeat it two or three more times. "Would you say that you don't have enough capacity?"

"Certainly," he aims his anger at me. "Do you think that I would have asked you for so much overtime otherwise?"

"So you have new bottlenecks?" I sigh.

"Yes, definitely."

Where are we going to find this army of people to deal with your rocks?

"Not true at all," Mason jumps in. "According to the existing order rates, we should have met the increase in volume without any overtime. We still have so much excess capacity."

Out of the corner of my eye I see Charlie nod. Thank God that Phil doesn't look at him. He just sits there quietly for a few seconds. Then he stands up saying, "Damn you, Mason. *You* run the shop if you are such a smart guy. Let's see you do it."

"Sit down," I tell him. "And you too. This attitude will get us nowhere." I wait for the tense atmosphere to settle down and then with a calm voice, knowing very well that I'm walking on eggs, I ask Phil, "Can you tell me what are the new bottlenecks?"

"The whole damn shop is one big bottleneck," comes the grumbling response.

"Come on, Phil, some resources must be more loaded than others."

"I'm serious, Gregg. You are probably unaware of what is happening now. Every two days, almost every shift, new bottlenecks jump out. I'm moving my people almost as fast as Mason is moving his priorities."

"Thank you, Phil," says Mason sarcastically. Then turning to me, "It's not bottlenecks. We didn't have and we still don't have bottlenecks. It's just rocks. Rocks that we have to remove from our plant."

"Ok," says Phil in a very challenging tone. "Suppose that we go your way. Where do you suggest we start? These damn rocks, as you call them, are popping up all over the plant and, besides, who will do it? We are so busy trying to keep our heads above water, where are we going to find this army of people to deal with your rocks? And our customers will kill us long before we've taken them out. You are totally unrealistic."

Mason just tightens his jaw, not answering back. No wonder, I think to myself, what *can* he answer back? But thanks to Charlie I'm ready now. "Mason, can we start from scratch? How exactly is the 'water in the lake' technique supposed to work?"

"Come on, Gregg. You

> *...there must be an area where it is more important and more beneficial to reduce inventory than another.*

— 31 —

know it by heart," comes the impatient answer.

"No, seriously, Mason. I thought I knew it, but I gave it some thought yesterday and I'm not sure anymore."

"It's very simple," Mason starts reluctantly. "You pick an area, you reduce the allowed inventory and, if you reduce it enough, trouble will appear and it will be difficult to meet the internal due date. Then you analyze the problem that surfaced, you solve it and you continue to reduce the inventory. That's basically what we did all last year. All of a sudden it's new to all of you."

"No, Mason, it's not exactly new. What you are describing is a very controlled process."

"And an ongoing one," Mason throws in a remark. "Yes, definitely."

"But there is something that has bothered me for a long time. How do you pick the area to reduce the inventory?"

"You just pick it."

"Come on, Mason, there must be an area where it is more important and more beneficial to reduce inventory than another. You know that the Pareto principle exists."

"You *know* where to pick it."

"In other words, what you are telling me is that there aren't any rules, you just have to pick it by intuition."

"Gregg, if someone knows the plant, he will know at any given point in time which area is the best candidate for the effort. It's not a big deal."

"Maybe you're right, but if we don't concentrate on the right area, the results will not be so dramatic."

"Come on, Gregg, look what we have achieved in our own plant. Don't you call an 85% decrease in work-in-process a dramatic decrease?"

"Yes, certainly Mason. But let's look objectively at what actually has happened in our

> *Bottlenecks are foreign to the JIT terminology.*

plant. We started by concentrating on what we thought were our bottlenecks and restricted the release of material according to their needs. Right?"

"We also dramatically cut the batches," says Mason. "I always maintained that if we just released what we needed in small batches that would be enough. Bottlenecks are foreign to the JIT terminology."

"Yes, Mason, you will probably be surprised that Charlie backs you on your last point, at least as far as our particular plant is concerned. But what I'm trying to describe may not be what we should have done, but was what we actually did. If I'm not mistaken, immediately after we took those actions there was a huge drop in inventory. Charlie, can you give us the numbers?"

"For what time frame, Gregg?"

"Let's say to about three months after we started those two drastic actions."

"In that period, work-in-process and finished goods inventory dropped by 71%," Charlie answers in his dry tone.

"And since then," I continue, "we have done exactly what you have described, Mason. We have reduced the size and the number of containers. We have reduced the area allowed for work-in-process. We have done it in a very controlled way. To solve the problems that surfaced, we introduced the techniques of SPC in a large way. We embarked on an ambitious and successful program for preventive maintenance and we extensively used set-up reduction methods. You can't say, Mason, that we did it halfheartedly. We've given it our all for more than a year already. Yes, lately, because of all the pressure we had to neglect it a little bit. Nevertheless, let's check what we achieved in terms of reducing inventory further...let's say in the twelve months following the big reduction. Charlie?"

"I would feel much better if we had a logical, sound process instead of just intuition."

— 33 —

"We have reduced it by an additional 12%."

"That's not shabby at all," Mason says. "That 12% means reducing a very low level by an additional one-third."

"Yes," I agreed. "But still the vast majority of the 85% total you refer to was done in the beginning by changing our policies and not by slowly taking the rocks out."

"What are you driving at? I don't see your point," says Mason.

"Just the fact that we can't be so sure that our intuition is good enough to pinpoint where we concentrate. I would feel much better if we had a logical, sound process instead of just intuition."

"What do you have against intuition?"

"Mason, the mere fact that we don't have a reference to compare to shouldn't be proof that we couldn't have done much better. But I'm troubled by something much more severe. You see, intuition stems from past experience and whenever a drastic change happens, our intuition becomes temporarily obsolete."

"Sorry, but I don't see your point at all."

"Ok, Mason, let's start again. The process that you have described is where we are in control. We reduced the water. We caused the rocks to emerge. Haven't you noticed that lately the rocks are emerging by themselves?"

"Shoot! The whole floor of the lake is elevated." Phil can't control himself anymore. "I can barely see any more water, just rocks."

"You see, Mason, if we had a logical procedure that would have directed us to which rock is the most important to take out first, which one second, and so on, then maybe we would have a chance. But now I have to agree with Phil."

> *"Shoot! The whole floor of the lake is elevated. I can barely see any more water, just rocks."*

"So what you are saying is that this way of attacking the problem is wrong?"

"Not at all Mason. As a

matter of fact, I regard it as the most important contribution of JIT to my thinking. Charlie credits JIT with changing his attitude about inventory. For me, personally, its most important contribution was how it changed my attitude about manufacturing problems, about problems in our process. Previously the first thing that jumped into my mind when I encountered a difficult process was how to bypass it. Today my attention is geared more to how to correct it, so I won't have to dance around it again in the future. In my eyes, this is a great contribution of JIT. Just as Charlie is not entirely happy with the formal approach of JIT toward inventory, so I am not entirely happy about how it drives process improvement. I think that our situation is the best proof that even though JIT has pointed us in the right direction, it did so without clearly pointing out the boundaries where this approach needs to be reversed."

With a broad smile I say, "JIT itself is a process and when we find defects in this process we should obey what JIT tells us; correct and refine it. It looks as if we need to use JIT philosophy on JIT itself."

The irony totally escapes Mason, and with an expression of a man having his back to the wall, he complains, "Just because of the flack we've gotten recently, you are ready to change all of JIT?"

"Mason, it's not a little flack and it's not happening just to us. If I'm not mistaken, it must happen to any plant that's embarked aggressively on JIT. It's unavoidable."

Mason looks utterly confused.

"Ok, Mason. Let's examine it step by step," I say, watching the interest on Phil's face and the big grin that Charlie is trying to hide.

"Come on, seriously—answer," I half encourage, half instruct him.

"To... increase... our... productivity." He stretches each word in an attempt to convey his opinion of this conversation.

"What is the purpose of implementing JIT?"

"Mason, if I allowed Charlie to respond, he would probably say that he really doesn't understand what productivity is. Why don't you use terms which are more precise?"

"Like what!?"

Mason is oscillating between anger and despair, but it's too important to let him off the hook now. So, without mercy, I keep on with what probably seems to him like pointless torture. "I gather that you didn't like *The Goal*, but. . ."

"I didn't say so," he immediately jumps in. "On the contrary."

"Okay," I continue, "so you agree that what really counts is only the bottom line—that the goal of the plant is to make money."

"Yes, of course. What's the big deal?"

"Nothing, except my request was that you answer in more precisely defined terms. Rather than using words like productivity or waste, do you mind if we stick to more tangible terms like Operating Expenses, Inventory and Throughput?"

"Okay, no problem," says Mason. Then after a small pause he adds, "Repeat your question."

It is clear that he is a little bit, just a little bit, more interested. "What is the purpose of implementing JIT?" I repeat in a calm, factual tone as if we were just starting the conversation.

"Multi-purpose I think," says Mason. "First and most important is to reduce inventory."

"So it seems," I say. "But is it most important? You see, Mason, after the first real reduction in inventory, which you may recall happened in just three months, the impact of further reductions has been—in absolute terms—very small. Yet most of our JIT effort occurred after the first three months. For what purpose? Just to achieve a small additional incremental inventory reduction?"

"Hmm," says Mason.

"The 12% further reduction," Charlie explains to Phil, "had an impact of less than

> *"Any successful JIT implementation should lead to an increase in sales."*

0.3% on our bottom line. It took a whole year of effort and now, in just the last month, we lost it all."

Phil nods his head in approval. It is not surprising that Mason is not trying to argue this point. He is much too knowledgeable for that.

"We also reduced Operating Expenses," he tries again, but it's obvious that his heart is not in this answer.

"How?" asks Phil. "We haven't laid off anybody."

"Yes," I say to Phil. "Nevertheless, Mason has a point. It is true that we didn't lay off, but we reduced head count through natural attrition. You know that we are now operating with 7% fewer direct workers that a year ago."

"Big deal!" says Phil. "Even without counting the overtime, let me remind you that our total direct labor accounts for no more than 10% of our expenses."

"9.6%," says Charlie, smiling.

Mason doesn't join the laughter. Rather, with a very thoughtful voice he says, "I'm beginning to see where you are going. After the big initial reduction in inventory, it looks as if the additional gains are negligible. It doesn't make sense. Maybe we have to look for the answer in the intangibles. But you and Charlie probably won't like it."

"What do you mean?" asks Charlie.

"We've achieved additional things," answers Mason. "You know, the remarkable improvements in due-date performance, in quality and in lead time. They must count for something. But never mind, you will probably claim that most of the gains were achieved in the first three months. . .and you are probably right."

"Not so fast," I interrupt. "Let's first clarify what you have pointed out. What is the impact of substantially improving things like quality, due-date performance and lead times?"

> *"The truth is that I only checked to see if we had enough capacity to handle all new orders."*

— 37 —

"They, I guess, should improve our competitive position. We should be able to sell more."

"Right," I say. "Or, if we try to put it in our new operational terms, it should improve our Throughput. Well, Mason, what is the purpose of implementing JIT?"

"You fox!" At last a broad smile breaks across Mason's face. "Yes, it is quite clear. The real purpose of implementing JIT is to bring the plant into a position where Throughput is increased. The Inventory and Operating Expense reductions are almost a side effect, or perhaps I should say a mean. Yes, I am starting to see your point. Any successful JIT implementation should lead to an increase in sales."

"This is exactly where we stand now," I summarize. "You see why I claimed that what has happened to us is not a fluke, but almost an unavoidable result of a successful JIT implementation. That's why I'm so puzzled by the fact that the literature on JIT does not talk about it."

"That is not necessarily true," remarks Mason. "Come to think about it, the originators of JIT—the Japanese—do mention the need to restrict increases in demand to a few percent per month. Now I understand it. Yes, they definitely have been in our situation and that is the answer they have reached. The answer is very simple and clear. We were too eager. We shouldn't have accepted all the orders. We're trying to chew too much too soon."

I try to digest this new development, while Mason continues.

"The answer or, if you want, the warning is spelled out in the literature. Maybe without an explanation, maybe as just a postulation, but nevertheless it is very clear. If you don't restrict the rate of increase in incoming orders, your entire logistical system will collapse and the plant will be thrown into constant frantic expediting. Sound familiar?"

> *I don't believe that a method whose main purpose is to increase sales should, once it's successful, prevent us from capitalizing on our success.*

I'm still trying to digest

the ramification of Mason's words and thus I'm totally surprised by the uproar raised by Phil.

"What are you boasting about? I can't believe my ears! Listen, fellow! You are telling us that all along you knew about the jam that we have now gotten into and you kept your mouth shut. What's going on here?"

Phil with his usual short fuse. At least the satisfied grin that was all over Mason's face disappears. It's as if someone wiped it with a wet cloth.

"Phil, come on, be fair," he tries to pacify the roaring lion. "I never claimed that I actually knew what was going to happen. This is only the wisdom of hindsight."

In a more calming tone, trying very hard to ignore the dirty looks that Phil blazes toward him, he adds, "The truth is that I only checked to see if we had enough capacity to handle all new orders. Maybe I've made an arithmetic error, but at the time it did look as if we had ample capacity."

After a short pause, he throws a question toward Phil. "Haven't you made this same, vital check?"

Now it's Phil's turn to be embarrassed—it's amazing at what speed the ball is zooming from side to side—"Yeah, I did. Of course. On paper it looked as if there weren't any problems. But reality certainly proved the opposite to be true."

"Yup," says Mason.

The last few sentences provide the clue so I forge ahead. "Well, what should we conclude from it?" I ask, waiting for a plausible hypothesis to solve the mystery of the vanished capacity—but, instead, what comes is a declaration.

"It looks obvious, doesn't it?" says Mason. "We should have obeyed JIT. We should limit the incoming orders immediately, and from now on we should restrict the increase in incoming orders to a few percent a month."

I don't know if it is my logic of the tone of my voice, but it seems now we agree on this point.

His authoritative tone irritates me, especially when Phil nods his head like a puppet on a string. When Charlie—et tu Brute—adds, "Yes, this is probably the solution," it's my turn to explode.

"No!!" I say as I raise my voice a little bit, "I don't buy it for one minute!! I don't believe that a method whose main purpose is to increase sales should, once it's successful, prevent us from capitalizing on our success."

They all look at me with blank faces. I try again. "The purpose of implementing JIT is to enable us to increase sales. Right?"

I succeed in squeezing out an agreement.

"We have done it," I continue. "Now we are in a position where the clients are practically banging down our door. Right?"

This time it's a little bit more difficult to gain agreement. Probably they are still shell shocked by the last two to three weeks, when the complaints about late shipments became overwhelming. This really gets to me.

"Can't you see the global picture?!" I almost roar. "If we are not in a situation where the clients are asking more and more from us, what are all these talks all about—this limiting the intake of new orders?! What are we talking about? We have succeeded in increasing demand beyond our wildest dreams. That's a fact!!"

I don't know if it is my logic or the tone of my voice, but it seems now we agree on this point.

"Now, when implementing JIT finally increases demand, are you telling me that because of JIT we cannot accept the demand that we have created? Don't you see the absurdity of it?"

Silence. No one volunteers to answer. After a short while I decide to press on.

> *...this solution does not explain why we are currently in a mess.*

"Well?" I say in a very demanding tone.

"We must limit the orders that we accept," Mason says in a very quiet tone. "Otherwise the entire JIT-pull-system collapses and we are thrown into a continual expediting mode."

"Yes—but why?" I'm trying to match his calm voice—without much success. "We have enough capacity."

"Even so," says Charlie, "we cannot support this increase in sales."

Like talking to a wall. They don't even start to see the problem. It's a very embarrassing situation. I've succeeded in stopping the fight among them. They are at last united in a uniform front, but this uniform front is aimed at me.

"Fellows," I start again. "Give me some credit. It's not that I don't see your point. I do. Yes, trimming the intake of orders will put us back on track. Even I can see it. But. . .yes, there is always a but. But what I see is that this way is a lousy compromise. We are sacrificing too much."

"A bird in the hand is worth more than a whole flock in the bush," mutters Charlie to himself.

"Granted, Charlie. But don't you see? There are many puzzling things that are left unresolved. To accept, in our situation, a solution that requires a huge sacrifice is, in my eyes, running away from the possibility of finding much better solutions. Do you all think that we have reached the final answer? Why? Just because we already found one feasible solution? What guarantees us that these unsolved puzzles will not come back in the future and catch us by surprise?"

Judging from the expression on Charlie's face I think that he moved maybe one inch. This is definitely not the case with Mason and Phil—they haven't budged at all.

At last Phil asks, "Why are you so unhappy? We've all agreed that this solution should work. Why not limit the incoming orders, rather than accept them and choke, as we are

. . . almost the entire difference between the selling price and the material price will hit the bottom line.

— 41 —

doing today?"

He speaks in a very pacifying voice. It is clear that he is trying not to provoke me. The result is just the contrary. He simply does not understand my position. So, much more calmly, even though much more disappointed, I try to explain again.

"Mason, we have identified a solution. That is certainly good, but we should not overlook two things. The first is that this solution does not explain why we are currently in a mess. The second thing is that if we adopt this solution we will have to sacrifice major benefits. You see, if the negatives associated with a solution are small we should adopt it immediately. But in our case, since the negatives are very large, maybe we should spend more time looking for a better alternative."

I see that I'm successful in persuading just myself. To go around again, where they repeat their position and I repeat mine, even if we try and use different words, doesn't look promising. Finally, I control my temper by reminding myself that if I didn't already have a better solution, I probably would react in the same way they are. I decide to try another angle—to expose the magnitude of the compromise inherent in the suggested solution.

"How much do you suggest we allow our monthly orders to increase?" I ask. They don't rush to answer. It is clear that it's the first time they have thought seriously about it.

Finally Mason volunteers a 'guestimate'. "I think that we should limit the increase to a maximum of 5% per month. That will give us enough time to remove the rocks."

"I'm not sure," replies Phil. "Right now I think we should use a more conservative number."

"Maybe you're right," agrees Mason. "Still 5% looks like a good starting point to me."

"On what basis do you make your estimate?" asks Charlie.

"Come on. Not everything should be so precise," responds Mason, and they both jump on him in unison.

This conversation more than irritates me, but I control my impatience and interrupt. "Never mind. Let's accept Mason's answer for the moment. Would you please calculate the ramifications of such a decision?"

When I see their expressions, I hurriedly continue since I don't want to hear another lecture about the need to trim the order intake. "Let's view it together. Suppose that we had been smart from the beginning, and used this policy when the orders started to explode on us. Where would we be today?"

"In a much better position and without so much white hair on my head!" Phil says with a broad smile.

"Don't give me that!" joins Mason, in a good mood. "You thrive on emergencies."

They don't even begin to see my point. I ignore these remarks, turn to Charlie and say, "How many months should we use for this analysis?"

Even though my question is not very clear, he doesn't have any difficulty answering. "The real increase in orders began about three months ago. If we had used a policy of accepting no more than 5% additional orders per month, we would be dealing with a volume today that is approximately 25% lower than the current monthly volume."

"That would have been nice," says Phil.

Mason certainly agrees.

Charlie—using words like 'about' and 'approximately'... giving rough estimates without being pressured into it? He must have already realized the other side of the coin. Counting on that, I keep my mouth shut and it isn't long before Charlie breaks Phil's and Mason's self-satisfied mood.

"Have you considered the financial ramifications of such a situation?" he snaps at them.

"Count on Charlie to give you the numbers side," says Mason in a good mood.

"Thank you, Mason," Charlie says, "but don't forget that the numbers sometimes represent the bottom line and

> *I don't mean in terms of finding a solution. We are not yet there in terms of defining the core problem.*

that's the only thing that counts. Seriously, if I relate to what we actually shipped as a measure of what we should have committed to, a very comfortable Monday morning quarterback trick, I can estimate quite accurately the impact of your 5% suggested policy on the bottom line."

He stands up and begins filling the large white board with numbers. Phil and Mason watch him very closely. I don't bother. It's not that I've already made these calculations, but the end result is very clear to me. Since this reduction in orders is not associated with a proportionate reduction in expenses, (the increased overtime expense is trivial compared to the total), almost the entire difference between the selling price and the material price will hit the bottom line. It must be a huge impact.

I wait patiently for about ten minutes. In this time, the clean white board turns into a magnificent rainbow of numbers—Charlie uses many colored markers to emphasize his calculations. Finally, the end result appears on the board and Charlie announces in a flat tone, "If we had taken your suggestion, Mason, we would have cut the net profit in the last three months by more than half."

You could have heard a fly if there had been one in the room.

"Will anyone volunteer to help me present a revised forecast to corporate, based on a policy of trimming intake of orders to just 5% a month?" I cannot prevent myself from rubbing salt in the wound—but it's really unnecessary. Phil's and Mason's eyes are glued on the board.

Finally, Mason speaks in a very quiet tone. "Yes, we forgot that the goal is to make money. I guess that we must devise a better way to evaluate the needed trim in the orders."

"No doubt," says Phil.

Charlie looks satisfied. I'm encouraged, but still far from satisfied. It is certainly a step forward, but we are not yet there. I don't mean in terms of finding a solution. We are not yet there in terms of defining

...what really is inventory—an asset or a liability?

the core problem. I am already tired, and I guess that the others are also far from fresh. What should I do? Maybe it's best to simply lay it out on the table.

"I'm afraid that we might go off on a tangent," I begin in a neutral voice, not directing my words to anyone in particular. "Let's summarize where we stand. We agree that accepting orders based on available capacity is not good enough. It brings us into a situation where our JIT-pull-system collapses. Before we begin breaking our heads on how to find the appropriate level of business we should accept, maybe we should ask ourselves if this pull system is the best one for us."

Before Mason begins again, I continue. "We have already identified three open questions. The first is what really is inventory—an asset or a liability? Let me remind you that we concluded that the negative ramifications of having too little inventory are as bad as having too much inventory. This conclusion is not exactly in line with the JIT-pull-system philosophy. The second point is the fact that we don't have a systematic way to identify which rocks have to be pulled out. Without it how can we hope to determine a proper level for accepting new orders, especially when we have all the reasons to suspect that this level is not a constant number but a variable. This JIT-pull-system treats every operation equally and it's hard to imagine how it can systematically point to the required local process improvements."

I take a deep breath and continue. "Above all, we must find out why our calculations are showing us that we have enough capacity and yet reality proves just the opposite. Without an adequate explanation, we are exposed. I hate to be in a situation where my only shield against unpleasant future surprises is just extensive prayer."

"Your last question reminded me of the story of the boy scouts described in *The Goal*," said Mason in a thoughtful tone.

"Yeah, that might be the key," says Phil.

I ignore these last remarks and instead say, "It's already quite late for a Saturday. I think that we have accomplished something and we still have the whole day tomorrow. Let's continue at 9:00 am sharp."

They all sigh and begin to stand up. Then I remember, "Phil and Mason, didn't you both work in an aerospace plant?"

"Yes," they say in unison.

"Why don't we begin tomorrow by having you show us how to implement a JIT-pull-system in an aerospace shop that produces heavy parts—parts that involve lots of operations?"

"It won't work there," Phil responds immediately.

"Mmmmmmm," says Mason.

Chapter 5

HOW COMPLEX ARE OUR SYSTEMS?

1. What Causes Complexity?

The complexity of a system is an expression of the number of things that have to be considered simultaneously — the greater the number of balls we have to keep in the air, the more complex the system. The things that must be considered are, of course, the factors that have the greatest impact on the desired performance of the system. We have already defined these factors as the system's constraints: anything that limits the system from achieving higher performance versus its goal.

It should be noted that the number of constraints does not determine the complexity of a system. Complexity is a result of the number of interactive constraints — constraints that impact each other. To better understand this statement, consider a system containing many constraints where none of them interact with each other. Such a system can readily be dissected into subsystems, each containing only one constraint. These subsystems are the simplest systems. Since the subsystems' constraints do not interact, the performance of the overall system is just the summation of the performance of all the subsystems. Thus, a system which has no interacting constraints is a very simple system, even if it contains a large number of constraints.

Whenever we address the question of constraints and the interaction between them, our attention is first drawn toward

> *Thus, a system which has no interacting constraints is a very simple system, even if it contains a large number of constraints.*

physical constraints. Physical constraints are market constraints, vendor constraints, and resource constraints. Let's examine each one in order to clarify the types of possible interactions.

2 Market Constraints

A market constraint exists when the market demand for a particular product — or a line of products — is less than the ability of the system to fulfill the market demand. This is a very common situation and sometimes is so widespread that market constraints exist for every product produced by the system (company).

Market constraints can interact with each other in two distinctly different ways: directly and indirectly. Direct interactions occur when increased demand for one product directly decreases the market demand for another product of the system. This situation exists when both products fulfill the same need for the same customers.

An indirect interaction exists when the increased demand for one product reduces the ability of the system to supply a second product to a level below its market demand, even though it doesn't necessarily erode the market for that other product. In other words, the interaction exists through another type of constraint.

The first case is very common but simple to handle. The need to deal with such a direct interaction exists when we consider introducing a new product, launching a promotional campaign for an existing product and, to a lesser extent, when preparing a bid. In all these cases, the complexity arises because of the common (and often devastating) mistake of using product cost considerations for making a decision. We should utilize cost considerations — or, more precisely, consider the impact of the decision on operating expenses — only when a resource constraint is involved. This is the situation in our second case, that of indirect interaction.

Actually, the difficulty in the case of direct interaction doesn't arise from complexity, but from lack of reliable information. The impact on the market demand of other products is usually only vaguely known and involves a lot of guesswork. Once the guesswork assumptions are made, the decisions should be straightforward, since they involve a tradeoff on just one measurement — throughput.

> *In such a case, the company should reexamine its market segmentation policies rather than constantly seeking other unsatisfactory compromises.*

It should be stressed that, in cases where it is known that direct interactions between market constraints are significant but hard to estimate, by definition a conflict situation arises whenever more than one product offered by the same company competes for the same demand of the same clients. This is a very clear indication that a policy constraint, which blocks an opportunity for more effective market segmentation, exists. In such a case, the company should reexamine its market segmentation policies rather than constantly seeking other unsatisfactory compromises.

In short, whenever direct interactions between market constraints gives the impression that the system is complex, the root problem is probably caused by how we are segmenting the market — a policy constraint. An entire chapter will be directed to the subject of market segmentation policies, but for now it's enough to note that for complex direct interactions of market demands we should actually examine the simple case of only one constraint — market segmentation policy.

By definition, whenever indirect interactions between market constraints are considered, we are dealing with a case where attention should be directed to another type of constraint: a vendor, a resource, or (once again) a policy constraint. No matter what the details of the case, it's quite clear that a market constraint is secondary to other types of constraints which interact with more

> *The performance of the system is entirely in the hands of an external entity. This is not a complicated case. It is a dangerous (almost suicidal) one.*

than one market constraint. Thus, this situation should be investigated by first analyzing the other physical constraints.

3 Vendor Constraints

Vendor constraints are the constraints that most plants are accustomed to complaining about, but which very few (luckily) really have. We should not use the term vendor constraint as an excuse for cases where, from time to time, a raw material or purchased part is missing. These problems are usually caused by internal policy constraints, such as purchasing policies or erroneous policies for setting the desired levels of material inventory.

Vendors are a constraint only when a material is constantly in short supply in the entire marketplace and the system cannot readily get enough of that material to supply its market potential. In such a case, the system isn't complex at all, it's just dangerously exposed.

When dealing with a system (and not just with a subsystem) that has a vendor constraint, every effort should be made to break this constraint. Engineering changes, expensive alternatives, even product changes or purchasing a vendor should be considered. Let's remember that, unlike any other constraint, it's impossible to buffer the system against a vendor constraint. The performance of the system is entirely in the hands of an external entity. This is not a complicated case. It is a dangerous (almost suicidal) one.

4 Resource Constraints

At this stage we have deduced that market and vendor constraints do not contribute to a system's complexity. It looks as if complexity stems, basically, from resource constraints. This conclusion stands to reason since, in any real life organization, there are many resources and the interactions between them occur through the products the organization produces and the tasks it does.

Thus it may seem quite surprising that it can be shown that no real life system can exist if it contains interactive resource constraints. This non-intuitive conclusion, once proven, leads to the realization that any system which exists in reality is a non-complex system. The impression of complexity is probably due to lack of proper analysis and not to any inherent complexity of our systems.

> *The impression of complexity is probably due to lack of proper analysis and not to any inherent complexity of our systems.*

The inability of systems to tolerate interactive resource constraints stems directly from the coexistence of two different phenomena — statistical fluctuations and dependent resources. Previous attempts to show that these two phenomena make the existence of interactive resource constraints highly improbable can be found in my article, "The Unbalanced Plant," [1] and in my more poetic attempt to describe this situation — the boy scout analogy in *The Goal*. However, the far-reaching ramifications of this conclusion impose the need to supply another, more rigorous proof.

Statistical fluctuations simply means that some factors which are inherent in an organization's activities cannot be determined precisely, but only by using averages. Examples of factors which are subject to statistical fluctuations might be run-time, future sales, or expected product development time. When we say that it takes five minutes to perform a certain activity on a certain part, we don't mean that it takes exactly five minutes, but only that it takes an average of five minutes. We are keenly aware that any one part might take four, or even seven, minutes. Likewise, when we predict the amount of each of our products we expect to sell during the upcoming quarter, we expect that the actual numbers

---

[1] Goldratt, E., 1981. The unbalanced plant. APICS 24th Annual International Conference Proceedings.

will only roughly approximate the estimated ones...Who really believes exactly in the forecast? Even firm orders have the tendency — from time to time — to be postponed or even canceled. Quoted product development time is certainly just a best evaluation or — as some claim — a best guestimation. All these factors, and many more, are subject to statistical fluctuations.

Dependent resources exist when some of the tasks that the organization has to carry out require more than one resource. In industrial companies someone has to design the product, someone has to convince the clients to order the product, someone has to talk to the vendors, someone has to accept material from them, someone has to start processing the material, someone has to finish it, someone has to ship it to the customer, and someone has to collect the money. There is a long chain of dependent resources.

These two phenomena exist, almost by definition, in every organization. As long as we don't have a crystal ball to give exact predictions, many factors are subject to statistical fluctuations. As long as we're dealing with an organization, and not just with a collection of individuals, the organization will always have tasks requiring more than one resource (dependent resources).

5 Analyzing The Possibility Of Having Interactive Resource Constraints

In order to analyze how the coexistence of these two phenomena (statistical fluctuations and dependent resources) impact interactive resource constraints, let's start with the simplest example where both exist. Then we'll replace the extremely simple conditions with ones closer to reality, while carefully tracking the resulting conclusions.

The simplest case of dependent resources is a case where only two resources are involved and one of them feeds the other. In other words, one resource is needed in order to start a task and another resource is needed to complete the same task. In order to turn both resources into system constraints so we have interactive constraints, let's assume that the first resource is capable of starting four tasks a day, the second resource is capable of completing those four tasks, no other resources are available, and the system's external clients demand more than four completed tasks a day. In such a situation, it is clear that both resources are constraints of the system.

When we look for the simplest case of statistical fluctuations, the first thing that comes to mind is a normal distribution. We have to remind ourselves that even though a normal distribution is the most well-known — you will find it in every publication dealing with statistics — it is definitely not the simplest distribution. Uniform or rectangular distributions are even simpler. But the simplest statistically significant distributions are binomial ones with equal probabilities, or — as they are popularly known — heads or tails.

This result is not a new revelation, (it was well-known even by the ancient Greeks), but modern industry has been stubbornly trying to ignore it.

In order to subject the performance of our interactive resource constraints to a head-or-tail type of statistical fluctuation, let's say that in our simple case each one of the resources is capable of doing (starting or completing) either three tasks or five tasks a day in equal probabilities. In other words, on about half the days each one of them can do three and about half the days they can do five tasks. This will fix the average of each resource at four tasks a day, as we agreed before. For the sake of simplicity, let's start with the ideal case (or what is considered today to be ideal) and assume that there is no inventory in the system. We'll start with a clean slate, carrying no sins from the past on our backs.

Now let's find out what the average performance of the total system is for the above scenario. To do that, we will have to examine all possible cases. One possibility is that, on a particular day, the first resource will begin three tasks and the second will complete three. The outcome of the system on this day will be, of course, three tasks. A second possibility is that the first resource will begin five, but the second will only complete three tasks. The outcome of the system remains the same — three tasks. Now let's examine a case in which the first resource only starts three tasks, but

> *Before we give up, let's remind ourselves that there is a huge difference between our real world and the world of mathematics.*

the second resource comes to work all charged up and can easily complete five that day. The outcome of the system — despite the increased capability of the second resource — will only be three completed tasks. The final possibility, when the first and second resources both do five tasks, will result in five delivered tasks for the system.

These are the four cases which have an equal probability of occurring. Thus, the system's average is simply the average of these four scenarios.

First Resource	→	Second Resource	=	Outcome
3	→	3	=	3
5	→	3	=	3
3	→	5	=	3
5	→	5	=	5
				14 / 4 = 3.5

The average turns out to be only 3.5 tasks a day. This result is not a new revelation, (it was well-known even by the ancient Greeks), but modern industry has been stubbornly trying to ignore it. The generalization we can make from the scenario above is that:

> The average of the system is smaller than the average of its components.

How bad is this situation? Not too terrible, since a closer look reveals that the above result cannot be a steady-state one. We assumed no inventory in the system at the start. However, if the average output is only 3.5 and the average input (the first resource) is 4, the unavoidable result is an accumulation of inventory in the system. This inventory will accumulate between the two resources and its iimpact will be to partially decouple the dependency between them. If, for example, we consider a later situation when a few partially completed tasks have already accumulated before the second resource, then the result of the third case (3 → 5) will not be three, but five. The extra inventory raises the average performance of the system towards four. (A passing thought . . . Maybe inventory is not always a liability?)

> *We can now understand, in a much more tangible way, Dr. Demming's crusade to reduce variability.*

The question now is how long will this devastating process last? How long will inventory continue to build up and throughput continue to be lost until the outcome of the system stabilizes at an average of four tasks per day? The mathematical answer is that it will take forever. The average outcome of the system will get closer and closer to four, but will never reach it. Before we give up, let's remind ourselves that there is a huge difference between our real world and the world of mathematics. In the mathematical world, three point nine nine nine . . . nine nine (and you can add as many nines as you want) is definitely not four. In our real world 3.99 is, for all practical purposes, four — or, if you want to be really picky, let's say that 3.999 is a good enough four.

The question remains . . . how long will the inventory have to accumulate — and throughput be lost — until we reach a "practical average" of four? This, of course, depends on our choice of "practical average," but simulations (and/or calculations) show that it's a relatively short period. In addition, the level of inventory that accumulates between the two resources is certainly quite reasonable.

6 The Impact Of The Variability Of Components

Before we drop the subject with a sigh of relief, we have to remind ourselves that we've only dealt with a very simple situation so far and we'd better continue to investigate this strange result of

3.5. Otherwise we might have some unpleasant surprises in reality. So, in the best scientific tradition, let's vary the starting conditions in order to investigate their impact on the final outcome. Let's change one thing at a time. If we change several things at once, the final result will probably change, but we won't know exactly what caused it.

Let's first change the magnitude of the fluctuations while keeping everything else the same. Our two resources will now be equally able to do either two or six tasks a day. The average of their individual performances is still four. That hasn't changed. Now let's repeat the same calculations to determine the average outcome of the system. Keeping the same starting point (zero inventory) in the system, we get the following results:

First Resource	→	Second Resource	=	Outcome
2	→	2	=	2
6	→	2	=	2
2	→	6	=	2
6	→	6	=	6
				12 / 4 = 3

We see that the average outcome has dropped from 3.5 to 3, and can conclude that:

> The average of a system is heavily dependent on the magnitude of the fluctuations of its components.

The bigger the fluctuations of the components, the smaller the throughput of the system. If we check further, we'll find that, in this case, the period during which the average inventory is increased rapidly is much longer. Inventory will accumulate to a much higher level before the loss of throughput can be reversed and brought up to a tolerable level (the "practical average" of four). We can now understand, in a much more tangible way, Dr. Demming's crusade to reduce variability. The variability of the system's components—and not just their average performance—dictates the level of inventories and the time required for buildup of the throughput of our systems.

7. The Impact Of A Skewed Distribution

The statistical distributions that govern our reality are far from being symmetrical distributions. They are skewed distributions ... skewed in a major way.

Still, even in this case, simulations will show that as long as we don't insist on reaching an average system throughput of exactly four tasks per day, the situation is quite manageable. To expose the magnitude of the problem, we'll have to change another one of our simplifying assumptions and bring the case being examined closer to a real world situation. So far we've assumed that the statistical fluctuations in our system are subject to a symmetrical distribution. Somehow, whenever we talk about statistics, we see in front of our eyes that nice bell-shaped curve, the normal distribution. It appears in almost every article and textbook that deals with statistical impacts on organizations. We almost take for granted that a symmetrical distribution is a good presentation of our reality. Is it really so?

Examine, for example, how much time it takes to set up a machine. Let's suppose that the average setup time is three hours. Will we be astonished if the next time it takes us seven hours to set up this same machine — four hours more than the average? I don't think anybody who has spent even a few months on a factory floor will be astonished by such an event. Disappointed and dissatisfied ... most probably, but astonished? Certainly not. But try to imagine that next time the set up takes four hours less than the average (which means the setup will take minus one hour). Now is the time to be astonished.

The statistical distributions that govern our reality are far from being symmetrical distributions. They are skewed distribution ... skewed in a major way. How much time will it take to process the next part when the established average is five minutes? If the worker talks with his friend it will probably that eight minutes. If

> *The fact that other links are stronger at that time does not compensate at all for the temporary weakness of just one link.*

the worker takes a nature break, it will probably take fifteen minutes. If the worker has a major disagreement with the foreman, it might take thirty minutes. If a tool breaks, it might take two hours. And if the machine breaks, it might take two days. While the probability of each of these happening is small, it certainly is not zero. In our real lives, statistical distributions more closely resemble exponential distributions. They are skewed to the extent that even events remote by more than 20 sigmas from the average have non-negligible probabilities. If skewed distributions more accurately depict reality, what is the impact of such skewed distribution on the performance of a system having interactive capacity constraints?

To examine this, let's subject our two interactive resources to a skewed distribution. Let's suppose that each resource is capable of doing five tasks a day on two-thirds of the days, but on one-third of the days it is capable of only two tasks per day. The average performance of each resource is still 5 x 2/3 + 2 x 1/3 = 4 tasks per day. We have changed just the statistical distribution, not the average performance of each resource. Here it's a little bit more complicated to calculate the average outcome of the system. Assuming the same beginning point of no inventory in the system, let's examine each of the possible cases. To simplify things, and not have to consider fractional probabilities, we can assume that each resource is subject to the following three equal probabilities, namely: 5 tasks per day, 5 tasks per day and 3 tasks per day. This will increase the number of combinations from four to nine, with each combination having the same probability. The results are:

First Resource	→	Second Resource	=	Outcome
2	→	2	=	2
2	→	5	=	2
2	→	5	=	2

```
5  →  2  =  2
5  →  5  =  5
5  →  5  =  5

5  →  2  =  2
5  →  5  =  5
5  →  5  =  5
           ─────
           30 / 9 = 3.33...
```

The impression of complexity is a result of not pinpointing these constraining policies, but rather trying to deal with their undesirable transient physical ramifications.

The average of the system is only 3 1/3 tasks per day. This is an alarming result. Even though the probability of each resource performing well (five tasks per day) is twice as large as its probability to perform poorly (two tasks per day), nevertheless the outcome of the system is closer to a poor performance than to a good one, forcing us to conclude that:

> The impact of the tail of the distribution is much larger than its probability.

(For those readers who would like to investigate the impact of a third dependent constraint resource, [three interactive constraints], the calculation is not too complicated. Only 27 equal probability scenarios are involved. The result is also not too surprising. The average outcome of the system plummets toward two tasks per day.)

8 Interactive Resource Constraints Lead To Bankruptcy

We all intuitively understand that the strength of a chain is equal to the weakest link at any given point in time. The fact that other links are stronger at that time does not compensate at all for the temporary weakness of just one link.

In our last case, once again inventory will accumulate, and this accumulation will again tend to decouple the dependency between the resources. But now — unlike the previous cases — the tail of the distribution requires an enormous accumulation and thus a very, very long time before practical decoupling is achieved. Simulations (or detailed calculations) show that, if we consider the very skewed distribution that exists in our reality, inventory will continually increase and a significant drain of throughput will occur — practically forever.

But what is the meaning of inventory continuing to pile up while throughput is continually lost? This situation leads, in reality, to only one scenario — bankruptcy. Since we are dealing with organizations that exist, we must conclude that at least one of the assumptions in our little example does not exist in reality. What is left to remove besides the assumption that we are dealing with interactive resource constraints?

What about those plants where people complain about resource constraints that shift from one department to another every two or three weeks? For now it's enough to highlight that, in such a case, there is probably not a single resource constraint in the plant and that, on average, all resources have more than enough capacity. This "floating bottleneck" phenomenon is caused by a policy constraint. The policy constraint might be the way performance is measured locally (efficiencies), or the work order policy (economic order quantities), or the devastating impact of using intermediate due dates. One (or two) policy constraints are probably responsible for the chaotic situation of the floating bottleneck. The impression of complexity is a result of not pinpointing these constraining policies, but rather trying to deal with their undesirable transient physical ramifications.

Whether the system is limited by physical constraints or directly by policy constraints, the number of interactive constraints is very limited. We all know it intuitively — the Pareto Principle does exist.

Looking Beyond the First Stage; Just In Time

Part Two

The sun is still hanging there, but it's quite chilly outside. Phil and I cross the plant's main parking lot on our way to the back entrance where we left our cars this morning. I feel very good with Phil. Not that he is a gentle or even a comfortable person. A smile spreads across my face when I try to visualize Phil as such. The truth is that he is very ill-tempered and I don't think I know anybody who has a shorter fuse. But if something has to get done, he is definitely your man. Of course, as long as you don't provoke him with nonsense, as long as you're practical and to the point, then I think you'd want Phil as a partner.

This is the third job I've had with him. Somehow whenever one of us decides that it's time to move, it doesn't take long before the other follows. Strange. I don't think I've ever had one-tenth of the quarrels with anybody else that I've had with Phil. There hasn't been even one week, in the last twenty years that we've worked together, when I didn't want to strangle him. Sometimes, in my effort to persuade this thick head to listen, I almost feel compelled to put my hands around his neck and shake — or maybe squeeze! That's a lovely thought! But putting nonsense aside, the truth is that Phil is the only person in the world with whom I feel comfortable spending quiet time.

As I open the car door he says, "Mason, it definitely would not work there."

"What?" I ask, totally puzzled.

"JIT," he answers.

"What the hell are you talking about?"

"Mason, wake up. Greg is right. JIT would never work in our former aerospace plant."

"I guess not," I sigh, a little bit annoyed with his sudden switch of subject.

But he doesn't let go. "Mason, what do you think about getting together tonight? For once in our lives, let's try to explain our intuition on our own rather than wait for Greg to squeeze it out of us."

I don't think this is the case at all, but maybe it's a good idea to prepare for tomorrow's meeting. Not that I feel bad now, but I realize that, in more than one way, I've made an ass of myself today.

"Nine o'clock, my place?"

"No," He replies in a very firm voice. "For a change let's meet at my place." And then in a softer tone, he adds, "Susan and the kids are at her mother's for the entire weekend, and I have the fridge filled with beer."

"Fair enough," I say and get into my car.

Today was a very special day. A rare one. Even though I was beaten quite badly on the head, I feel refreshed. The day's discussions, as harsh as they were, have somehow removed a veil that was obliterating my sight. They helped to bring into the open doubts that I've had for quite some time but hadn't admitted even to myself. It's not that I'm totally clear about where it's going to lead me, but it feels like I'm on the verge of a new beginning. It's the same feeling I had a few years ago when I started to abandon my

> *Compared to me, people from Missouri are not skeptical enough. It's not sufficient to show me. I have to understand what I see.*

old love, MRP, for the simplicity and the challenge of JIT.

Am I so shallow . . . falling wholeheartedly in love with one method, just to abandon it after a while, to become a crusader for another? I don't think so. My opinion of myself — and I hope the opinion of everybody else who knows me — is quite the opposite. I'm very methodical and cautious. Before I support anything, I have to investigate it in depth. The enthusiastic opinions of others — even people whom I personally respect — just cause me to double check the evidence and to spend even more time clarifying the underlying logic to myself. Compared to me, people from Missouri are not skeptical enough. It's not sufficient to show me. I have to understand what I see.

To tell the truth, I would sometimes prefer to be a little bit less skeptical. This trait of mine is not restricted to new concepts, but also affects my attitude towards new people. That's probably why I don't make friends easily. As a matter of fact, all my friends are people I've known for quite a long time, people with whom I've covered a substantial distance. Since Marion left me more than six years ago, I haven't fallen in love even once. It's very lonely to be like that. But it's okay, as long as I have my adorable little kittens.

Yes, I was once into MRP, even more than I'm into JIT now. How many nights I spent with the books, charting diagrams to fully absorb the difference between dependent and independent demands! And those long, late hours — or maybe I should call them very early ones — that I spent trying to figure out a systematic way to manipulate the Master Schedule. It was like flirting with a woman — nothing about it was too difficult; no hours were too late.

But then this new JIT lady arrived . . . so gorgeously attractive in her promise of . . . of what . . . of releasing me from the mountain of 20-digit part numbers? Actually it didn't. I still use all those part and operation codes each day. I smile bitterly when I

The details of these transactions were, and are, a finance requirement—to enable them to calculate the actual product costs.

recall that I still to struggle with manipulating the Master Schedule. And in the last few weeks . . . I don't know who is manipulating whom anymore. Am I driving the Master Schedule or is it driving me . . . nuts?

Seriously, what was so attractive about JIT? It certainly didn't use the same terminology that we were all used to. It didn't mention Bills of Material or Routings. But, in retrospect, that didn't mean that we could get rid of them. We are still using them to the same extent as before. Moreover, JIT didn't even reduce the effort of reporting transactions from the floor. The need for all this elaborate, detailed reporting was not even because of my work. All I needed before, and still need, is to know how much inventory we have and where it's located. The details of these transactions were, and are, a finance requirement — to enable them to calculate the actual product costs.

"Never mind," I say to myself as I maneuver the car into my too crowded garage.

Lying on the carpet, I stare into two emerald slits only an inch away. To stabilize them, I put my hand on the fur ball. Sharp nails endanger my bare leg. With a roar, I turn slowly and pick up the humming intruder. It's so relaxing to play with this beautiful and uncomplicated creature. Kittens are not bothered by — and do not bother you with — annoying, abstract concepts. They are interested in tangible things like water and food. They certainly will never be bothered with a question like, "What is so compelling about JIT?"

Blowing into its nostrils, I try to make Red sneeze, while my mind, as if on its own, is stuck on the last question. Why is it that during the last three years I talked so enthusiastically about JIT while downplaying MRP? Come to think of it, I really can't find a logical explanation. It cannot be the facets of JIT that deal with preventive maintenance or setup

> *Let's not forget that inventory reduction was the most emphasized result of our successful MRP implementations.*

reduction techniques. First of all, they really don't belong to my field of logistics. They belong more to production or process engineering. Secondly, these techniques were definitely known a long time before this tidal wave of JIT swamped the U.S.

As for the *quality* aspects of JIT, the same reservations are certainly valid. I took a course in Statistical Process Control from Juran long before I heard the name JIT. To tell the truth, I don't see even the slightest difference between what I learned then and what is advocated today. Quality was always important, even though we talked about it less. Maybe it's new in the boardrooms, but not to people who had to answer customer complaints.

Can it be that what I really like about JIT is just the fact that it gives me a legitimate reason to blame others? "It's not the schedule that is too complicated. It's your environment. Reduce the ridiculously long setups, eliminate scrap, streamline the operations, and then I'll be able to give you simple and stable schedules," I can almost hear myself saying to Phil and his superintendents.

No, I don't think I'd be able to deceive myself to that extent. What attracted me to JIT must be connected directly to my work, to the materials management field. What is it? The thrust to reduce inventories? This might be a good excuse for Charlie, but not for me. As the material manager, I'm very keenly aware that this was also the thrust of MRP. I can still remember the phrases that I used so zealously to persuade my former president to invest in a very expensive MRP software system — and even more expensive hardware to run it. What were everybody's words then?..."let's put order on the floor, so that we will be able to deliver what we promised and do it with less chaos and less inventories." Sounds identical to today's JIT phraseology. Right?

Today we are even more extreme — we call it "Zero-Inventory." What a joke! I laugh into the face of the innocent kitten who responds by wetting my nose with his red, quick tongue. With zero inventory you will have zero production. Yes, I know, we just wanted to emphasize the desired trend, but that's okay for the masses, not for us — the professionals. Let's not forget that inventory reduction was the most emphasized result of our successful MRP implementations. So what the hell drew me into it?!

My irritation forces me into a sitting position. I throw the soft ball and watch the two little creatures chase it. I'm always amazed at the sight of two kittens struggling to win some imaginary victory over a ball. I guess they pretend that the ball is a mouse, but I'm sure they've never seen a mouse in their short lives. A mystery of the genes?

Watching their intense game sparks an answer in my mind. It's push versus pull . . . It's obvious...I made the switch to the JIT camp when I realized the basic fallacy of MRP. . .the fallacy of *pushing* material to the shop floor, rather than pulling it, as JIT is advocating. Satisfied, I stand up to open some cans for my kittens and to fix myself a drink.

Holding a big glass in my hand, I sink into the armchair. Yes, it was this drastic difference in the logistical method...pull, do not push. That's what makes all the difference in the world. I sip slowly from my glass, rolling the spicy liquor on my tongue while rolling "push-pull, push-pull" around in my head. Push is certainly wrong. We were pushing material onto the floor according to the Master Schedule, and the inventories were piling up all over the place. No wonder. In constructing the Master Schedule, I couldn't take into account temporary shortages of capacity. True, I tried to level the load, but there is a limit to what can be done. To foresee all the interactions and to level the load to the extent that no more than one job is scheduled for each work center at any given point in time is not only beyond human capability, the daily fluctuations put it beyond the computer's capabilities, too.

The end result is all too well-known to anyone who has spent time on the factory floor. Inventories accumulate everywhere, expeditors fight constantly with foremen, we are swamped with everything that we don't need now, and at least one of the things that we can't do without is always missing. It reaches the point where you just put plugs in your ears, push everything to the floor

> *. . . but something else left a dramatic and lasting impact on him—our supermarkets.*

that you think is needed, and use your expeditors to pull the few things you really need out the other side — in short, the usual madhouse of the "push" environment.

Compare this to the beautiful calm and orderly fashion of the pull method. I cannot forget the time that the simplicity of the idea struck me. No, it wasn't when I first heard about it. It wasn't even when I heard it for the tenth time. At that time — I hate to admit — my response was just the opposite. I was certain that it would never work in our plant. The light bulb went on when I read how the idea was invented here in America. Dr. Ohno was sent from Japan to the United States to learn how we manage our plants. He was not too impressed by what he saw in our factories, but something else left a dramatic and lasting impact on him — our supermarkets. At that time, in the early fifties, supermarkets did not exist in Japan. They had only the traditional shops where customers didn't have direct access to the merchandise. His observation was almost naive. What struck him as an overwhelming revolution was the fact that only a relatively small portion of the merchandise was displayed on the shelves, with the bulk of it stored in an adjacent "warehouse" area.

"It makes sense," he probably said to himself. "Why should we dump everything onto the shop floor. What will it do besides block all the aisles and cause problems for the customers? What they do in these supermarkets makes much more sense. For each product they decide on a suitable shelf space. They fill up this space and keep the remainder of the stock in the back room. Only when a customer takes a product do they fill the shelf again. The fact that the supermarket people have some time on their hands — either because they re-stocked faster than usual or because sales in the last hour were a little bit slow — is not considered a good reason to bring out more products and block the aisles. Only when the shelves are less than totally full is an action triggered."

Big deal. I've no doubt

Big deal. I've no doubt seen it at least a thousand times without getting excited. But I'm not Dr. Ohno.

seen it at least a thousand times without getting excited. But I'm not Dr. Ohno. He immediately saw the relevancy to a plant environment. "What is the difference between a work center in a plant and a supermarket?" I can almost hear him talking to himself. "Both have customers they have to service. Does it really make such a big difference that in the supermarket the customers come from the outside, while the customers for a plant work center are the next work centers? In both cases, the resources providing the service should not consider what they prefer to do, but should concentrate on satisfying the needs of their customers."

Once we accept this line of reasoning — that a work center is actually a service center — the parallels to a supermarket are obvious. For each work center we have to determine the equivalent of the allotted shelf space. In other words, we will have to determine how many units of each product (or partially processed product) a work center should hold in a "finished" state, so that its "customers" can take them whenever they see fit. To hold more than this number should be viewed not just as filling the shelves, but blocking the aisles. More product than the allocated amount does not improve the overall service. It jeopardizes it. Thus each work center has to make sure that its "shelves" are totally full, but under no circumstances should it cause them to overflow.

It sounds very simple, almost intuitively obvious, but actually it isn't. As a matter of fact, this mode of operation implies a drastic change.

I empty my glass, letting the liquor send another one of those warm waves that slowly spreads from my toes upward. Yes, the magnitude of this change was the most difficult part to fully recognize. The *real* change is not at a procedural or technical level. It's a change in the work ethic itself.

> *The real change is not at a procedural or technical level. It's a change in the work ethic itself.*

Currently, and in the past hundred years, our work ethic demanded that people should work, not stay idle. From the point of view of management, I believe that it is best summarized the phrase, "If a worker does not have anything to do, let's find something for him to do." Everybody must work all the time. That's why we pay them.

Contrast this approach with our conclusion that under no circumstances should a work center cause its "shelves" to overflow. This last idea mandates that a worker produce only whenever its work center's "customers" have taken some products, causing the "shelves" to be partially empty. Otherwise, the worker should not produce! That is the concept of Just-In-Time. It's definitely a different work ethic. Don't produce unless it's needed. Don't fill the entire plant with inventories just because you happen to have some spare time on your hands.

How difficult was it to implement this cultural change in our plant? I don't think that what happened in our plant is representative. We didn't go about implementing it in the usual way. Our approach was very awkward and affected by some unusual coincidences. I was trying to convince everybody to adopt JIT, but nobody wanted to listen. Then Greg came one day, all excited about *The Goal,* and things started to move — you know, identifying our Herbies and managing everything according to them. So instead of starting by establishing the proper "shelves," I had to start by choking the release of material to the floor according to the needs of our bottlenecks — or at least what we thought our bottlenecks were then.

Surprisingly, we didn't have any real problems with the hourly workers. They were easily convinced that what we were doing made a lot of sense — the bottlenecks were very well recognized by everybody. The only resistance came from the foremen who were still trying, for a while, to make their efficiency numbers. But a synchronized multi-front attack overcame their resistance in a surprisingly short time.

Greg played the Dice Game with all of them. The superintendents (headed by Phil

> *The only resistance came from the foremen who were still trying, for a while, to make their efficiency numbers.*

who became a Goal addict) used the two-by-four technique a few times. I watched our storerooms with hawk-like eyes to make sure that my people didn't release anything that wasn't needed. It wasn't easy. Too frequently they were tempted to do a favor for a foreman-friend who was desperately trying to boost his efficiencies. This part was a real battle, but a short one. Maybe two or three weeks, no more.

Within a few months, it became apparent that we had broken all our bottlenecks, and I was able to convince everybody (including Phil) that it was about time to move to the next step and to institute the Pull-JIT System. The transition was much smoother than I had expected. The most troubling step, the one that I felt most unsure about, turned out to be a no-brainer. I wasn't clear at all about how we should go about fixing the proper size for the various "shelves" but, as it happened, Phil and his superintendents decided on them at one relatively short meeting. I don't know how they actually did it, (it looks to me like they used their gut feel and space limitations as their guidelines), but I was very careful not to peer too closely into it. The important thing was that, a few days after the decision, the Pull-JIT System was already functioning.

It never fails to amaze me how well it works. Whenever assembly draws a container of parts, an entire string of work centers is at once awakened for action. The work center whose shelves were tapped immediately gets busy processing a new container of parts to replenish the missing one. This new container is drawn from the "shelves" of the preceding work center, which in turn becomes active to replenish its shelves. The process repeats itself from work center to work center — according to the routing of the particular item drawn — until a container of material is released to a gating work center, and peace is restored. No, the word peace is not suitable, especially when you consider that these waves of activity are initiated

> *It's more accurate to think of the whole plant as one huge spring, exerting enormous pressure from material to final assembly.*

at very short intervals. It's more accurate to think of the whole plant as one huge spring, exerting enormous pressure from material to final assembly. It's like a dangerous snake just waiting for a chance to attack. Whenever a container is pulled by assembly, the entire beast responds immediately.

Yes, we had some initial difficulties, and nobody escaped the learning curves, but they were relatively minor. In some places, where it was a long distance between work centers, we had to establish light signals to notify a work center that a container was being taken from its remote shelves. In a few rare cases, the number of different parts involved was great enough to force us to use the original KANBAN card technique. But, for the most part, it wasn't necessary; especially in light of the fact that, in some cases, we used this opportunity to streamline the work centers in a more logical way. This meant that, for some groups of machines, we had to split them into two or even three smaller groups so that major families of parts could be produced by work centers that were in close proximity, rather than traveling long distances to and fro across the entire plant. Even Phil said, once it was done, that this way made much more sense.

Lately he is starting to bitch and moan that, because we split up the old groups of identical machines, he is running into problems. We're finding, more and more, that one such machine is overwhelmed with work, while two other identical machines, which are in another "flow-line," stand half utilized. But I think this is just a symptom and not a real problem. As we pointed out in today's discussion, we simply were too eager and accepted too many orders too quickly.

It's quite obvious what is happening now. When just one or two containers are pulled from the "shelves" of a work center, that work center doesn't have any problem replenishing them. But now, too often, many containers of different parts are drawn within

> *. . . one such machine is overwhelmed with work, while two other identical machines, which are in another "flow-line," stand half utilized.*

a short period of time, and the priority problem (which one to replenish first) becomes a real headache. Greg is issuing more and more, almost desperate, instructions on which are the hottest orders. Phil is shuffling people and parts between the "flow-lines," and my people and I are trying to put some logical order into this mess.

We should reduce the demand — it's obvious. When a work center has to jump to respond to too many demands, the entire flow is disrupted, especially when there is a set-up involved. Yes, in spite of the major progress that we've made in the last year, setup on some machines still takes more than half an hour, and it takes over ten minutes on a much bigger bunch. This amount of time may sound small, I know, but not when you have to jump very frequently from producing one type of part to another. Phil and his superintendents are already demanding that we double the size of the containers. These men will never understand.

I'm staring angrily into my empty glass. I need another drink. On second thought, maybe it's not such a good idea. I need to eat something. The sandwiches we had at noon now look very small. Eat or drink?

Red ends my internal debate when he jumps onto my lap. I call Her Majesty to join us, but she just raises her tail and elegantly marches into the other room. Women! Absentmindedly I stroke Red's fur. Once I start to move my fingers under his chin, he closes his eyes and starts to hum. This is the most beautiful sound — totally relaxed satisfaction. I feel my tension slowly dissipate. This is even better than another drink.

> *... service is almost a four-letter word to our production people.*

"A work center should be viewed as a service center." Nice words, but the last few weeks have shown me how much we fail to implement this attitude in our own plant. Every work center is just looking at its own performance, at its own difficulties, and the hell with its "customers." And still this idea is so simple and so powerful. If they just could absorb it!

Service. The client is always right! What a joke. You just have to witness some of the fights that go on between the expediters (who represent the customer's needs) and the foremen to realize that service is almost a four-letter word to our production people.

Absentmindedly I continue to stroke Red's fur, remembering the times when I was forced to accompany Marion to buy a new dress. She always insisted that I come along so she could choose "a dress that you will like." Even now I clearly remember that, when it came to the final choice, she never considered my opinion. "What do you know about today's fashion?" she used to say. "You'll see. When I put on the proper makeup and matching shoes, you're going to love it." As it turned out, she was always right because, in the end, I was always babbling with praise. Besides, who is going to argue, after spending a couple hundred bucks, just to find himself in a pointless fight?

Why this sudden nostalgia? Ha, service. That was the thing that never ceased to amaze me. The endless patience of the clerks in the shops. Marion was a hard client to satisfy, I can tell you. She never bought in the first shop that we went into and not even in the fifth one. In every shop she would try on almost every outfit, or that's the way it looked to my impatient temper. The clerks were always smiling, always cooperative, with so many different 'lovely' bullshit remarks. It almost made me sick. "Try this one blah . . . blah . . ." Marion would go into the small cubicle and out again. . "How gorgeous it looks on you . . ." and another one, and another one. And all this time you can bet that the customer, Marion, (not neglecting me, of course) is, at least, the Queen of England. Then in the end, we'd leave without buying anything. "I have to give it some more thought." Even after all these years my ears burn when I recall it, especially when the same warm, polite words always followed us. "No trouble. I hope that next time we'll be able to satisfy you." That's SERVICE!

> *"No trouble. I hope that next time we'll be able to satisfy you." That's SERVICE!*

I sink another inch into my comfortable armchair — by now I'm lying more than sitting — and close my eyes. I try to visualize a work center in a plant with the attitude of a true service center. Slowly it starts to dawn on me. JIT is not just a bunch of unconnected improvement techniques. It all stems from this idea of SERVICE. Take the small containers for example. "Yes, Mister Customer, you want only one part? So sorry, you'll have to take the entire work order. It's only one hundred parts. You don't need them now? It's okay, you'll probably need them sometime in the future. What? No, excuse me, but I'm serious. If you want one, you'll have to take the entire batch, all one hundred." That's not service. That's not looking at the client's needs, but at your own comfort. That's work center mentality, not service center mentality. No wonder JIT's ideal is to strive to reach a production batch of just one item everywhere.

Or take, for example, the attitude toward setup of machines. "You want a red part, dear client? So sorry. We are producing white parts today. What about tomorrow? So sorry. . . but you see, we save setup time by going from white to green and only then to red. Why don't you come back next week? Then we will be delighted to serve you." You see what I mean? Reducing the time for setup to improve response to clients is essential . . . not to save costs, but to improve response.

With all the effort we've put into setup reduction, I don't think we've really grasped this. We look at setup reduction as something good because we think it reduces production cost. That's the wrong approach. It leads to enormous resistance when we want to "waste" the saving in setup time by cutting batch sizes; which, of course, necessitates more frequent setups.

Somewhere I read that Toyota had reduced setup times to ten minutes on processes which still take four hours here. Yet they

> *We look at setup reduction as something good because we think it reduces production cost. That's the wrong approach.*

devote sixteen hours a week to setup where we devote only eight. No wonder. They reduce the setup time in order to reduce batch sizes, and they use such small batches that their process time is probably only half an hour. Here, if it takes four hours to set up a machine, you can bet that we'll run it for a minimum of two days. That's no longer the case in our plant, but every time I want to cut the size of the containers further, it's a bloody fight.

Take another example — preventive maintenance. It's so obvious now. "Oh, dear client, we're so sorry, but the machine is down. Yes, we know the same thing happened two days ago, and last week, but what can we do? They don't make them like they used to anymore." Service isn't polite excuses. Service is giving the clients what they want, when they want it, and of satisfactory quality. "What? The dress shrank to half its size in the first wash? Let me see it. Yes, it's dreadful. We'll replace it with this identical lovely dress. Will it shrink as well? I don't know. Why don't you try it?" No wonder "Quality at the Source" is one of the foundations of JIT.

Everything falls so nicely into place when derived from the same concept. Service, service, and once again SERVICE! I find myself almost standing up. Yes, it's very exciting when isolated pieces fall into place all of a sudden and expose one beautiful, homogeneous picture.

I'm hungry. It's time to put some food into my belly. Fresh salad and a juicy steak, carefully cooked to medium-well, will certainly do.

Holding a beer can in one hand, Phil opens the door.

"Down?" I ask.

"Yes, definitely," he answers, and gestures the way with his free hand.

I much prefer to go down to Phil's family room, rather than sit in his living room. It's not that the living room is uncomfortable. On the contrary, it's heavily

... but everytime I want to cut the size of the containers further, it's a bloody fight.

decorated with dignified, mahogany furniture and silk curtains. Its atmosphere almost demands respectable behavior. I can't imagine sitting there holding a can in my hand. Pilsner glasses would be mandatory. Dragging a flip-chart into that room is totally unthinkable.

Here in the basement it's much cozier. I stretch myself out on the sofa which has seen much better days, and accept with gratitude the cold beer that Phil is so quick to furnish from the tiny fridge hiding in the corner.

"Listen, Phil," I say while stretching a lazy hand toward the big bowl of popcorn, "I must tell you about the interesting new insight into JIT I found this evening."

Before I can continue, I see a sour expression spread across Phil's face. "What's the matter?" I ask.

"Mason, Mason." He repeats my name in a voice which sounds like an old man about to give up trying to teach a teenager a lesson.

"Stop patronizing me," I respond. "Do you want to hear it or not?"

"No, Mason. I don't want to hear your new insight into JIT. I've gotten sick and tired of hearing it over the last three years." He mimics my voice, "Every two or three months `a new in-depth.'" And then, probably as a response to my apparent irritation, he raises his hand and says in a louder voice, "And don't give me this crap of `If you had only listened, we would have gotten these results a year earlier.' It doesn't work anymore, not after the madness we've faced recently."

That gets to me! That attitude is totally unfair. "What's wrong with you?" I respond, my voice rising. "Do you want, all of a sudden, to ignore the fantastic results we've gotten from JIT?"

> *I don't want to hear your new insight into JIT. I've gotten sick and tired of hearing it over the last three years.*

"No. What's wrong with *you?*" Phil is practically shouting now. "It's as if today's discussions didn't occur at all. They must have washed over you like water off a duck's back. And besides," he continues to roar, "we didn't implement JIT. We identified bottlenecks and worked according to them. You can't take credit for that. You yourself said today that the word `bottleneck' is foreign to JIT terminology."

This really gets on my nerves. "Phil, you forget all the effort we put in after the initial first steps...the pull system, the flow-lines, statistical process control . . . all the efforts toward preventive maintenance and setup reduction."

This has some impact on him. He lowers his voice a bit. "Yes, Mason, but you forget that all the additional gains we achieved through those efforts have been lost during the last two, chaotic months."

He has a point, but I have to straighten him out. "Not true!" I answer confidently. "They weren't lost at all. We simply took too many orders. The minute we trim the intake, it will all come back. They are all there — the shorter setup time and the better quality. If you just keep your mouth shut for few minutes, I'll tell you what's wrong. I'll explain the meaning of service."

Phil looks at me in silence but, when I'm about to continue, he starts talking again, "You're right. We shouldn't begin the evening this way. But, Mason, do me a favor. Save your thoughts about service for yourself. We're not a service company. We're a production company."

"That's the trouble!" I burst in, but I'm talking to his back now. He's near the open fridge, and I'm just wasting my breath.

After a while he turns around, hands me another open beer, and then sinks into the armchair again. He says calmly, "Mason, let's stop this idiotic debate. We've had it too many times in the past, and we know it leads nowhere. We have something to do, remember?"

"Okay," I sigh and accept the cold beer. "Let's start to analyze how we would have

> *. . .'bottleneck' is foreign to JIT terminology.*

— 31 —

implemented JIT in our previous company."

"It wouldn't have worked there!" he says.

"Stop this nonsense." I start to lose my infinite patience. This guy could even provoke an angel! "Do you want to analyze it, or do you just want to voice your final conclusion?"

"Okay, okay." Phil smiles. "No offense. Let's do it slowly. Where do you want to begin?"

I take my time and try to put some order into my thoughts. Phil waits for my answer, and I let him wait for a while. Why not? He himself said to take it slowly. "Why don't we start with the sheet-metal parts?" I finally suggest.

Phil smiles and responds in a good mood. "Mason, this trick won't work. You know that the real difficulties are always in the heavily-machined parts. Don't try to avoid the issue just to protect your beloved JIT. Besides, we are trying to prepare ourselves for tomorrow's meeting, and Greg has asked specifically about the heavily-machined parts."

It's obvious that Phil hasn't been wasting his time. He is well prepared. It's not going to be easy, but I didn't expect it to be. A little bit irritated, I say, "It looks as if you've already given it some thought, so why are you asking me to start? You go ahead!"

Phil doesn't lose his composure. He finishes swallowing his beer, wipes his mouth with the back of his hand and, in a very confident tone, starts to lecture. "First, we must define what we call heavily-machined parts. If we're referring to our previous plant, I think we can adequately define them as parts which require at least sixty different operations to process. Or, if I use your terminology, they are parts whose routing doesn't fit on just one computer sheet. I would say that, since the routing of most heavy parts covers several pages, we should consider that they take an average of one hundred

> *"Do you want to analyze it, or do you just want to voice your final conclusion?"*

operations to process."

His confident, lecturing tone really bugs me. "Phil, you're not talking about now. You're still living in the past," I say in a not-too-friendly voice. "Since we left that company over four years ago, they have probably tripled the number of Numerical Control machines. You know that these NC machines permit considerable consolidation of operations. I'd say that we should use a number below fifty as the average number of operations per part."

Of course, this doesn't fly with Phil. "Most of the part's routings were re-engineered before we left," he opposes. "I still say that my numbers are pretty good. But you know what, Mason? I'll settle for your ridiculously low number anyway — let's say sixty operations — okay? Anything to prevent you from avoiding the issue. Then can I continue?"

"Okay, sure," I gesture with my hand, waiting for Phil to start dancing on the subject of the average number of times a part has to return to the same machine. That was once a nightmare for me, but I think I've already found an acceptable solution. I figure Phil is in for a surprise, but he surprises me instead. He doesn't return to the subject of routings, but instead asks, "What would you estimate was the yearly usage of those parts?"

I don't hurry to respond, trying to figure out where Phil is heading. After a short pause he continues, "I would say the largest program we had needed about fifty to hundred parts per year, but most were in the range of considerably less than two dozen per year."

"Yeah," I say. "A good average would be about two or three pieces a month."

"That's reasonable," he agrees.

Then the real attack begins. "Suppose now that we'd implemented JIT and refined it to an ideal level. How many containers would we hold for each

... they have probably tripled the number of Numerical Control machines.

part between every two operations?"

"In an ideal case, there would be only one container per part after each operation and only one item in each container," I reply. To reach such a level would have taken a very long time, if possible at all, but Phil didn't ask about my realistic estimation, he asked about an ideal case. Now he's probably going to be stuck. So what?

Phil, in his stubborn way, just continues. "This means that, under the ideal JIT implementation, we would always keep sixty pieces for every different part on the floor." Not giving me anytime to absorb this, he elaborates. "Remember, we agreed to use sixty operations per part as a good estimation. You said that in order to have the JIT-Pull System work — assuming even an ideal situation — we'd need one piece after each operation. This means that, for each part, we would have sixty pieces of work-in-process."

"Yes, I know how to multiply sixty by one," I say, more than a little bit annoyed. It's obvious now where Phil is heading...There's an enormous amount of material on the floor. But he doesn't spare anything.

"So Mason, we just agreed that the average consumption is about two pieces per month . . ."

"Two to three," I break in.

"Okay, two to three per month. Which means that, under ideal JIT implementation, we would have to maintain twenty to thirty months of inventory on the floor." In a triumphant voice he brings his argument to its final conclusion: "This is much more work-in-process than we ever had, and nobody would say that we were even close to being good."

> *"In an ideal case, there would be only one container per part after each operation and only one item in each container,"*

I'm a little shocked. Swiftly I scan the numbers in my mind, but can't find any loophole. Yes, I can argue the numbers, but it won't help to change the final conclusion. Phil definitely has a point.

"I told you it wouldn't work there," he chortles, pouring more salt on my wounds.

"I didn't say you're wrong," I reply, getting up from the sofa to get another beer from the fridge. "JIT is supposed to work in a mass-production environment, and heavy aerospace parts are certainly not that," I throw over my shoulder.

Coming back to the sofa, I try to organize my thoughts. Phil looks like he's ready to continue, but I stop him. "Wait, Phil. You've made your point. Let me digest it before you continue. What do you think is the main difference between mass-production and heavy parts?"

"One big difference is the number of operations a part has to go through," Phil answers cooperatively.

"Yes. I suspect you're right, even though for some automotive parts it might not be true. The main difference, I think, is probably in the daily usage. Two or three pieces per month is certainly not mass-production. I can't imagine anybody calling mass-production something that is consumed in quantities of less than hundreds per day."

We sit in silence for awhile. "What really counts," I say slowly, "is probably the ratio. For the Pull-JIT System to work, the daily consumption of most parts must be larger than the average number of operations per part."

"Yes that's probably so," agrees Phil. "Otherwise the production is certainly not just-in-time."

"What do you mean, not just-in-time?"

"It's obvious, isn't it," says Phil, and then, noting the expression on my face, he hurries to explain. "If we examine our heavy

"This is much more work-in-progress than we ever had, and nobody would say that we were even close to being good."

parts environment, assuming even the ideal implementation of your Pull-System, what will we find? When the assembly is pulling one container, every work center along the route of that item will start to work almost immediately, causing a container to be pulled from raw material inventory onto the production floor. Right?"

"Yes, Phil, that's absolutely right. Finally you've grasped my meaning," I smile back.

"If we concentrate on that last container," (he ignores my last remark) "the one that was just pulled to the floor, how long will it take for it to be processed through all operations and finally be assembled?"

"If we use your previous numbers," I answer, "it's quite easy to calculate. If the monthly consumption is three, that means assembly will draw only three containers a month. Thus our container will move through only three operations per month. And if it has to be processed through sixty operations, it will take . . . twenty months."

"So if we release a part to production today, and this part takes more than a year and a half until it's assembled, that is not exactly what I'd call Just-In-Time," Phil concludes, with a straight face.

It hurts. That's for sure. It's quite tempting to ignore it and just repeat that JIT is valid for mass-production, but there must be a different reason. I learned long ago that running away from such dichotomies is running away from a chance to gain deeper understanding.

> *"For the Pull-JIT System to work, the daily consumption of most parts must be larger than the average number of operations per part."*

"Let me think about it for a minute," I request. "If Just-In-Time turns out to be producing `in more than one and a half years,' there must be a good reason."

"Come on, Mason. We

used to do it in less than eight months. You're trying to find a reason to justify JIT in spite of reality."

"Phil, will you shut up for a minute! That's not what I meant at all, and you know it. Come on, old buddy, give me a real hand. In the Pull-JIT System, we determine the number of containers that we would like to hold after each operation...like the shelves allotted to a product in a supermarket. Each work center is trying to keep its shelves totally full. So, whenever the succeeding work center takes a full container, the previous one immediately starts to process a new container to replenish its shelves."

"Mason, wait. You say that the supplying work center is going to work on a new container to replenish the shelves. What if this new container isn't needed until a week from now?"

"It doesn't matter," I reply. "The concept is that the shelves must be full at all times." The dichotomy is starting to be obvious even to me, but Phil's verbalization is making it clearer.

"So what is really meant by Just-In-Time is not PRODUCE just in time, but rather REPLENISH just in time."

"I guess you're right," I answer. "And in a mass-production environment, the difference between producing and replenishing is negligible for all practical purposes. It's probably less than an hour. But, with heavy aerospace parts, this same difference can easily be more than a year." And, to myself, I bitterly add, "What do you expect from an idea that was invented in a supermarket? Replenishing is the name of the game there. Production is a foreign word."

After a while, I recognize that Phil can't possibly stop at this point. He's much too practical for that. "So what is your suggested solution in the heavy parts environment?" I ask.

"Before I answer, let me ask some more questions," he says and leans forward. Oh, oh, here comes another blow. But what

I learned long ago that running away from such dichotomies is running away from a change to gain deeper understanding.

can I do? Phil is now moving ahead full speed. "Let's suppose, just suppose, that a real disaster occurred in the last work center. You know, one of those catastrophes that causes us to lose a machine for an entire month. What effect would that have on the assembly schedule and, consequently, on the shipping schedule?"

"It's obvious," I reply. "Since there is only one piece of each part ready for assembly, that month won't end up well. But, Phil, your question is totally unfair. We have considered an ideal case. If there is a chance of such breakdowns, we wouldn't hold just one container between each two work centers, but much more."

"Not so fast, Mason. Don't try to turn your Just-In-Time production system into a Just-In-Case shipment system... maintaining many containers for each part between each two work centers when the consumption is just a few a month! No. Let's examine it slowly. Suppose that only the last work center is prone to breakdowns."

"Fair enough. I see what you mean...let's consider a case in which only the last work center might be down for a whole month and where the monthly consumption is, let's say, three per month. Then we have to hold at least three complete parts after that work center. Every prudent material manager would do this, even if the chance for such a breakdown is relatively small. For large aerospace assemblies, the ramifications of not having a part is huge. It might hold up a multi-million-dollar product."

"Fine," says Phil.

I don't actually like the way he is leading me by the nose, but what can I do? I should have concentrated on Greg's specific question rather than occupying myself with general thoughts about JIT. Now it's too late, and I must follow Phil's lead.

> "... Suppose that only the last work center is prone to breakdowns."

"Now," he continues, "suppose that the feeding work center — the second from the end — is also subject to such

— 38 —

breakdowns."

I try to avoid the question. "That's a horrible situation."

"Horrible, I agree, but it's not uncommon, as you well know."

Phil isn't letting me off the hook.

"In such a case," I force myself to answer dejectedly, "I suppose we don't have any choice but to maintain an additional three pieces right after that work center, too."

"Mason, cheer up. It's not as bad as that," Phil responds surprisingly. "Suppose we don't increase the inventory allowance between the last two work centers, (it's still one), and the feeding work center is down for a whole month. What is the damage to assembly? Remember, we're talking about an environment where no bottlenecks exist. Otherwise, forget your JIT. If there are bottlenecks, we'd better go back to the solution discussed in *The Goal* and *The Race* — the Drum-Buffer-Rope method."

"Yes, yes," I respond impatiently, realizing my mistake. "All work centers have, on average, excess capacity compared with the demand, so they can catch up without hurting assembly... as long as we have those three completed pieces at the end."

Phil opens his mouth to continue, but I don't let him. Something's bothering me. I think I may have found a glitch in Phil's arguments. Anyway it won't hurt to try. He is too damn satisfied with himself tonight.

"Wait a minute. This is important. Let's examine it one more time," I say loudly.

Phil has no choice but to agree. "Well, go on," he urges.

My thoughts are not yet clear enough, so I get up slowly from the sofa and start to pace up and down the room. After some time, I approach the flip chart, draw

I think I may have found a glitch in Phil's arguments. Anyway it won't hurt to try. He is too damn satisfied with himself tonight.

two circles connected by an arrow, and start to talk...anything to buy some time. I'd better be onto something or Phil will rightfully explode.

"Let's suppose that the last work center is down for a month." I start slowly, basically feeling my way as I go. "By the time it's up again, assembly has depleted its buffer. Remember, we hold enough complete parts for only one month's consumption."

"Right," Phil replies, nodding his head.

"Now suppose," I continue, still not certain where I'm really aiming, but letting my hunch carry me forward. "Suppose that before the last work center. . ." and I point with the marker to the right circle. . ."Suppose that before it had sufficient time to replenish its buffer, the preceding work center. . ." and I shift the marker to the left circle, "this second work center from the end also had your horrible disaster, and it broke down for a whole month. In such a case, when one disaster follows another, assembly will be out of parts."

"Yes." Phil breaks into my drawn out explanation. "Of course, in such a case the shipping schedule will be missed. But. .."

"Don't interrupt me, please. Be patient or I'll lose my train of thought."

"Okay, okay, carry on," Phil sighs.

"Now, suppose the second work center breaks first. At the time of the break, the last work center cannot fully replenish its buffer because it doesn't have material to work on. So, if one of these work centers (it doesn't matter which one) breaks again before the final buffer is replenished, the shipping schedule will deteriorate. I think, Phil, that we need to add the additional three pieces between the two work centers."

"I think, Phil, that we need to add the additional three pieces between the two work centers."

"Can I say something now without breaking your train of thought?" Phil asks in a sarcastic tone.

"Be my guest," I gesture, feeling much better. At least I'm giving him a run for his money.

"I think that you've made your usual nice attempt to confuse me, but I'm afraid it won't work this time." He grins at me. "Don't tell me that you're treating the chance of a work center breaking down as something that can be determined exactly. You know that we're talking about probabilities. The word `chance' implies that. We protect the plant, by keeping the three pieces at the end, against the slim chance that the machine will go down for a long time. We are willing to do it, as you yourself have said, because the damage which would occur in such a case is very extensive. But, of course, we're still evaluating the cost (the need to hold three prices for each part) versus the probability and the magnitude of the damage. When we say that we protect against a one-month break, we don't mean that a two-month break is an absolute impossibility. We just mean that the chances for even an extended breakdown are so slim that it's not reasonable to pay the price to protect ourselves against such an improbable occurence."

He stops to take another long gulp from his fifth, or maybe sixth, can. It's very clear what he intends to say now, but I decide not to interrupt him. Let him dig himself a nice deep hole. I'm already prepared to counter his argument. So I just keep quiet and concentrate on my beer until Phil continues.

"Your argument about holding an additional three pieces between the last two operations is based on the assumption that two such breakdowns will follow one right after another. Mason, who are you kidding? You know very well that the chances that two breakdowns will occur one after another is incredibly slim. If people had worried about protecting themselves against such ridiculous odds, nobody would live in California."

> *When we say that we protect against a one-month break, we don't mean that a two-month break is an absolute impossibility.*

I don't get excited or even insulted. I just look straight into his eyes, and, trying to irritate him by using a seemingly pacifying tone, I say, "You're using strong words like `incredibly slim' and `ridiculous odds'. Let's not turn this discussion into an empty political battle. Let's put aside these empty words and coldly examine the situation. Can I assume that we would both consider the chance that a particular machine will go down for a long while once a year a slim chance, but something still worth taking precautions against?"

When Phil nods in agreement I continue, keeping the same level, calm tone. "For the sake of simplicity, let's round off the numbers and say that we're protecting against a ten percent chance that a machine will go down for an entire month during a ten-month period."

"Fair enough." Phil picks up the ball. "That's exactly my argument. We're protecting against a ten percent chance, but the cases you have brought up have a much smaller chance of occurring. The chance of two machines breaking one after the other are only about one percent."

He hurries to correct himself when he sees that I'm about to object. "Okay, okay. Since the sequence in which they break doesn't alter the negative impact on shipping, let's agree that the chances are higher than one percent, but still lower than two percent. That's still much too low to be bothered with."

"I can't agree with you," I reply.

"What? You're saying that we should protect ourselves against something that has a only a two percent chance of occurring?" Phil starts to show his temper.

"Damage will occur as long as the second breakdown happens before the buffer of finished pieces is restored to the level of three pieces."

"No, no. Calm down. I simply don't agree that the chances are only two percent. Phil, don't jump out of your skin. Let me explain. You see, you assume that damage will occur only if the second break occurs *immediately* after the first one.

This is not necessarily the case. Damage will occur as long as the second breakdown happens before the buffer of finished pieces is restored to the level of three pieces."

"Right." He starts to calm down. "But I still don't see the difference."

"I think we should examine how much time it takes to restore the buffer." And, before he has a chance to respond, I continue, "Remember we agreed that no work center is a bottleneck, but that still doesn't mean they have unlimited capacity. Suppose, for example, that the machine under consideration has five percent excess capacity. If such a machine has a one-month breakdown, how long will it take before it can catch up? Remember, after the breakdown this machine is an entire month behind, and it has only five percent spare capacity for catching up."

"Hmm . . ." says Phil. "I see what you mean. What you're asking is how many months it will take until this machine catches up on a backlog equal to 95 percent of its monthly capability." He quickly scribbles on a piece of paper and continues. "The answer is 39 months . . . I see what you mean. The chance for damage to occur due to a second breakdown can be quite high, since the recovery time might be very long. I see . . ." he muses as he sinks into a long silence.

I just lay on the sofa sipping beer and enjoying life. All in all, Phil is a nice chap.

Phil stands up and goes to make more room for additional beer. I turn on the TV to watch . . . commercials . . . commercials . . . commercials. Just when I decide to give up and turn off the TV, he returns.

"Listen, Mason, what are you trying to do . . . persuade me that the JIT-Pull System is even worse than I say? The huge amount of sixty pieces of work-in-process is not enough? Are you trying to prove that, under normal conditions, the pull system will need even more? I think some-

" . . . From the beginning of the process. Why the hell do we have to freeze containers at those stages?"

how we've switched positions."

My good mood disappears. Of course, he is right. I allowed myself to enjoy a hollow victory. But Phil doesn't stop there. Probably offloading some liquid has enabled his brain's wheels to turn much faster.

"And besides," he continues, "this miserable situation is a direct result of the fact that you insisted on restricting the number of containers held between each two work centers to just one. According to this scheme, we are forced to hold over sixty containers — a very large quantity — on the floor . . . and we're still exposed. What we should do is allow these same containers to accumulate near the end, then the damage due to multiple breakdowns would be negligible."

"That's exactly what I claim," I answer with a smile. "We have to add more containers toward the end of the process."

"No!" Phil almost explodes. "We already have too many containers in the process."

"But we agree that we need them to protect against breakdowns, so where are we going to get them from?" I'm totally puzzled.

". . . From the beginning of the process. Why the hell do we have to freeze containers at those stages?" Phil is getting emotional now.

> . . . *remember that in MRP we allowed two whole days for each operation, even though the actual processing time was less than an hour.*

"But I don't understand." I've really lost him. "How can we do it? The Pull-JIT System must have at least one container between each two operations. Mechanically, it can't work otherwise."

"That's what I've claimed all the time. Your JIT-Pull System doesn't make any sense. For its sake, we've been holding inventory where we don't need it at all. I thought that JIT stands for decreasing inventory, not *increasing* it."

What an attack! It's almost physical. "Wait, Phil!" I'm trying to stop the avalanche. "Without the pull system we are going to swamp the entire plant with inventory."

"Why?" Says Phil. "Why do you say that? If we just behave logically, of course we won't do it."

"Come on!" is my only disgusted response.

Phil switches to persuasion. "Mason, I certainly don't want to leave it as just a generality. Of course we need a procedure. Otherwise we'll swamp the plant with inventory. But that doesn't mean that the only procedure is the JIT-Pull procedure. Why don't we construct one that makes more sense?"

"Well, well, Mr. Phil Ohno. Okay, genius, what do you suggest?"

Phil throws me a nasty look, but nevertheless continues. "First we have to establish a good estimate of the average lead time for producing our heavy parts. I know that it varies but, still, Mason, give me an estimate."

"Estimate . . . forget it. It's impossible to give any sensible number."

Phil doesn't say anything. He just continues to lean forward and stare directly into my eyes. A muscle starts to jump high on his cheek. I start to feel really uncomfortable.

"Phil, you know it depends on many things. If we expedite it, and Murphy is miraculously asleep, it might take just one week. But, realistically, I will never personally guarantee any number below three or four months. And, Phil, you know how dangerous it is because breakdowns and scrap are commonplace. In the past,

> *Whenever assembly uses a complete part, we'll release a new one for production. One for one.*

remember that in MRP we allowed two whole days for each operation, even though the actual processing time was less than an hour. Still, there was a lot of fighting between my poor expediters and your production gorillas. No, to give any number is too dangerous."

"Mason, we're making some progress. To make things easier, let's say that we will not consider any major catastrophes at this stage." Seeing my expression, he hurries to add, "Of course we're going to take them into account before we finish, but right now give me an estimate of the lead time. Forget any major catastrophes, but consider the routine, smaller disasters. And yes, another thing...try to answer on the assumption that my people and I are no longer concerned with making high-efficiency numbers. So I'm not forcing you to release material just to supply work for my people and thus the work force is now free to work on what is really needed."

I smile back and say, "Under the assumption that production is headed by the new Phil and we're not considering major catastrophes...I guess a good estimate on lead time would be about four months."

"But Mason, we agreed to take sixty operations per heavy part as an average. Even an inflated MRP would use a lead time of 120 days. And what about my promise, and the elimination of major catastrophes? You're unfair."

"Phil, you forget that in actuality we had eight months' inventory. No, I still say that four months is a good number. I'm standing firm on that one."

"You're just stubborn," says Phil, "but okay. Now suppose we hold enough protection against catastrophes for three whole months. That should be more than sufficient, right?"

"Yes, sure," I agree.

"Okay," says Phil, "let's summarize. Four months lead

"Mason, it was never pull to start with. Your JIT system is just an exaggerated case of PUSH."

---

time at a consumption rate of three per month is twelve pieces. An additional three months' protection against major catastrophes adds another nine pieces. In total, we should release twenty-one pieces onto the floor. We should not release more until assembly uses a part. Whenever assembly uses a complete part, we'll release a new one for production. One for one. This will give us tremendous protection, and we'll still be holding only twenty-one pieces...which is much better than your ideal case of sixty pieces plus who knows how much more to protect against the usual disruptions."

What the hell is happening here? I expose my confusion by blurting out, "But, Phil, what makes you believe there will be any completed parts for assembly to use?"

"Your estimate of four months lead time," he answers calmly. "I should have about nine pieces ready. Major catastrophes will reduce this number from time to time, but as you yourself have estimated, unless the roof falls in on our heads, this number will never be reduced to zero."

After a short pause he continues, "And, Mason, I don't have to argue with you about the four month number. I just have to watch the number of completed pieces we have. If, on the average, this number is significantly higher than nine, as I suspect it will be, then your estimate of the lead time is actually inflated. If that happens, we'll just pass up a couple of releases of new parts to the floor. It's quite neat and simple."

I don't answer, and Phil doesn't continue to talk. I just replay in my mind what he's said. Yes, it definitely will work. At last I sigh, "There goes my pull system."

"Mason, it was never pull to start with. What I'm suggesting is PULL. Your JIT system is just an exaggerated case of PUSH."

That's a little bit too much. "You're going to have to explain such a blunt and arrogant statement," I say, looking desperately for a fight.

"Of course," says Phil, "but on one condition."

"Which is?"

"That you will listen objectively and not just in order to find a chance to get at my throat. It's not a personal struggle, remember?"

"You're right." I calm down. "Please explain."

"You see, Mason, you gave me the key when you highlighted for me that . . ."

I stop listening. The sky is falling on my head, and Phil seems to have all the answers. "It's too stuffy in here," I interrupt. "Can we go out for a short stroll?"

"Of course," says Phil, playing the role of the perfect host.

Chapter 6

THE PARADIGM SHIFT

1 | The Historical Process

Many times, in the history of science, a situation arises where the existing knowledge in a particular subject is no longer satisfactory. When this happens, we witness a movement that cannot be described in any other way, except as a renaissance. In many places, independent and autonomous efforts begin to break new ground. In the beginning, when these efforts are still in their infancy and resemble new "beliefs" much more than substantiated, valid approaches, I the user community, extrapolating from the accepted body of knowledge, views these new "beliefs" as too avant garde. The ideas seem strange, almost ridiculous and certainly of doubtful value. It is no wonder that their originators, convinced of the validity of their intuition but still lacking a clear verbalization, respond with an attitude that can be rightfully referred to as arrogant or even fanatic.

This attitude of the originators - and the pockets of people that have become convinced - tends to put them on a war path. Unfortunately, the fight is not just against the established body of knowledge but also against the equally new ideas of other originators. Some - but certainly insufficient - precautions are taken to recognize the good parts of the existing know how. Half hearted attempts will be made not to throw the baby out with the bath water.

> *. . . start to explore ways to mold the new ideas, . . .into a new and uniform body of knowledge.*

This sound attitude towards the existing body of knowledge does not usually characterize the relationship between the originators of the new and different ideas. Each has a very good understanding of the existing body of knowledge. Having analyzed it in depth, their new insights give them a very deep understanding. But, this is certainly not the case when they are relating to each other's ideas. The information at this stage is quite limited and the new ideas have not yet matured to the degree where they can be clearly explained. It's no wonder, in retrospect that it looks as if these people, in the name of open mindness, are attacking each other's approaches with the zeal and biased logic of a fanatic.

Most of the new approaches usually provide a significant contribution. They may emerge from different angles and may be based on different facets of the established base of knowledge. This does not mean that only one of them is valid and all others are wrong. It certainly doesn't imply that we have to choose one to the exclusion of the others. It is no wonder that after some time the consolidation process begins. People start to explore ways to mold the new ideas, which have now passed the test of reality, into a new and uniform body of knowledge. We find less and less articles and presentations entitled "this or that method - which is better?" Rather, synergetic attempts start to be voiced.

At this stage, an attitude of compromise begins to dominate the subject. Unfortunately the main driver of these "synergetic" efforts is territorialism. We try to accommodate all the new approaches by dividing up their applications - "this method is most suited for such a case, while this other method is more suitable when dealing with such symptoms." These compromises, even though calming the heated environment and providing the necessary conditions for meaningful communication, at the same time open artificial gaps between the various, valid new methods. This compromising approach does not lead to a proper synergism. It only results in co-existence, and as such postpones the most beneficial stage, that of molding all of the existing methods into one extremely powerful body of knowledge. A body of knowledge, in which internal conflicts have been resolved and where a foundation is laid that can support a new explosion of ideas.

> *... each one of these movements encompasses much more than was envisioned.*

I believe that in order to achieve a meaningful synergy we should also strive to highlight the underlying differences, rather than just emphasizing the similarities. Only in this way are the different basic assumptions exposed and analyzed, so that there is a realistic chance of achieving a single uniform theory. The different contributions of each of these methods can then be amalgamated into one theory, which is more powerful than just the summation of all the individual methods. The previous article (Theory of Constraints Journal, Vol. 1, Number 5), which explains the ramifications of the existence of statistical fluctuations and dependent resources, provides the framework in which such a powerful analysis can be carried out. An analysis of those new movements that have shaken management science for the last two decades.

2 The Change in our Perception

It is quite obvious to everybody, that Just In Time (JIT), Total Quality Management (TQM) and Theory of Constraints (TOC), all aim toward achieving the same objective, namely; to increase the ability of a company to make more money now, as well as in the future. What is not so well understood, is that what is different about them is not the basic assumption that they attack. They all attack the same erroneous assumption, moreover, they all use the same new assumption in place of the old one. The main difference between them lies more in the realization of the depth of the change which must stem from the new assumption they all use. Thus, we will find the biggest difference in the

> *... being satisfied with broad statements like - "overall management philosophy" - certainly doesn't provide a feasible starting point.*

techniques they have, or have not, developed to cope with the resulting change.

The first step in the analysis should be the removal of existing misconceptions. The biggest misconception is what the primary problem is that each one of these movements is struggling to solve. This and other misconceptions arise from the impressions that we have gotten when these new movements were in their infancy and only vaguely understood. Today, we have grown to learn that our initial impressions were much too limited and that each one of these movements encompasses much more than was originally envisioned.

Still, it's very hard to overcome our inertia and realize that a broader understanding of each one of these movements clearly indicates that they are all dealing directly with exactly the same problem. These movements have caused our perceptions to change over the last few years, and in all cases our perceptions have also evolved in basically the same direction. To realize the magnitude of this change it might be worth while to put into one paragraph, what we are saying sporadically.

"It's not enough to state that Just In Time's primary focus is not the reduction of inventory. It's not just a mechanical KANBAN system. It's definitely an overall management philosophy." "It's not enough to state that Total Quality Management's primary focus is not to increase product quality. It's not just a procedural Statistical Process Control system. It's definitely an overall management philosophy." "It's not enough to state that Theory of Constraints' primary focus is not elevation of bottlenecks. It's not just a mechanical Drum Buffer Rope system. It's definitely an overall management philosophy."

I don't think that anybody has a quarrel with the above statements. But what must be emphasized is that, in spite of the fact that we have come to realize the broader scope of these movements, no significant efforts have been made to restate the problems that they focus on. Saying, that our original understanding of the focus of these movements was much to narrow is important, but it does not, by itself, clarify what their primary focus is.

Which avenue offers the biggest opportunity?

Leaving the situation unchanged and being satisfied with broad statements like - "overall management philosophy" - certainly doesn't provide a feasible starting point from which to consolidate these movements.

The mere fact that no such restatement of their primary focus has been suggested clearly indicates that it's not a trivial task. I believe that the obstacle to such a restatement resides in the fact that even the original problem, which all have tried to resolve, cannot be found within the old body of knowledge. We can see this problem only when viewing the situation from the new framework provided by the new movements.

3. The Traditional Scale

In order to precisely restate the problem these new movements have addressed, it's obvious that we have to state the desired objective. A problem exists only when we encounter something that prevents or limits our ability to achieve a desired objective. In our case we don't have to differentiate at this stage between the various movements, because as we already noted, they all have exactly the same objective. To improve the ability of a company to make more money now as well as in the future.

How can we improve the ability of a company to make more money? The Theory of Constraints states what is obvious to everybody; there are only three avenues to increase making money. They are to: (1) increase Throughput, (2) decrease Inventory and (3) decrease Operating Expense.

Which avenue offers the biggest opportunity? If we look at just the short term, the answer is that Throughput and Operating Expense are equal in importance and both are more important

> ...most of the factors impacting our ability to increase Throughput are currently called intangibles.

than Inventory. This impression stems from the way Throughput (T), Inventory (I) and Operating Expense (OE) appear in the relationships most often used to judge "making money." Throughput and Operating Expense are both inherent in Net-Profit and in Return-On-Investment calculations, where as Inventory appears only in the latter. In both relationships, Throughput and Operating Expense are considered to have the same degree of importance, since they effect the calculations by the difference between them.

$$NP = T - OE \quad ROI = (T - OE) / I$$

Actually, our traditional scale of importance is quite different. In the short run, it looks as if our ability to reduce Operating Expense is much greater than our ability to increase Throughput. We don't control the market, but we do run our own show. This perception, by itself, is enough to place Operating Expense on a higher level than Throughput, but this tendency is intensified considerably by other measurements that we currently use.

The measurements that dominate our short and medium term behavior are cost accounting procedures. What is "cost" if not Operating Expense. The mere fact that cost considerations are used for every type of short and medium range decisions makes Operating Expense more emphasized than Throughput. Let's remember that most of the factors impacting our ability to increase Throughput are currently called intangibles.

The impact of cost accounting on the importance of Inventory is even more dramatic. The way we evaluate material inventory enables us to disguise a part of this "period" Operating Expense as Inventory. This mechanism - usually referred to as added value - completely obliterates the importance of reducing Inventory. We no longer know if by reducing Inventory we actually help "make money" or whether we achieve just the opposite.

Thus until these new movements appeared on the scene in a significant way, despite top management's healthy intuition, the reality of our companies has been such that Operating Expense firmly holds the drivers seat. Throughput in most cases was just a second contender, while Inventory trailed way behind, giving the impression that maybe it wasn't even in the race.

> *...to increase the ability of the company to make money on an on-going basis, T definitely takes a first and foremost position.*

4 The New Scale

Since their conception all three movements, TQM, JIT and TOC, have not accepted these rankings. They all recognized that for the long run (making money also in the future) it is essential to adopt an entirely different scale. This recognition as initially only at the intuitive level, as can be easily deduced from examining the early publications. I certainly can attest to it personally, as far as the Theory of Constraints is concerned. But the struggle to convince the market of the validity of this new approach lead to a better verbalization. Today, after years of struggle, the new scale of importance has become widely accepted. In a few years we will all probably have a hard time remembering that there once was a time when we actually accepted the old scale.

When we come to evaluate which avenue - T, I or OE - presents more opportunities for improving, the answer is obvious. In striving to decrease OE and I, the magnitude of the available improvement is, by definition, limited since neither of them can exist in the rage of negative numbers. But this is not the case for T. This measurement, which we strive to increase, is inherently unlimited. When it comes time to judge the performance of a specific period, T and OE are on the same level of importance. Nevertheless, when we wish to evaluate what should

> ...to enable an increase of Throughput in the future, it is vital to reduce Inventory in the present.

we do in order to increase the ability of the company to make money on an on-going basis, T definitely takes a first and foremost position.

What about the relationship between OE and I? Which one of them is more important? At first sight it looks as if there is no valid reason to change our previous analysis. But this is definitely not the case. In our previous analysis, we considered only the direct impact of these measurements on the bottom line. What we neglected was the parallel indirect impact Inventory has on them. Even in the traditional body of knowledge it was recognized that such an indirect channel exists. The carrying cost of material and the depreciation of assets have always been taken into account. In other words, it is very well recognized that Inventory does have an indirect impact on Net Profit through it's impact on Operating Expense.

What all the three movements were fighting so zealously to formally bring to the attention of management was the importance of a new, indirect channel. A channel through which material Inventory impacts not only Operating Expense but more importantly, future Throughput. All the new movements have claimed that this long neglected channel is immensely important and should not be discarded, where our future ability to sell is concerned.

I believe that the way all three movements regard this indirect channel - the impact of Inventory on Throughput - is well documented in *The Race* (pages 34-67). In those pages, it is proven that the work-in-process and the finished-goods portions of Inventory, have a dramatic impact on the future Throughput of a company.

The future Throughput of a company is determined mainly by it's ability to compete in the market. The parameters that dominate a company's competitive edge are: its products (both the quality and the engineering aspects), its price and responsiveness (due-date performance, as well as quoted lead times). All three movements point to the fact, that material inventory has a devastating impact on all of the above parameters. Thus to enable an increase of Throughput in the future, it is vital to reduce Inventory in the present.

> *Otherwise we would have continued to justify investments to improve Throughput, primarily on the incorrect basis of cost savings (OE).*

We see that the scale of importance that all the new movements are using is drastically different from the one that was assumed by the previous bodies of knowledge. Rather than considering OE as the number one avenue for improvement, T as number two and I as a doubtful third, the more correct scale is: T is definitely first, I is second (due to it's indirect impact on future T) and OE is just a modest third.

The uncompromising stand that all these movements have taken to highlight the importance of this scale is what caused a distortion in the perception of the main message these movements tried to advocate. Only recently have we succeeded to break these all too narrow perceptions.

For several years we were misled into believing that the main objective of Total Quality Management was to improve customer service and product quality. Now it's objective is more understandable. If Throughput is number one, these types of actions are by far more important then previously perceived. We can also understand very well why TQM was so zealous about those issues. Otherwise we would have continued to justify investments to improve Throughput, primarily on the incorrect basis of cost savings (OE). We would have been justifying actions done for the most important avenue by calculations based on the impact on the least important one.

The same thing happened to our perception regarding JIT. It wasn't too long ago that the crusade to move companies along the lines of this method was called: "zero inventory." Even today JIT is still described as the method that regards inventory as

> *All three movements, being extremely pragmatic, did not take the short cut of just stating blindly, "reduce inventory"*

a liability. I wonder how anybody was led to believe that JIT advocates reduction of inventory even at the expense of jeopardizing current customer service — which is what zero inventory would do. Now it's obvious to everybody that the emphasis placed by JIT on inventory reduction was done solely for the purpose of improving future Throughput.

As for the TOC - it took a slightly different punishment. In its efforts to put OE in its proper place of importance, this movement launched a crusade against the accepted principles of cost accounting. The undesirable result was, that until recently, this crusade was regarded, by many, as the main thrust of TOC.

5. The Inventory Dichotomy

Now that we clarified that all three movements agree on the same goal and on the same (new) scale of importance for the measurements, the ground is set to verbalize the common problem that triggered them all. The problem stems from the realization of the important role that reduction of material inventory plays in the ability to increase future Throughput. All three movements, being extremely pragmatic, did not take the short cut of just stating blindly, "reduce inventory" (even though many of their followers have mistakenly espoused this idea).

Like every practitioner, they were keenly aware that the primary way to protect current Throughput is through the build up of material inventory. What are the KANBAN cards of JIT and the TIME-BUFFERS of TOC, if not a deliberate effort to build material inventory? "Zero inventory" is synonymous only with zero production, and thus zero Throughput. Not having inventory buffers is equivalent to the ridiculous declaration that Murphy does not exist.

The recognition of the two conflicting influences that material inventory has on Throughput surfaced a new challenge. The Evaporating-Cloud diagram clearly displays this problem.

Reduce variability and the need for maintaining inventory is reduced.

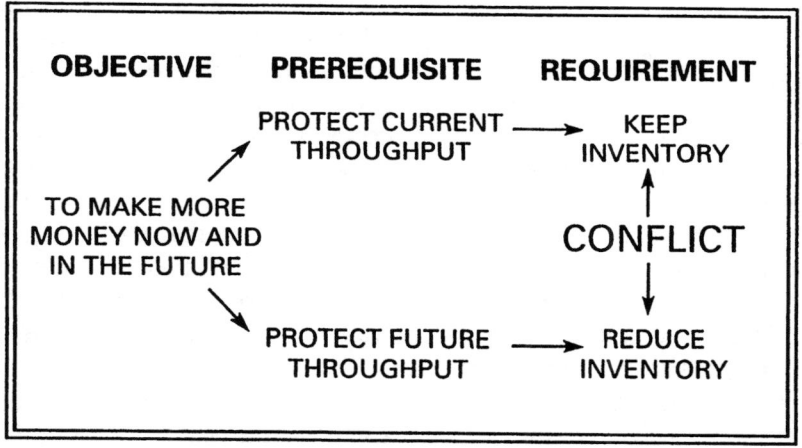

Rather than wasting time and effort in the attempt to find a "suitable" compromise, all three movements concentrated on attacking the foundations which gave rise to the conflict. Why do we need inventory to protect Throughput? The answer is now very well understood. As long as a system contains both statistical fluctuations and dependent resources, there is a trade off between Inventory and current Throughput. In the previous article, we showed that even when we start with zero inventory, inventory will accumulate to restore Throughput.

No wonder that Total Quality was developed by statisticians. If statistical fluctuations cause a need for inventory, then let's concentrate on reducing statistical fluctuations, or variability as they called it in their attempt to use a more common terminology. No wonder that SPC (statistical process control) became a cornerstone technique of TQM. Reduce variability and the need

> ...the amount of resources involved is restricted either by physical allocation (flow-line) or logical allocation (finite schedule).

for maintaining inventory is reduced. The conflict is "evaporated" without any compromise.

Even a superficial knowledge of JIT is sufficient to recognize that this movement also recognizes the same solution. SPC is renowned for reducing the direct variability of a process, while JIT is better known for its contribution to set-up reduction and preventative maintenance procedures. From a global point of view, set-up and breakdowns are just very big fluctuations in process time.

What is probably less known is the fact that the developers of JIT have concentrated even more on another way to "evaporate" the conflict. Statistical fluctuations are not the only necessary condition creating the need for inventory, dependent resources are also a necessary condition. So it's no wonder that JIT is so zealous about streamlining the operations. Flow-lines are an excellent way to reduce the amount of resources involved in the production of one product family.

But JIT didn't stop there, it advocated the use of U-Cell configurations, where one worker moves with the processed piece from one machine to another. This technique, even though it results in a very large reduction in equipment utilization, drastically reduces the number of dependent resources and thus provides a significant reduction in the level of inventory needed to protect current Throughput.

Initially, the Theory of Constraints concentrated on attacking both of the above necessary conditions. Predetermined schedules reduce both statistical fluctuations and dependent resources. The mere fact that a particular type of resource has, on the average, excess capacity is still far from a guarantee that when a particular part has to be processed by that resource, it will be instantly available. It might, at that exact moment, be busy processing another part.

The reduction in the amount of resources that need to be involved, is similar in effect, to that of flow-lines, except for the reduction in resources needed to move the parts from one remote work center to another. This additional material handling capacity is more than compensated for by the resulting greater immunization against product mix variability. In effect, the amount of resources involved is restricted either by physical allocation (flow-line) or logical allocation (finite schedule).

The change from the "cost world" to the "Throughput world" is grossly underestimated.

As long as the three movements were primarily concerned with their attempts to remove the "inventory dichotomy," it made a lot of sense to compare them with each other. At this level, it is important to try and sort out where they complement each other and where a choice has to be made. That was the situation in the early 80's, but it is no longer the case.

6 New Overall Management Philosophy

Still, as important and as practical as these new local solutions may actually be, their contributions certainly do not deserve to be called a "new overall management philosophy." First, the application of their suggested solutions is mainly geared to the factory floor. The factory floor is very important, but is it really that more important than design, distribution, sales or marketing? Can we then use the term "overall?" Second, the new local solutions are all of a mechanical nature: correcting processes to improve quality, rearranging the physical layout or using a different mode of material release. Is it really justified to refer to such techniques as a "management philosophy?"

The realization of the need for a new overall management philosophy came when the effort of reducing inventory clearly revealed that current inventory levels do not stem from the need to protect current throughput. The main reason for their existence, and also the difficulty in reducing them, certainly lies in erroneous

> *We have added to it what can only be called "the beginning of the month improvement project."*

policies. That is when all three movements started to zealously preach the obvious.

What can cause TQM to go on a campaign preaching: "it's not enough to do things right, we must do the right things?" Unless the wrong things are being done on an overwhelming scale.

What can cause JIT to go on a warpath, under the banner of: "don't do what is not needed?" Unless unneeded things are being done on a grand scale.

What can cause TOC to constantly wave the flag of: "the end result of many local optima, is certainly not the optimum of the total company?" Unless almost everywhere we are striving to achieve local optima.

The clear vision of the enormity, the magnitude, of the mistakes that we make, stems directly from the realization that these wrong actions are geared primarily towards reducing costs. There is apparently a world of difference in almost all management actions if the most important measurement is no longer "cost", but Throughput. The change from the "cost world" to the "Throughput world" is grossly underestimated. Actions which are a must in the "cost world" are regarded as totally devastating when judged through the prism of the "Throughput world."

Where exactly do the three movements differ? Not in their new philosophy, they all advocate the very same new philosophy. Not in the way they judge actions, but in the tools, procedures and systems that they offer management to adjust to this entirely different world.

JIT is telling us "don't do what is not needed." Fine, but what are the exact type of actions, the mode of operation, that leads to do things which are not needed? Here JIT stops short. TQM is warning us to "do the right things." Fine, but what are the guidelines to identify those illusive "right things." What are the procedures that will allow us to identify them. TQM only tells us that to answer this question we must have something mysterious called "profound knowledge."

No wonder that with such ridiculous answers, we find ourselves floundering. JIT and TQM certainly open our eyes to the fact that we are living in a different world, the "Throughput world." But they have stopped on it's border, without providing a map or even a compass. The result today, is that it looks like we are no longer satisfied with the excitement of "the end of the month syndrome." We have added to it what can only be called "the beginning of the month improvement project."

> *The "cost world" is a world in which almost everything is important.*

Today, we are totally exposed to the absolute need to switch gears into the "Throughput world" and at the same time we don't have a clear road map of what it actually is or how to methodically reach it. The common result is that we just jump from one piece of the puzzle to another. From one worthwhile "project" to another. In this way, as the last few years clearly demonstrated, results can be achieved only very slowly and quite painfully. This is definitely not the proper way to join the pieces into a holistic picture.

Only the Theory of Constraints has struggled directly with the global ramifications of putting Throughput as the number one avenue, while tumbling Operating Expense (cost) from it's previous dominant position to the modest role of being just number three.

What is actually the paradigm shift that results from changing the priority scale of the measurements? If Operating Expense is number one, we should consider as important every point where Operating Expense occurs. But Operating Expense is paid at an enormous number of places. Every worker, engineer, clerk, salesperson, manager, are outlets of Operating Expense. As a matter of fact, every consumption of disposable material or consumption of energy is an Operating Expense outlet. The "cost world" is a world in which almost everything is important.

Even is we are lead to believe that everything is important, we still remember that some things are more important than others

> ... it is no wonder at all, that more than half of their time is required to put out fires.

- the Paretto principle. Almost everybody has heard about the Paretto principle in one form or another, but what is less known is that this principle is strongly dependent on the nature of the given system.

Placing Operating Expense as the dominant measurement creates the impression that our organization is composed of independent variables. The Paretto principle for a system composed of independent variables, is known as the 20/80 rule. Twenty percent of the variables are responsible for eighty percent of the end result. For example, 80% of the money that we pay to our material vendors goes to only 20% of the items on the list. Or look at the money that we collect from our clients - 80% of the receipts are for 20% of the products.

No wonder that under this management philosophy of running the business that a classification is desperately needed to put some order into the maze of numerous details. The classification used is the "product cost" classification, which was once totally in line with the dominant concept of Operating Expense. Managers that work today under this improper principle will find themselves wrapped in so many details that it is no wonder at all, that more than half of their time is required to put out fires.

7 The Throughput World

When we finally awaken to the realization that Throughput is the dominant measurement, the picture drastically simplifies. What is our reality? Our organizations are definitely not a system of independent variables. Exactly to the contrary, many resources have to carry many tasks in concert for quite a substantial time before a sale to a client is made. Throughput is not connected to any one action or any one resource, it's achieved only when the actions of many are completed. Putting Throughput as number one, forces the realization that our organizations operate as an assemblage of DEPENDENT variables.

The degree to which we are unprepared to manage according to this commonplace, undebatable realization, can be easily demonstrated by the fact that almost all believe in the validity of the 20/80 rule. In configurations of dependent variables, the Paretto principle takes the form of a 0.1/99.9 rule. Just a fraction of a percent is responsible for almost all the end result.

> *"The strength of a chain is determined solely by the strength of the weakest link."*

In common practice, unobliterated by fancy sophistication, we have always recognized that: "The strength of a chain is determined solely by the strength of the weakest link." As long as the links are not exactly identical (as long as statistical fluctuations exist) there is only one "weakest" link. The number of constraints are limited by the number of independent "chains" in our organization.

Of course switching from a perception of a 20/80 world to a 0.1/99.9 world takes us into a new dimension when we think of focusing. This by itself is sufficient to cause a "new overall management philosophy. This switch definitely effects every manager and every type of decision. It is no longer primarily the concern of production, distribution, sales, design engineering and finance are no less effected by this concept. Such artificial barriers between the functions must be tumbled down.

The various functions participate in the same "chains" (products) and thus each must consider the impact of a weak link, no matter where it is in the organization. Managing a part of an organization as if it were an isolated kingdom was possible when Operating Expense was dominant, but it's impossible when we realize the dominance of Throughput.

It is quite obvious that once we understand that the constraints — the weakest links — determine the end results, that they should become the focal point for management. The previous tool that served us for years, "product cost," can now be safely discarded. It actually stopped to serve us when it became obsolete — when we stopped to pay workers based on pieces produced and

> *If nobody is to be fired, how can cost be reduced?*

switched to hourly pay. It became devastating when our "overheads" grew to be much larger than direct labor. It becomes unnecessary now.

Today, when most companies are declaring that jobs will not be lost as a direct result of improvements, it is quite ridiculous to find that the same companies are engaged in "cost reduction programs." If nobody is to be fired, how can cost be reduced? Some will say that they refer to reduction of "cost per unit produced," but then it is obvious that these programs intend to increase Throughput without a commensurate increase in Operating Expense. If that is the case, these programs should not waste effort in chipping away at costs, but instead should focus on opening the constraints. The grip of the old concepts is so strong that even the originators of JIT and TQM didn't succeed in breaking away from it.

It is amazing to what extent TQM and JIT have not realized the major ramifications of the evolution that they themselves helped to create. In the world of Throughput it is impossible that every quality problem, every set-up reduction, every pile of inventory, can possibly be considered of top importance. This way of relating to things is a residual of the "cost world." It's no wonder that the only way to focus the implementation of the much needed JIT and TQM techniques, is through the verbalization of their own philosophy by TOC. It is about time to change the diffused, arbitrary way we approach the latest "monthly improvement program," is quickly eroding the good will of our people.

8. The Focusing Process

"Focus on everything, and you have not actually focused on anything." Focusing means: "Under my responsibility, I have this big area. I elect to concentrate most of my attention on a small fraction of my area." Spreading attention equally to all portions of the area means no concentration whatsoever, no focusing.

In the "cost world," focusing is very hard to do. At best, we have to focus on a very large portion of the details. This is not the case in the Throughput world. What should be the first step? Where should we concentrate? That's totally obvious, isn't it? On the weakest links, on the constraints. They are the ones that determine the overall performance of the company.

"Focus on everything, and you have not actually focused on anything."

In light of the above, what is your suggestion? What should be the first step? Yes. We must first of all find the constraints of the system.

Are we guaranteed to find something in every case? In other words, is it mandatory that every system must have at least one constraint? Maybe the answer will be clearer if we ask the same question using different words; Have you ever seen a company with no constraints whatsoever? The intuitive answer is obvious — never. In any chain, there must be a weakest link. But let's try to substantiate it a little further. If there is a company with no constraints, what does it mean? Nothing limits it's performance. What must therefore be the performance of this company? What must be its Net Profit and ROI? Infinite. Have you ever seen, or heard of a company with infinite net profit?

The conclusion is obvious, every system must have at least one constraint. On the other hand, any system, in reality, must have a very limited number of constraints. Thus, the first focusing step of the Theory of Constraints is intuitively obvious:

1. Identifying the System's Constraint(s)

We put the 'S' in the word constraints in parenthesis, because there might be systems that have only one constraint.

Identifying a constraint means that we already have a very good appreciation of the magnitude of it's impact on the overall performance. Otherwise, we might also have some trivialities on in the list of constraints. Or as I call them, "chupchicks."

Is it important to prioritize the constraints according to their impact? Not necessarily so. First of all, let's remember that at

> *... every system must have at least one constraint.*

this stage, we do not have precise estimates. The second thing to remember, is that the number of constraints is very very limited. Anyhow, we have to handle all of them, so let's not waste time with fruitless efforts. Identifying the constraints, that is what counts.

What should be our next step? We have just identified the constraints. We find those points, those things, that we are so lacking that they limit the overall performance of our entire system. How should we manage them?

The intuitive response is to get rid of them. But you know as well as I, to get rid of a constraint takes a lot of time. For example, if the constraint is the market, to break this constraint might take many months, or even a year. Or if the constraint is a machine and we have decided to buy another one, the delivery time might be more than six months. What are we going to do in the meantime? Sit on our rear, doing nothing? That does not seem like good advice for a second step.

How should we manage the constraints, the things we do not have enough of? At least, let's not waste them. Let's squeeze the maximum out of them. Every drop counts. To put it in more civilized form, the second step of the Theory of Constraints, is thus:

2. Decide How to Exploit the System's Constraint(s)

Exploit simply means, squeeze the maximum out of them. I have deliberately chosen a word with slightly negative connotations. EXPLOIT. No matter what it takes. Let's understand something. I do not believe that we can have job security in a company that loses money. In a company that loses money, job security is threatened, no matter what the top management is saying. Here are the constraints, the ones that limit the overall performance. The job security of everyone in the company depends on the performance of these points. No mercy, squeeze the maximum out of them.

For example, if the constraint is the market. We have enough capacity, but not enough orders. Then, exploit the constraint means: One hundred percent on time delivery. Not ninety-nine, but one hundred! If the market is the constraint, let's not waste anything.

Okay, we have now decided how we are going to manage the constraints. What about managing the vast majority of our resources which are, by definition, non-constraints? Should we leave them alone? Within a very short period of time, they will become constraints. How should we manage them?

> *The job security of everyone in the company depends on the performance of these points.*

The answer is, intuitively obvious. In the previous step, we have decided on a course of action that represents the maximum that we can do under the current situation. But the constraints need to consume things. If the non-constraints do not supply more than the constraint can absorb? This will not help anyone. On the contrary, it will hurt. To summarize it, let's write the third step of the focusing process.

3. Subordinate Everything Else to the Above Decision

Now we are in a state where we are managing the current situation. Is it the final step? Of course not. Constraints are not an act of God, we can do something about them. Now is the time to do what we were tempted to do before. Let's open the constraints, if we do not have enough, it does not mean that we cannot add. The next step is intuitively obvious.

4. Elevate the System's Constraint(s)

Elevate means, lift the restriction. This is the fourth step, not the second step. So many times we have witnessed a situation where everybody was complaining about a huge constraint. But when they exercised the second step of exploitation, of not wasting what was available, it turned out that there was more than enough. So let's not hastily run to approve subcontracting, buy a new machine, etc. When the second and third step are completed, and we still have a constraint, that is the time to move to the fourth step.

> *I have never seen a company which has a market constraint. I have seen many that have marketing policy constraints.*

By the fourth step, we have also taken care of the issue of moving the company forward. Can we stop here? Or must we add a fifth step? The answer is once again intuitively obvious. If we elevate the constraint, if we add more and more to the things that we didn't have enough of, there must come a time where we have enough. The constraint is broken. The performance of the company will rise, but will it jump to infinity? Obviously not. The performance of the entire company will be restricted by something else. The constraint has moved. Thus the fifth step is:

5. If in the Previous Steps, a Constraint has been Broken, Go Back to Step 1

But this is not the entire fifth step. We must add to it a very big warning. You see, the constraints impact the behavior of every other resource in the company. Everything must be subordinated to the constraint's maximum level of performance. Thus, from the existence of the constraint, we derive many decisions or even rules, sometimes formally, many times just intuitively. Now the constraint has been broken. It turns out, in most cases, that we do not bother to go back and examine those decisions and rules. They stay behind. Now, we have policy constraints. Thus, the fifth step must be expanded to:

5. If in the Previous Steps, a Constraint has been Broken, Go Back to Step 1, But Do Not Allow Inertia to Cause a System's Constraint.

I cannot exaggerate the importance of this added warning. In most companies that I have analyzed, I have not found physical constraints. I have found policy constraints. I have never seen a company which has a market constraint. I have seen many that have marketing policy constraints.

It is very rare to see a company with a true capacity constraint, a true bottleneck. But very often we see companies with production and logistical policy constraints. This is, by the way, the case described in *The Goal*. Was the oven a capacity constraint? Did Alex Rogo buy a new oven? Not at all. He just changed some internal production and logistical policies, and before long, capacity was coming out his ears.

Except for one single case, I have not seen vendor constraints, even though many companies complain about their vendors. I have seen devastating purchasing policy constraints.

What happens every time we dig down to find the reasons for these awkward policies? Sometimes, to tell the truth, we almost have to launch an archaeological dig. We find that thirty years ago or so, when these particular policies were put into practice, they made perfect sense. All the reasons are now long gone, but the policies are still with us.

Five steps. A very intuitively obvious and simple procedure of focusing. Everybody knew them before. Everybody understands that they ring true. Nevertheless, do managers really use them? In cases of emergencies, yes. But otherwise? The grip of the "cost world" is so strong, despite our clear common sense intuition. It turns out that our actions are much more directed by the formal "cost world" procedures than the straight forward, totally obvious, steps that have just been laid out.

Looking Beyond the First Stage: Just In Time

Part Three

Rocking gently in my bamboo armchair I'm slowly sipping on my first cup of coffee. Waiting patiently for the silhouettes of the woods to take on more details. This is my time of day, when the sun is just about to rise. When, with each moment, the light intensifies. The world becomes richer. The woods are no longer just a big black lamp. The individual trees are already quite clearly distinguishable. Now the branches are starting to emerge out of the background. Soon the small twigs are going to be noticeable. The intricate, but still so simple, picture of my backyard will soon be illuminated against the pink new sky.

The birds are starting to add sound and movement. Somehow this just adds to deepen the silence. This is the time to be with yourself, yet without being alone. This is the time to be deep in thought and still be one with the surroundings. The cold breeze caused my bare arms to develop goose bumps. It just adds to the feeling of freshness. In the last minutes I've located Phil's major snake. His scheme can not possibly work in our plant. Now it's just a matter of finding a method that will work. No rush, there is still ample time. Our meeting is not due for several hours yet.

I continue to rock and to sip from my coffee. My eyes are glued to the trees, while my mind is floating. Quite a team we have back there in the plant. If anybody can dig us out of our frantic situation, it's definitely us. We have put ourselves in it, we can climb out. What we need is just the time to pause to think, to re-evaluate. Greg forced such a pause on us. Bless his soul.

I play back what Phil told me last night. Even though his arguments have many tiny flaws, he is basically right. Just-in-time is not a pull method, quite the opposite.

Yesterday I was too intimidated to argue. It's for the better. Otherwise I would have immersed myself in pointless detailed arguments, just to win an empty victory, and by this I probably would have blocked myself from seeing the obvious. No, what counts is not Phil's particular words but his message. Somewhere, if I can just strip it to its elementary concept, the answer for our problem, which is definitely hidden, can be discovered. What is it? It seems that the only way is to dive in to it once again. Right now is certainly the time. My mind is not fogged with beer and my mood is peaceful.

No, Phil's scheme is too over simplified for our situation. It might work in the heavy metal parts of aerospace, where the demands are stated as a few units per month. Where assembly is not done at that plant. Where the number of different parts are less than two hundred. But in our plant? Phil was so immersed in trying to solve Greg's question, that he totally forgot that what we actually must solve is our plant problem.

In our plant we must deliver specific orders which are due on very specific dates. Not just "so many per month." Moreover, the quantities per order range all over the map. Some orders are for onesies and twosies, some are for hundreds or even thousands. Some orders are known a month in advance, some are urgent, to the extent that we have to supply them within days. Yes, days. And the fact that most of our products involve a few levels of assembly?

> . . . *that he totally forgot that what we actually must solve is our plant problem.*

How can I use Phil's scheme when my bill-of-materials is some five levels deep?

Still, what he said last night certainly has a lot of merit. There must be a way to turn the concepts into a workable procedure. The conventional way of MRP definitely is not one. The Just-In-Time method already backfired on us. There must be another way and it is probably along the lines that Phil has described. But what is it? Maybe the best way to find it, is to go over and reveal why the other methods didn't work. Not just to testify to the fact that they didn't.

"Push-Pull." That is probably the root of it all. I must understand what these two words really mean. Phil's explanation, that JIT is not a "pull," was quite farfetched. It was more emotional than logical. Here I will have to rely on myself. But why not, in the end, who has a better understanding of those concepts, me or Phil? Let's face it, everything that he knows about it he learned from me. Learned, I practically hammered it in his head. With a smile I stand up for a refill of coffee.

Moving back slowly, trying not to spill anything on the floor, the words "push-pull," "pull-push" echoes in my head. Why do I have to fill the cup to the rim? I pause to sip as my progress toward the porch is remarkably faster. Too late. I have to go back to the kitchen to bring a mop to wipe the floor. "Push-pull," "pull-push." To repeat endlessly, these words are certainly not going to lead me anywhere. What deeper understanding can I add to what I've already found. How did I describe the plant yesterday. The words start to surface in my mind: "under JIT it's more accurate to think of the whole plant as one huge spring, exerting enormous pressure from materials to final assembly. It's like a dangerous snake just waiting for a chance to attack. Whenever a container is pulled by assembly the entire beast responds immediately."

Somehow these words

"Push-pull," "pull-push." To repeat endlessly, these words are certainly not going to lead me anywhere.

sound a little bit different today. I roll the last few sentences over and over in my head. "A dangerous snake". . . "The entire beast responds immediately. . ."No, that's not the important phrase. I shouldn't be distracted by my own metaphors. "From material to final assembly"..."From material to final assembly". . .Wait, that's the opposite of pull, the pressure is pushing from material toward final assembly. Phil is right. The pull is not achieved by the KANBAN cards. They are just the trigger. I have stepped on something. But let's face it, I don't understand it, it's too diffused.

Again. Try again, I'm encouraging myself. What are the tasks of the KANBAN cards? To signal a worker to process a container, so they actually cause the pull. I'm starting to go in circles. Something does not click. If it wasn't for my stubborn nature I would probably give up by now.

Her-majesty jumps on my lap and brushes my cheeks with her tail. Absent minded I start to stroke her thick white fur. KANBAN is definitely the opposite of "push." On the other hand, whenever I try to claim that KANBAN is '"pull" I run into trouble. But what is the opposite of "push" if it is not "pull"?

Red tries to join the party. A swift response from Her-majesty's sharp paw nails, quickly changes his mind. Graciously, he jumps back from my lap and with his tail high in the air, he retreats into the house. I laugh loudly when it dawns on me. There is another opposite to "push." It is not necessarily "pull." It's simply-"do not push." What one can learn from the mouths of babes or for this matter from the paws of kittens.

Yes, now it's much clearer. The KANBAN cards are the mechanism by which we *stop* the "push." If you don't have a KANBAN card do not produce. There is enough inventory in the pipe, don't push any more into it. The "pull" is not given by the cards, it exists in the plant all the time. It is simply generated by the understanding of the workers that they are called into the plant in order to produce, not just to stay there to twiddle their fingers in idleness. When the

"Tell me how you measure me, and I will tell you how I'll behave."

KANBAN cards limit the push of material to a level lower than the capacity of the work centers, idleness is forced from time to time. Then the inherent eagerness to pull is revealed. "It's more accurate to think of the whole plant as one huge spring, exerting enormous pressure from materials to final assembly." Now it makes perfect sense.

When we respond to the natural tendency of pulling by pushing materials, the workers are pulling and everybody is busy. But what they pull is not necessarily what is needed to be pulled. When we block the push, allowing only what is needed, then of course the situation improves remarkably. Stop the "push," do not allow the "pull" to be wasted on what is not needed, then you will not need expeditors to guide the "pull."

Who is pushing to the extent that we must block it? It's certainly not the workers. A worker could not care less what is done with the parts that he/she completed. It's us management. We want to get our monies worth. We pay good money, they have to get busy to ensure a return. But that cannot be the full answer. In our plant, it was too damn difficult to stop the foreman from doing things, just so that their workers will be busy.

Then it dawns on me. It's the measurements, they create the "push." We measure our workforce by efficiency and variances. That forces them to get busy all the time. "Tell me how you measure me, and I will tell you how I'll behave." That's it. It's so embarrassingly simple.

Is KANBAN the only mechanism to stop the push, I ask myself. I'm getting a little bit annoyed because I can not escape the answer. KANBAN is definitely not the only way to stop the push. What the hell did we actually try to do with MRP? Exactly the same thing. Impatiently I push Her-majesty to the floor and stop rocking the armchair. I lean forward, put my head between my hands and concentrate. What was the original thinking behind MRP, before we buried ourselves with oceans of tiny details?

The major contribution of MRP was to include the time factor.

We took the orders...and

the forecast, if firm orders didn't stretch far enough into the future. No, forget the details, I remind myself. We took the orders for the various products and calculated the amounts of material that we needed to release, to satisfy those orders. In calculating the quantities, we were careful not just to take into account the details of the bill-of-materials, we were careful to net the already existing stocks in the pipes. But all this was just the first step. "Net" Requirement — as we call it — was done much before MRP software became available. The major contribution of MRP was to include the time factor.

We backed off from the required due date, the time to produce the product in order to determine the release date. How many efforts were invested to evaluate, as precisely as possible, the process time per unit? How many stormy debates were conducted in order to pin-point the set up times? Not to mention the endless (and still on going) discussions to get reliable numbers for the various queue and wait times. All this mammoth effort so that we can arrive at required release dates for materials. What for? Yes, ask yourself what for? So that we will not release work before it's actually needed! So that we can restrain the push!

I lean back and start to rock again. We were not so stupid after all. We were doing the right things. I snap my fingers to call the kittens again. The sun is already up. It looks as if it's going to be another gorgeous day.

So why didn't it work?

If everything was done right, why didn't it work?

It's quite obvious, isn't it. We developed quite a good mechanism but the way that we used it was appalling. Rather than using it for what we intended—to block the push, we actually used it to legalize the push. I smile bitterly. Yes, that is exactly what we have done.

"Master-Schedule." These two words say it all. Here lies the Achilles heel of the entire method.

"Master-Schedule." These two words say it all. Here lies the Achilles heel of the entire method. What is "Master-Schedule"? Why using firm orders and forecast was not sufficient? Now it's so obvious. All those long nights, frantic pacing and agony. For what? Just to accommodate the erroneous concept of "push." I'm almost disgusted with myself. What was my main concern when I devised a master schedule? To make sure that everybody has enough work! When did I deviate the most from the actual requirements; when a whole department was due to run out of work! This is a little bit too much for me to swallow. I'm the one who has made my own life miserable? I've got to roll it over once again.

We have tried to satisfy two masters. Our clients — meeting the due-dates, and our local efficiencies — supplying enough work to the floor. The mechanism that enabled us to ignore the apparent conflict was the "Master Schedule." Did we have to do it? Certainly not. How did Phil describe his new attitude? "My people and I are no longer concerned with making high efficiency numbers. So I'm not forcing you to release material just to supply work for my people and thus the work force is now free to work on what is really needed." Those were his exact words. He actually said it all in a nutshell.

KANBAN worked better than MRP just because it was less flexible. The Japanese method is too rigid to be distorted. You simply can not "push" just to achieve high "efficiencies," even if you want to.

I'm embarrassed. That's the only way in which I can describe what I now feel. Me, a hard nosed professional, to ignore the obvious for so long. To bury myself in the endless mechanical details so that I no longer saw the entire picture. How could I have ignored it, when everything was pointing to the bare conclusions.

MRP stood for Material-Requirement-Planning. The planning of how much and WHEN to release the materials to the floor. In our time estimations, especially in the queue and wait times, we took into account that things would not go smoothly. That machines will not always be available, that workers will sometimes be absent, that break-

> *KANBAN worked better than MRP just because it was less flexible.*

ages will occur. In short that Murphy does exist.

We took all that into account and said; in spite of all of these misfortunes, if we need to deliver this and this order on this and this date, there is no need to release materials for it before this and this point in time. We generated exactly what was needed to stop the unnecessary push. And then...we went and ruined it all. By concerning ourselves with local workcenter efficiencies. By playing not our client's game but our own internal numbers game.

I continue to look into it, not in order to find more understanding but as if I'm in some type of addiction. In some state of mind that imposes self punishment.

The MRP mechanism itself didn't allow for push. So we added — as an integrated part — the mechanism of the Master-Schedule. We created the additional mechanism that enabled us to accommodate the push. Then we simply could deceive ourselves by deliberately feeding misleading data into the MRP system. Not the actual dates of the orders and the forecast, not when they actually are needed to be shipped, but artificial dates. We could "legitimately" pull forward orders just so that everybody would be happy. Everybody would have enough work. MRP didn't work as a shop scheduler because of the way the shop was measured. Because of the mandatory demand that everybody be busy all the time. Enough. I tell myself, but then another question pops; and KANBAN?

Yes, of course we could add many more KANBAN cards between each two workcenters. But the whole environment under which we usually implement KANBAN is the environment which is saturated with phrases like "Don't do what is not needed" or "Inventory is bad," "Inventory is a liability." Under such conditions it's almost impossible to just continue to add more cards.

MRP didn't work as a shop scheduler because of the way the shop was measured.

It is interesting to note that even under JIT we didn't directly attack the devastating core policy. We didn't openly claim that measuring workcenters by local efficiency and variances is wrong. No, we went in a round about way. Rather than openly condemning the local efficiency measurements, we just ignored them and concentrated on exposing one of the resulting bad symptoms — excess inventory.

Was it a more effective way to get the desired change? I doubt it. In our plant — due to *The Goal* — we attacked local measures directly. It speeded up the implementation. Maybe we, in the western world, use the more subtle way because we just copied it from the Japanese, and they are famous for avoiding internal, stormy clashes. Maybe. I really don't know.

But really, what bothers me now is another disturbing thought. Once we recognize the fallacy of local measurements, like we clearly do in our plant, will MRP work? Moreover, once we understand how not to distort the use of MRP under these conditions, which is actually better for scheduling: JIT or MRP? What a question! It's about time to have breakfast, my stomach needs some filling.

Flap, flap, flap. The fork is clicking against the plate as I scramble the eggs. Small pieces of onion are already sizzling in the frying pan. In a few minutes Mason's famous gourmet omelette is going to be ready. I love having breakfast. I love mornings, especially Sunday's, even if as today, it doesn't mean rest but work. Not exactly work. I can not possibly call the challenge of a decent brain-storm work. Especially when it's done with people that I respect, and they are well prepared. Am I? I don't think that they will appreciate another "deep insight" as Phil calls my ideas. No, I better come up with something more tangible. With a workable procedure. Yes, this is what they really expect from me.

JIT or MRP, who is better? Who cares. Both are not good enough for our plant. I move everything to the table sit down and start to stuff myself. No. Any good procedure should stem from understanding the previous methods. How can I hope to

> *I don't think that they will appreciate another "deep insight." No, I better come up with something more tangible. With a workable procedure.*

devise something totally from scratch, especially when in one hour I have to drive to our meeting. And besides, what did Sir Isaac Newton say: "I can see to such distances, only because I stand on the shoulders of giants," or something similar.

Both methods have tried to stop the unnecessary "push," I start to think systematically. They definitely used different techniques, but is there something more generic that distinguishes between them. Let's see. JIT uses KANBAN cards to signal that the local buffers are full. MRP does not use any intermediate buffers. What does it use...local time estimations. So what? I spread more butter on my toast. So everything! Don't you see the huge difference?

They both understand that the only way to guarantee on-time shipments is by acknowledging Murphy. JIT was never "produce at the last minute" it is "replenish immediately." MRP never used just the bare process-times, it always added the much bigger queue and wait times. Both JIT and MRP use inventory to protect the throughput. But what a world of difference in the manner that they relate to inventory. They treat inventory differently to the extent that they actually use different units. KANBAN uses pieces (or containers) as the unit of measure of the local buffers. MRP, when it comes to regarding inventory as protection, uses units of time. That's how the individual protection is expressed, not in pieces but in time.

Which choice is superior? It's obvious — time. Just try to imagine one particular workcenter that is capable of producing, during an entire year, 100 different part numbers. Under JIT it will have to constantly carry, in its buffers, 100 different type of containers. What for? If we suspect that misfortunes (breakages, etc.) can impair the performance of this workcenter, the question that we should ask ourselves is: how long will the misfortune last? And if the answer is, for example, up to two days, let's protect it with inventory which is sufficient for two days work - that will be enough.

Yes, where protection is our concern the dominate unit is certainly not containers or pieces,

Both JIT and MRP use inventory to protect the throughput.

but time. MRP on this point is definitely more appropriate than KANBAN. Phil's healthy intuition, like every prudent production professional, has led him along the same path. Time — that's the unit of protection.

I chew slowly on my delicious omelette. So, where does it lead me? For a few minutes I continue to chew on my breakfast. My mind is empty. As if I'm standing in front of a brick wall. I don't even have a clue on how to proceed. Slowly a particular word starts to surface. Almost unnoticeable at first, but then it becomes stronger and stronger. "Protection," I say loudly to the empty kitchen. "Protection against misfortune. Whom do we try to protect?" And everything becomes clear.

I stand up to clean the table and thoughts are rushing in my head like an express train. Yesterday, when Phil described his scheme, about scenario did he talk? On a scenario that contains a lot of misfortunes. Even major catastrophes, as he referred to them. His major concern was to deliver in spite of these catastrophes. He did not use them as an excuse for poor performance. He struggled with the problem of how to deliver promptly in spite of them. Whom did he try to protect? Each individual worker. This thought didn't even cross our minds. He was trying to protect just the assembly plant — our client. Just what really counts in the long-run. The performance of the total plant!

Now the mistakes of both MRP and KANBAN are, at last, totally exposed. What does MRP try to protect? The performance of each individual workcenter. That's why we put such large queue times in front of every operation. It's not just the Master-schedule that is concerned with making sure that the local performance will be high — that the internal number game will be adhered to — it's also the way that we feed "data" to the system.

We are trying to make sure that each operation will be done "on time," as if it really matters. What does matter is that the order will be shipped out of

. . . where protection is our concern the dominate unit is certainly not containers or pieces, but time.

the plant on time. We are trying to protect each and every workcenter. We try to protect everybody's ass. That's what causes us to spread the protection everywhere. The end result is that the total system is exposed.

As for KANBAN the same lousy end result exists, even though because of a slightly different reason. What was the basic concept of JIT? Service! Each workcenter has to service the next workcenter. No wonder that this concept leads to the need to protect each workcenter we spread much too thin, the limited protection that the total system can afford. Who do we have to service? The plant's clients. The artificial internal clients are causing us, at the end, to impair our service to the actual clients.

We have to protect the performance of the plant as a whole. Trying to protect each unit of the plant causes us to spread protection everywhere. Let's face it, we can afford only a limited amount of protection. We can not fill the plant with unlimited numbers of containers, we can not release material years before we have to ship the order. We can not be too generous with protection, we can not waste it. We must reserve the protection for what really counts. We must concentrate protection on what really matters. And in our plant it's crystal clear, we must protect our clients. We must deliver to them on time.

I look around. The kitchen is now perfectly tidy. Now what to do? How can I devise a mechanism that will protect the customer's orders? The first step is quite obvious. Since time is the dominant unit — as long as protection is concerned — I will have to use MRP. But rather than spreading the time estimates along each entry in the bill-of-materials and along every operation in the routings, I'll have to put all of it just before the order. On the last entry of each product. And everywhere else I'll have to set the times to zero!

And everywhere else I'll have to set the times to zero!

I swallow hard. To enter zeroes for all time estimates! The process and assembly times? The queue and wait times? That's exactly the opposite of what I was trained to do. And how will we know how much time it takes to process? How will we track the actual performance? "Who cares." I firmly remind myself, and climb upstairs to get dressed. We are not tracking it today anyhow. And besides tracking after the fact does not have anything to do with scheduling, that must be done before the fact.

Yep, that's what I'll have to do. To make a copy of the data, and zero all the time estimates. In this way we still keep track of the time estimates for all other purposes. Courageous move. One in a long list of courageous things that we have already done in our plant. I start to get used to it.

One cheek covered with foam, I'm gently working on my chin. Nine times out of ten I succeed to do it without staining the towel red. How am I going to find the right amount of protection. I still have to put one time estimate per product.

How will it actually work? MRP will be fed only with firm orders and the forecast. I'm not going to do any "Master-schedule." Just the bare data of the quantities that have to be shipped to the clients and the dates on which they have to be shipped. Then MRP will take each order...will subtract from it the amount of stock that we already have in finished goods (if we have any)... and will shift the date back by the protection time. Maybe I should call it Buffer-Time, to give my compliments to JIT as well. Or maybe even better; Shipping-Buffer-Time. I smile at my shaved face in the mirror. It's a good sign that I can afford to play with names. I'm definitely making progress.

And then, I think as I enter my bedroom to get dressed, MRP will then do the usual. Diving down the product structure, netting stocks along the way — if there are any. Until it reaches all the raw materials. Then what I will have to do is just to instruct the computer to print out the end results. The list of material that has to be released. Each with the needed quantities — which will be the quantities required to satisfy

> *... but this time without the bad side effect of unnecessarily blocking containers near the gating operations.*

the order, netted from already released stocks. And the dates of release, which will be the original due-date of the order minus the Shipping-Buffer-Time. Exactly what I need.

My people will release these exact quantities. No more, no more is needed. And they are going to release them close to the specified dates, not before. They are not needed before, even if things will go wrong. Protection is already taken into account. Phil's people will have to process what is available. And if at a given point in time a workcenter will find itself with nothing to do? So what. It's exactly equivalent to the current situation, when a workcenter finds itself without any KANBAN cards.

I'm achieving the exact same effect, blocking the "Push," but this time without the bad side effect of unnecessarily blocking containers near the gating operations. The permanent accumulation will occur not between each two workcenters — like in KANBAN — but only before shipping. And if the clients are willing to accept early shipments — which some do not — even better. Phil is going to like it, for sure.

The open question is how to determine the protection time? The Shipping-Time-Buffer, excuse me. It is basically the estimated time to produce and assemble a product. Not the average time, but the estimation of the — almost the worst case - of the elapsed time. What determines this time? First of all, of course, the actual time to produce the product. The time to process the various parts by the machines plus the time required to do the assemblies. Not the summation of all these times but just the longest route.

I shiver. That will necessitate using standard process and setup times. These numbers were never accurate to start with, and in the last two years I've neglected the tedious task of sitting on top of them. Except for a few workcenters, those that don't have, from time to time, enough capacity. It might be quite risky to use this garbage. It might lead to very big mistakes in the estima-

The process time of an item is absolutely negligible in relation to the total elapsed time.

tion of the Shipping-Buffer-Time. How big? I ask myself as I enter my car. I turn the ignition and wait. These lousy diesel engines. At the time I bought the car it seemed a good idea, saving on gas etc. But every time I have to wait, the two minutes or so, before I can start driving, I become quite impatient.

How big a mistake can the erroneous estimations of process time cause? Basically nothing. Why do I worry about them? Everybody knows that most of the time that inventory is on the floor is just spent in queue. Queues in front of machines or waiting in front of assembly until the machined parts are also available. The process time of an item is absolutely negligible in relation to the total elapsed time.

"Forget it," I'm telling myself as I maneuver the car out of the garage. I stop for a moment to close the doors. What a comfort these electronic remote control devices are. As I turn into the street, I chuckle. Nulling the process times will prevent MRP from adding artificial lead-times by multiplying the time by the quantity of the entire order. For large orders the time to process the entire order on some workcenters are quite large. But it's not lead-time, since we start the process much before the entire quantity is ready and we start to transfer to the next operation, much before the entire quantity is finished. We certainly learned something from the small containers of KANBAN.

No, the actual process time has very little to do with the elapsed time. All this effort to feed the data accurately to MRP, just to distort the end result. Amazing. How many more grand scale mistakes are we going to expose before the plant will really exploit all its potential? Is there an end to it? I wonder.

I'm now on the interstate. The traffic is very light. What do you expect on Sunday morning? The lead-time is mainly determined by Murphy. That's for sure. What number should I choose. It seems as if I don't have a clue. No, that is not really the case. I definitely know that I have to choose a number which is higher than one day.

And besides such level of expediting will turn the plant into a madhouse.

One day is not enough even with fierce expediting. You know personally taking the pieces from one workcenter to the other, throwing everything else out of their way, forcing additional overtime shifts and so on. Even with such drastic measures one day is probably not enough for many orders.

At the same time I know that six weeks is certainly out of line. Even an "Orphan" order, which runs into a series of problems, will be finished in less than six weeks. How can I determine a suitable Shipping-Time-Buffer? I must examine, more closely, what is meant by protection time, by my concept of Shipping-Time-Buffer.

If, for example, I decide on three days. That means that for each order I'll release the appropriate material just three days before it is due to be shipped. Some orders will make it... Maybe 30 percent of the orders, maybe 40 percent, but certainly less than half. What chance do I have to succeed in expediting all others, so that everything will be delivered on time? Not even a chance that a snowflake stands in hell. And besides such level of expediting will turn the plant into a madhouse. It will be worse than even the current frantic situation. Three days is definitely too short.

One week? Now we start talking. Yes, if we release everything one week before we have to fulfill the order, more than half of the orders will be shipped on time without any problem. Maybe even 80 percent. Yes, still a lot of expediting will be needed. This means quite a lot of people devoted to this task, overtime from the production side is probably unavoidable. And expediting 20 percent means that not all orders will be shipped on time. On the other hand, the average response time of the plant will be very fast, the total WIP and finished goods inventory will be very low, and cash situation will be improved.

> *How many plants do I know where this extremely important decision if actually made by the forklift driver?*

Let's go to the other extreme. Let's choose three weeks. Three weeks will almost ensure very high due-date performance. Probably over 98 percent of orders will be ready on time without any expediting. But inventory will be quite high, demand on cash will be more severe and more importantly the plant's average response time to its clients will be impaired.

I'm totally relaxed now. It's obvious that the decision as to what number to choose must be done by all of us together. No, a decision that impacts, customer service, expenses, investments and cash, must be taken by the one responsible for the overall performance of the company. By Greg. We can recommend, we can help in clarifying the pro's and con's but it's certainly his decision. How many plants do I know where this extremely important decision is actually made by the forklift driver? Strange world.

Anyhow I'm ready now. I signal for a right turn and go off the interstate. Usually, it's not done so easily. This is the main exit to the town and on weekday mornings I'm usually stuck here for a very, very considerable time. But now it's Sunday, no delays. I'm so immersed in my work that I start to think about myself as work in process. But it's true. When I'm driving, trying to go from one place to another, I and my car, are work in process. The resources are the roads. Not exactly. The roads are the equivalent of moving material from one workcenter to another. The junctions, not the roads, are the equivalent of the workcenters.

At the junction, that I just passed, I usually spend considerable time every morning in the "queue." But not today. Today is Sunday. And I definitely take it into account when I determine how early should I leave my house if I need to be in the plant at a certain hour. I intuitively adjust the Shipping-Buffer-Time. It is much-much larger than the net driving time. In the early hours, when I can average 50 miles per hour, I cover the distance between my house and the plant in less than fifteen minutes. Yet, every normal weekday morning I step out of the door about one and a half hours ahead of time. And when there is an important meeting, one that I can not afford to be

Having excess capacity does not guarantee instant availability.

late to, maybe two hours before I need to arrive.

What determines it. What determines the Shipping-Buffer-Time? It looks as if it is composed of three different components. One is the actual process time, which for the material in our plant is even more negligible than in the driving example. The second is the time spent competing with the other cars on the roads, and especially at the junctions. Yes, this is definitely a major time factor. Even though a resource has — on the average — more than enough capacity, there is no guarantee that it will be free to work on a specific part, at any given point in time. Having excess capacity does not guarantee instant availability. It's like this damn junction. I'm sure that its average utilization during the entire week, considering nights and weekends, is very low. Never the less, in the mornings it's definitely a bottleneck.

A major factor that affects the size of the Buffer-Time is definitely "non-instant availability of resources." The third component is pure Murphy — that's clear. Forgetting something at home and having to go back and get it, a flat, or even taking a wrong turn by mistake. Which one is bigger; pure Murphy or non instant availability? I imagine that it depends on the environment. In our plant I feel that the latter is dominant. Certainly it's the case since we improved considerably the reliability of our processes.

Can I make a good prediction of the impact of the non-instant availability of resources? I'm doing it with my driving—taking into account the time of day, the weather conditions and major events like a football game. In the plant I have an even better knowledge to start with. I have the orders, I have the product structures and I can make a good estimation of the process times. Those are the parameters that determine when a resource will be over loaded — will not be available.

How to do it? I don't have the foggiest idea, but it must be possible. As I turn, following Charlie's car into the plant parking lot, I realize another dichotomy. Process times do effect the lead-time. But their dominant effect is not their direct effect but

> *How to do it? I don't have the foggiest idea, but it must be possible.*

their indirect effect. The direct process time of a particular part is a negligible portion of its lead-time. The indirect effect of loading the resources — creating non instant availability — is the major contributor to the lead-time. MRP is busy computing the negligible direct impact, while totally neglecting the ability to use the same information (how?) to compute the major non direct impact.

With a broad smile I open my car's door. "Good morning Charlie."